W9-BKK-576

SKYGODS

SKYGODS

The Fall of Pan Am

ROBERT GANDT

WILLIAM MORROW AND COMPANY, INC.

New York

Library of Congress Cataloging-in-Publication Data

Gandt, Robert L.
  Skygods : the fall of Pan Am / Robert Gandt.
    p. cm.
  Includes index.
  ISBN 0-688-04615-0
  1. Pan American World Airways, inc.—History. 2. Airlines—United
    States—History. I. Title.
  HE9803.P36G36 1995
  387.7'06'573—dc20   94-39832
                                                 CIP

Printed in the United States of America

First Edition

1 2 3 4 5 6 7 8 9 10

BOOK DESIGN BY MICHAEL MENDELSOHN/M&M DESIGN 2000, INC.

To the pilots of Pan American World Airways

ACKNOWLEDGMENTS

At the death of any great corporate enterprise, it is tempting to assign blame. In the case of Pan American World Airways, there has been no lack of denunciation of the decisions, executives, and agencies that abetted the fall of the airline.

In this account there are no culprits. It is recognized that the officers charged with the direction of Pan Am struggled to the extent of their individual abilities to save the airline. That they failed is less a reflection on them than it is a statement about the complex life and times of Pan American.

This book is drawn from the author's twenty-six years as a pilot for Pan Am and from the contributions of over two hundred Pan Am airmen and employees. All the dialogue, thoughts, and impressions in the book are construed from those recollections. My sincere thanks are owed to each who dug into his trove of memories and gave life to the Pan Am story. Any errors of transcription or interpretation are my own.

In certain instances the names of characters have been altered for reasons that will be apparent to the reader. All the stories are true.

—R.G.

CONTENTS

PART I: APOGEE

Chapter One: That's Why We're Here   3

Chapter Two: Trippe   10

Chapter Three: Skygods   18

Chapter Four: Jets   27

Chapter Five: The Empire   39

Chapter Six: The Man from Camelot   44

Chapter Seven: New Hires   54

Chapter Eight: The Everyman Airplane   69

Chapter Nine: On the Line   80

Chapter Ten: Succession   92

PART II: DESCENT

Chapter Eleven: Crash   103

Chapter Twelve: Vietnam   117

Chapter Thirteen: The Boy Scout   122

Chapter Fourteen: Besieged   129

Chapter Fifteen: Just Call Me Jeeb   136

Chapter Sixteen: A Place Where You Never Have to Grow Up   149

Chapter Seventeen: The Cold War Gladiator   162

Chapter Eighteen: The Children's Crusade   173

Chapter Nineteen: Deep Pockets   184

Chapter Twenty: The National Caper   190

Chapter Twenty-one: Orange Pukes and Blue Pukes   198

Chapter Twenty-two: The Crown Jewels   206

PART III: IMPACT

Chapter Twenty-three: The Texas Huckster   215

Chapter Twenty-four: How Sweet It Is   224

Chapter Twenty-five: Strike   235

Chapter Twenty-six: Pacific   243

Chapter Twenty-seven: White Knights and the
   Maximum Skygod   251

Chapter Twenty-eight: Mister Nice Guy   261

Chapter Twenty-nine: A Village in Scotland   271

Chapter Thirty: The Coyote's Last Leg   282

Chapter Thirty-one: The Yawning Abyss   296

Chapter Thirty-two: Delta   304

Chapter Thirty-three: Tango Uniform   312

Index   319

For I dipp'd into the future, far as human eye could see,
Saw the Vision of the world, and all the wonder that could be;
Saw the heavens fill with commerce, argosies of magic sails,
Pilots of the purple twilight, dropping down with costly bales . . .
                    —ALFRED, LORD TENNYSON

If we went into the funeral business, people would stop dying.
                    —MARTIN R. SHUGRUE,
                        pilot and vice-chairman,
                        Pan American World Airways

Pan Am can go to hell.
                    —ALFRED E. KAHN, *chairman,*
                        Civil Aeronautics Board

PART I

APOGEE

CHAPTER ONE

THAT'S WHY WE'RE HERE

The image would remain fixed in Rob Martinside's memory for the next twenty-seven years: burnished aluminum fuselages, sleek tails slanting skyward, blue-on-white paint schemes gleaming in the morning sun. New Boeing 707s, the cutting edge of commercial jet technology, covered the ramp at the San Francisco International Airport. Each bore on its tail the round blue logo of Pan American World Airways.

As Martinside made his way across the ramp to the Pan Am complex at the south end of the airport, he paused to gaze at the polished beauty of the jets. He was twenty-six years old, the youngest in his class of newly hired pilots. It was his first day at Pan American.

Martinside met his fellow new hires. Despite the differences in height and shape, they seemed cast from the same mold. Freshly released from military service, each still wore the ubiquitous crew cut, a PX-bought polyester business suit, an enormous wrist chronometer.

But there was something besides haircuts and clothes that distinguished them from their contemporaries of the mid-1960s. In their walk, in the way they bantered among themselves, in the appreciative look they cast on the nearby jet airplanes, there was a *cockiness*. To a man, they walked with a discernible swagger. It was an acquired trait—the body language of the fighter jock, the astronaut, the test pilot.

Each knew he could have gone to another airline. There was Delta, for example, if you wanted to live in the South. There was Braniff, Texas-based and expanding very fast. American was also Texas-based, with a large domestic system. TWA was a leaner version of Pan Am. With TWA you could live in middle America—Kansas City was its headquarters. If you flew for Eastern Airlines you were based, not surprisingly, near the Atlantic shore.

But those were *domestics*, like Greyhound Bus. This was *Pan American*. No bus driving for them. No miserable lunches in places like Des Moines or Cincinnati or Boise. For them it would be sushi in Tokyo, *petit déjeuner* in Paris, tea in London. Pan Am advertised itself as "the world's most experienced airline." Well, sure, thought the new hires. That was the kind of airline they *ought* to be working for.

Pan American was the world's most glamorous airline. It was also the most snobbish. Pan Am's response to pilot applicants went something like ". . . if you *truly* believe that you possess the credentials to fly for the world's most experienced airline, then present yourself to our offices at . . ."

It was a time like no other in the history of the airlines. Traffic growth had doubled in the early sixties and was forecast to double again before the end of the decade. Expansion was so rapid that airline recruiters were predicting that the supply of new pilots—military *and* civilian—would be used up and the airlines would have to hire college kids and train them from scratch. Promotion would come so fast they would barely get settled into a new seat before the next became available. Boeing and Douglas could not build jetliners fast enough to fill the orders of the airlines.

Navy, Air Force, and Marine Corps pilots had an edge in the hiring order. To the airlines, military aviators were a known quantity. They were trainable, it was assumed, and they could probably even take orders.

Between 1964 and 1968 a steady stream of hopeful airmen flowed through the front door of Pan Am's operations complex at Kennedy Airport. Each of the crew-cut young men (no women pilots were being hired by the major airlines in the sixties) carried a briefcase containing his most precious documents—his military flight logs and pilot licenses.

They joked about the physical exam and the rubber-gloved flight surgeon who checked for everything from hernias to hemorrhoids—*Don't turn your back on the guy with the gloves*—and kidded each other about branch of service—*Are you Air Force or did you have formal flight training?* Each felt obliged, under the scrutiny of his peers, to flirt with the pretty blond nurse.

Mike Denham was a good-looking kid who had flown a Navy jet up from Pensacola just for the interview. Denham was a fighter pilot, cocky and good-humored, who wanted it made clear he was *not* a transport or a patrol plane pilot—one of the multiengine pukes.

Chuck Kraft, who *was* a multiengine puke, knew exactly why he was there. He had spent the past four years eating box lunches and drinking bug juice and flying Air Force C-130 transports around the world. During his missions a scene had begun to repeat itself. At each layover—Madrid, Paris, Bangkok, Hong Kong—he would head directly for the hotel where the airline crews stayed. At the swimming pool he would observe the same curious sight: *Pan Am stewardesses* —Swedish, German, French, American—gorgeous in their bikinis, frolicking around the pool. Frolicking with them would be smiling, suntanned, obviously overpaid *Pan Am pilots*.

One day in Bangkok, standing there in his evil-smelling, baggy flight suit, B-4 bag in hand, his gaze riveted on the scene at the pool, Chuck Kraft suddenly fathomed an immense truth: *They're doing the same goddam job I am.* And in the next instant, with his new clarity of vision, he made a career decision: *Screw the United States Air Force. Screw their box lunches and bug juice and baggy flight suits.* The next day he mailed his application for employment to Pan American.

At thirty-one, Cale Boggs was the oldest of the group. Son of a Maryland senator, he had already been out of the Marine Corps for a few years, made a pass at law school, and worked for General Motors in the industrial relations department. While there, he made a discovery. Boggs discovered that he hated *all* forms of employment that had nothing to do with flying. So here he was, contrary to his father's high hopes, standing in his boxer shorts in a drafty hallway at Pan Am's medical department, about to become an airline pilot.

Before Rob Martinside left the Navy, he had investigated other careers—business, law, teaching—and dismissed them all. Martinside realized that he had no burning ambition to do *anything* except fly airplanes.

The commanding officer of his Navy squadron understood this facet of Martinside's nature. "Martinside," he advised the young officer, "you happen to be the laziest naval officer I have ever observed in my entire career. You should consider being an airline pilot."

In addition to the physical exam, there was a torturous four-hour written test called the STANINE (a military-invented acronym for "STAndard test with a perfect score of NINE"). The same test was administered by most of the airlines, and extracts of the quiz had already been transported back to Navy and Air Force ready rooms around the world. The point of the STANINE seemed to be to separate both extremes on the cerebral spectrum. The airlines wanted bright pilots, but not *too* bright. It was okay to be smart, but not goofy. To the untutored, the STANINE was a confounding array of questions ranging from the names of the Beatles to the chemical composition of basalt to inquiries about how you felt about God and whether you had ever coveted your neighbor's wife. One section of the exam required the candidate to analyze a pattern of lights, under pressure of time, and then punch appropriate buttons to extinguish the lights.

The moment of truth for the applicants, though, was the interview. The interviewers were crusty old Pan Am captains with eyes like spark plug sockets. There were usually three interviewers, and they sat behind an elevated table, peering over their half-frames at the presumptuous young men in the PX suits.

The questions didn't lead anywhere in particular. The old pelicans mostly wanted to see the kids squirm, listen to them talk, find out if their veins carried any of the sacred juice of the Skygods.

"Why do you want to work for Pan American?"

"I want to fly for the best airline in the business, sir."

The interviewers nod. *Standard suck-up answer. No surprise.* "Yes, but why do you think Pan American is the best in the business?"

"I read a lot of aviation history. I know that Pan Am was the first to pioneer the ocean routes and to fly the newest airplanes. Ever since I was a kid, I knew that I wanted to fly for Pan American."

More nods. *Okay, the kid has done some homework.* "Tell us about yourself. What kind of a pilot are you?"

Here the candidate might pause a second, considering how much to lay it on about his personal skills. If he was a fighter jock, he might insert a little gentle bragging. Multiengine pilots tended to shrug and let their thicker logbooks testify to their accomplishments. "I have always been regarded as an excellent pilot by my commanding officers. . . ."

"Why are you getting out of the service?"

"Because I want a career as an airline pilot. It's a stable, satisfying profession that suits me and my family."

Good answer. He has a wife and, probably, kids, which implies a measure of maturity. Less likely to be a skirt-chasing gadfly. "How do you think you'll like having a seniority number and taking orders from more senior crew members?"

The interviewers lean forward to hear the answer. This is the real nitty-gritty.

The interviewee clears his throat. "I'm very conscious of the chain of command, sir. I have no problem taking orders. I know that at Pan Am the captain is *absolutely* in command."

The ancient pelicans exchange glances over their half-frames. *The applicant has obviously been coached to say the right thing. But what the hell, he understands the most fundamental truth about Pan American World Airways. Hire the kid!*

It took a couple of weeks to score the tests, do the background checks, and follow up on the applicants' references.

The commanding officer of Attack Squadron 36, based at Cecil Field, Florida, received a telephone call from the Pan American personnel department. Afterward, he summoned Lieutenant Rob Martinside to his office.

"Martinside, I have just performed one of the noblest services of my entire naval career."

"What was that, skipper?"

"I just told some guy from Pan American World Airways that you were a distinguished officer and an asset to the Navy and that your leaving would be a severe loss to the service. The dumb shit believed me. Please accept my congratulations."

And so it happened. Three days later came the telegram:

TO: LT. R. D. MARTINSIDE, NAS CECIL FIELD, FLORIDA
YOU HAVE BEEN ACCEPTED BY PAN AMERICAN FOR PILOT EM-
PLOYMENT AND ARE ASSIGNED TO TRAIN AND OPERATE AS A
COPILOT FROM THE SAN FRANCISCO BASE STOP PLEASE REPORT
TO THE CHIEF PILOT/PACIFIC CAPT. DON KINKEL AT SAN FRAN-
CISCO INTERNATIONAL AIRPORT STOP BRING LICENSES FLIGHT
LOGS AND BIRTH CERTIFICATES STOP CONGRATULATIONS

SIGNED CAPT. SAM MILLER MANAGER FLIGHT OPERATIONS

In the indoctrination room the newly hired pilots helped them-selves to the coffee and began getting acquainted. They wisecracked about being Navy pukes or Marine jarheads or Air Force wienies and indulged in a little bragging about numbers of carrier landings or mis-sions flown in Southeast Asia.

But mostly they talked about Pan Am:

"Did you know they're buying a whole fleet of 727s?"

"They're opening a base on Guam. . . ."

". . . flying freighters to Saigon . . ."

"We'll make captain in five years. . . ."

"Pan Am will be the first to get the SST. . . ."

Someone said he had seen a mockup of the American SST. The tail of the proposed supersonic transport bore the Pan Am blue ball.

On this, the morning of the first day of their new careers, a eu-phoria pervaded their chatter. It was the sweet, contented certainty that they had *arrived*. By some stroke of fortune, they had been plucked from the vast ocean of faceless and futureless aviators and deposited here in aeronautical heaven.

Pan Am had been the first to fly the Pacific, first across the Atlantic, first around the world. It was the first American carrier to fly jets. It had more international destinations than any other carrier. Pan Am jet freighters carried more cargo than any other airline.

Now there was talk of SSTs—supersonic transports—and even commercial space travel. With just a touch of theatricality, Pan American was accepting reservations for its first commercial service to the moon. The lunar flight list had swelled to 93,005 names.

Into the classroom of newly hired airmen strode a craggy-faced man in a business suit. "I'm the chief pilot of the Pacific Division," he said. He had crinkly eyes that looked as if they had peered down at the world from a thousand different cockpits. The new pilots took their seats. A respectful silence fell over the room.

The chief pilot surveyed the young faces over the tops of his half-frames. And then he told them exactly what they had expected to hear. "Congratulations, gentlemen," he said. "*You*"—he paused for effect —"are going to be SST pilots."

The pilots glanced at each other, nodding. *Supersonic transports? At Pan American?*

A young man in the first row spoke for them all. "Yes, sir, we know," he said. "That's why we're here."

CHAPTER TWO

TRIPPE

If anybody ever flies to the moon, the very next day Trippe will ask the Civil Aeronautics Board to authorize regular service.

—JAMES M. LANDIS, *former chairman, Civil Aeronautics Board*

Pan American World Airways was ruled from the forty-sixth floor of the world's largest corporate office building. From this aerie, Juan Trippe presided over a global enterprise employing more than forty thousand workers. It operated 143 jet transports and had another billion and a half dollars' worth on order. Pan Am spent $31 million a year just on advertising. Besides the airline operation there was the Intercontinental Hotel chain, a business jets division, a missile range, and, of course, the Manhattan skyscraper.

Juan Trippe had been the first airline tycoon. Now he was the last. Smith at American was retired. So was Patterson from United. Eddie Rickenbacker had given up command at Eastern.

Trippe and Pan Am. More so than at any other airline, the two entities—founder and airline—were indivisible. Pan Am was *Trippe's* airline. It was his creation, his life's work, his only passion. The airline's corporate persona bore Trippe's own peculiar personality—imperious, aloof, guileful, dynamic.

They called him the Great Dissembler. Juan Trippe could answer a question with such vagueness, digressing and rambling, that no one could remember the original topic. This was usually taken as a sign of his preoccupation with the burdens of managing his empire. Many, though, were convinced it was Juan Trippe's way of deflecting questions he preferred not to answer.

In his earlier life his abundant energy had made him appear younger than his years. At sixty-nine, he had a stoop and a paunch and he walked with an old man's gait. His legendary absentmindedness had worsened, and he'd become increasingly vague. He relied on secretaries and assistants to remind him of meetings and lunches and appointments.

Names had always been a problem for him. Trippe had learned to greet people, even his closest associates, in a halting, hesitant way, expecting them to offer their names. He would smile his angelic smile and his brown eyes would twinkle as though he were enjoying a private joke. But this, too, was thought by some to be a cover-up. They believed Trippe was a self-centered autocrat who simply never bothered to learn anyone's name.

The Latin-sounding first name always fooled people. Juan Terry Trippe's name came from a maternal aunt—Juanita Terry. The Trippe family, in fact, could trace its lineage back to 1633, when an English ancestor landed on the Maryland shore.

In 1909, just after Trippe's tenth birthday, his father took him to an air race in New York, around the Statue of Liberty. It was a grudge match between Glenn Curtiss and his archrivals, the Wright brothers.

The day belonged to Wilbur Wright. He made three successful flights in the gusty air, swooping around the Statue of Liberty in a figure-eight pattern, enthralling thousands of spectators. None was more enthralled than Juan Trippe. Standing there, fixated on the clattering biplanes, the boy knew from that day on what he would do with his life.

Trippe's father was a banker. Though not wealthy by the standards of his old-moneyed friends, Juan Trippe grew up among a privileged class. Like the scions of advantaged Eastern families, he was sent to prep school, then off to Yale. Photographs of the period show a serious, athletic-looking young man with aquiline features and clear brown eyes. He was an undistinguished scholar and a good football player. Above all else, he learned at Yale the value of having the "right" connections.

In 1917, during Trippe's freshman year, the United States entered World War I. With most of the football squad, he quit college and volunteered for military service. Despite his less-than-perfect vision, he finagled his way into Navy flight training by memorizing the eye chart in the preinduction physical.

He first soloed in a Jenny biplane over Long Island. Perhaps peering into the future, Trippe declined an assignment to tiny, single-engined pursuit planes. He volunteered instead for flying boats. But he never saw action. Before he could embark for Europe, the news came that the Great War was over. Trippe went back to Yale.

On Trippe's twenty-first birthday, his father died. At the same time, the Trippe bank failed. So when Trippe graduated, with only a meager inheritance from his father, he took a job that befitted a Yale man and a banker's son: He went to work as a bond salesman with the Wall Street firm of Lee, Higginson & Co.

He hated it. After two years, Trippe renounced Wall Street. Win or lose, he announced, he would make his living in the aviation business.

In 1922 there was scant evidence that such a business existed. Trippe invoked his Yale connections, making the rounds of old classmates, selling them stock in his new airline, which he called Long Island Airways. At an auction he bought seven Navy surplus Aeromarine float planes for $500 each.

The Aeromarines were single-engine aircraft that normally accommodated a pilot and one passenger. Trippe found that by replacing the Aeromarine's 90-horsepower engine with a 220-horsepower engine, he could modify his float planes to carry *two* passengers. Thus did Juan Trippe, early in the game, seize on a tactic that he would use for the next half century: *Increase capacity by whatever means and you increase revenues.*

That summer he dispatched his ramshackle fleet on round trips to the Long Island summer homes of the rich. He sold flights to Atlantic City. He chartered his float planes for trips south to the Caribbean and north to Canada. He worked as bookkeeper, scheduler, pilot, baggage handler, and janitor.

But by 1924, despite the long hours and hard labor of its founder, Long Island Airways went broke. No matter how much revenue Trippe managed to draw into his little airline, the bills always exceeded the take. He was forced to sell off, piece by piece, most of his assets. But Trippe still had reason to be cheerful. He had managed to pocket a small personal profit. And he had learned much about the complexities of commercial aviation—meeting payrolls, maintaining airplanes, raising capital.

Trippe was convinced of one thing: The airline business, to have any chance at a profit, would have to be semiregulated, like railroads and shipping lines. An airline had to have routes. And it had to have some sort of privileged status to fly its routes.

The next year a piece of legislation—the Airmail Act of 1925, called the Kelly Act—provided that privilege. The Kelly Act gave the Post Office authority to negotiate with private companies for the carriage of airmail. That meant *subsidy*—a dirty word in America's capitalistic society. America's fledgling airline industry would be subsidized by postal revenues.

To Juan Trippe, it meant the rules of the game had just changed: Money *could* be made in the flying business.

The new airmail routes drew applications from hundreds of speculators and investors. Through a consulting business formed by Juan Trippe, a corporation called Eastern Air Transport was created on paper. Trippe's corporation merged with another, better-financed company called Colonial Air Transport. On October 7, 1925, the new route—and the airmail contract—was awarded to Colonial Air Transport.

Trippe was vice president and manager of Colonial. He hired employees, rented facilities, ordered new airplanes. From his list of old school chums, he recruited investors and directors. They represented some of America's greatest fortunes: men like John Hambleton, war hero and son of a wealthy banker; Cornelius "Sonny" Whitney, air enthusiast and playboy heir to a banking fortune; and William A. Rockefeller, who had flown with Trippe in the Yale Aero Club.

It was inevitable that Juan Trippe's brash style would rankle the older, conservative directors of the company. Trippe was a young man in hurry. He wanted Colonial to expand, to move into new markets. He saw airmail not as Colonial's real purpose but only as a means to become a *passenger-carrying* airline. He committed the company to buying large, trimotor transport airplanes—two from Dutchman Tony Fokker, who had emigrated to America and was building aircraft in

New Jersey, and two from Henry Ford, who was building his own all-metal trimotor transport, the famous "tin goose."

The showdown between Trippe and the directors came when Trippe tried to extend Colonial's routes into the Chicago–New York market. The nervous board of directors was more interested in getting the airline into the black. Colonial was losing money by the plane-load—over $8,000 a month. The airline's cash had dwindled to less than $100,000. In a stormy shareholders' meeting, the majority voted against Trippe.

Trippe cleaned out his desk. It was the spring of 1927. He was out of a job, again. But he had reason to be optimistic. Things were happening in aviation. Whitney and Hambleton were ready to join him in a new venture called Aviation Corporation of America. They intended to bid on a proposed airmail route between Key West and Havana. Another young man, a lanky airmail pilot named Charles Lindbergh, had just proved the feasibility of transoceanic flight.

And in Florida a new airline was being formed for the purpose of flying into Latin America. It was called Pan American Airways.

Pan American was the dream child of Major Henry "Hap" Arnold of the Army Air Corps. With his colleague Major Carl Spaatz, Arnold had raised an alarm in Washington about a German-operated airline in Central and South America called SCADTA (Sociedad Colombo-Alemana de Transportes). SCADTA was extending its routes through Central America, as far as the Panama Canal. The Germans even intended to fly to the United States.

A *German* airline operating an air service in the Americas? Only seven years after the Great War? It had to be stopped. Arnold and Spaatz decided they would resign from the Army. With a former naval aviator named John K. Montgomery, they would form their own airline to confront the Germans. Montgomery, who was already a civilian, began recruiting investors. For their first route, they wanted the airmail contract from Key West to Havana.

But in the autumn of 1925 the Billy Mitchell affair exploded like an aerial bomb in the Army Air Corps. General Billy Mitchell, commander of the American expeditionary air force in France, was the outspoken proponent of American air power. Mitchell was also contentious and undiplomatic. In 1921 he proved his point—and enraged the military brass—by sinking a number of captured German warships with his bombers. When he publicly attacked the War and Navy departments, calling their leadership "incompetent, criminally negligent and almost treasonable," he was court-martialed, found guilty, and suspended for five years from rank, command, and pay.

Hap Arnold and Carl Spaatz were Mitchell's lieutenants. Both testified in Mitchell's behalf and assisted with his trial strategy. With Mitchell out of action, the two officers felt honor-bound to remain in the Army and carry on the fight.

Montgomery took over the airline scheme. In 1927 he incorporated Pan American Airways and filed its application for the Key West–Havana airmail route.

Meanwhile, yet another consortium, headed by a financier named Richard F. Hoyt, chairman of Wright Aeronautical Corporation, applied for the Havana route. This group, Atlantic, Gulf and Caribbean Air Lines, was the resurrection of a defunct airline, Florida Airways, founded by war ace Eddie Rickenbacker.

That made *three* applicants competing for the Key West–Havana route, including Trippe's Aviation Corporation of America. At the urging of Assistant Postmaster General W. Irving Glover, the three groups were persuaded to merge. On July 19, 1927, the U.S. Post Office awarded FAM 4, the foreign airmail route from Key West to Havana, to Pan American World Airways. After much backroom finagling and manipulation of stock, Hoyt emerged as chairman of the board. Twenty-eight-year-old Juan Trippe became president and general manager of the airline.

Only one serious obstacle remained: The airmail contract carried with it a deadline for service to commence on October 19, 1927. There was still no runway at Key West that would accommodate the new airline's trimotor Fokker land planes. There was only an old washed-out military strip. For weeks, construction crews had been grading and filling and laying the new surface. Then the rains came and washed it all away.

The construction crew laid new gravel. Again the rains came.

This went on, night after night. Time was running out. There was still no runway at Key West. Pan American stood to lose not only the contract but the $25,000 bond posted with the application.

Juan Trippe put on his angelic smile and went to Washington to plead for an extension of the deadline. The Postmaster wasn't moved. He refused to grant any extension. If Pan American could not commence service on the 19th, the contract would be forfeited. The new airline would be out of business before it ever left the ground.

On October 17, the first of the new Fokker trimotors ordered by Trippe landed in Miami, ready to proceed to Key West and inaugurate the service to Havana. All that was needed was a runway in Key West. Trippe, still in Washington, received the report that the construction crews were working around the clock. Don't worry, they said. The new runway would be ready.

That night the rains came. Torrents of Caribbean rainwater carved the new runway into an obstacle course.

It seemed hopeless. The gloom could be felt all the way from the gullied airfield at Key West to the chilly bureaus of Washington. Pan American Airways seemed to be finished.

And then appeared an unlikely hero.

Cy Caldwell looked just like any other member of the 1920s breed of barnstormers, rumrunners, and fly-for-the-hell-of-it adventurers. He wore riding breeches and an oil-stained flying jacket. But on this day, October 18, 1927, Caldwell had in his possession an item of incalculable value—*a float plane*. It was a Fairchild FC-2 named *La Niña*, which Caldwell was ferrying to the Dominican Republic. Equipped with its pontoonlike floats, the Fairchild was independent of washed-out quagmires like the runway at Key West.

To Pan American's manager in Key West, J. E. Whitbeck, Caldwell looked like an angel dispatched by Jehovah. *A float plane!* Whitbeck pounced on the barnstormer. Would Caldwell consider *diverting* his airplane to Key West, and then flying Pan American's first load of contract mail to Havana?

Standing there in his wrinkled flying togs, the flier looked over the scene. He wasn't particularly interested in the new airline's plight. Havana was out of his way. And he was supposed to be in Santo Domingo the next day.

Never mind all that, said Whitbeck. *How much?* How much would Caldwell charge for his services?

That threw a new light on the matter. Caldwell reconsidered the matter. How about, say, $175?

A sigh of relief was heard all the way to the District of Columbia.

The next morning, Whitbeck and his crew loaded seven bags of mail containing thirty thousand letters aboard the Fairchild. Cy Caldwell took off, and one hour and twenty minutes later he landed *La Niña* in Havana harbor.

After that single flight, Caldwell flew off into obscurity. But his name became a part of the Pan Am legend. It was Cy Caldwell who saved Juan Trippe's airline.

CHAPTER THREE

SKYGODS

sky·god \'ski-'god\ *n* **1** *cap* : a being who reigns supreme while aloft in man-made flying contrivance   **2**: an aeronautical creature endowed with godlike attributes and worthy (in his or its own estimation) of human worship

Back in the boat days . . .

The new hires heard a lot of that during their training. Whenever someone talked about an event that happened in the first half of Pan Am's existence, his voice took a reverential tone: "Things were different in the boat days, you know. Back in the boat days we used to . . ."

Everything of consequence happened back then. Those were the days when Pan American took to the skies, and oceans, in its great flying boats—lumbering, deep-hulled leviathans that took off and alighted on water. To the old-timers, everything that happened *after* the boat days was anticlimactic. Then came the coldly efficient, unromantic land planes like the Douglas DC-4 and DC-6 and the Boeing Stratocruiser and then the antiseptic, kerosene-belching jets.

The flying boat was a hybrid—neither fish nor fowl—born of the notion that because two-thirds of the planet happened to be covered with water, it made sense to use the stuff for taking off and landing airplanes. And for a while that was the *only* option. Conventional land planes required long runways of thick concrete in order to take off with a heavy load. Until the late thirties, no such hard-surfaced runways existed anywhere in the world. Only the flying boat, using miles of sheltered harbor and lagoon, was able to lift the vast store of fuel required to carry a payload across an ocean.

There was also a psychological factor. Passengers took comfort in the knowledge that should calamity strike and the flying boat be no longer able to fly, it could become, in fact, a boat.

Juan Trippe, it was said, had a nautical fetish. On the walls of his home hung paintings of clipper ships, the fast full-rigged merchant vessels of the nineteenth century. It was Trippe's dream that his airline, Pan American, would become America's airborne maritime service. Pan Am flying boats would be the clipper ships of the twentieth century.

So he called his flying boats *Clippers*. Aircraft speed was measured in *knots*. The pilots who commanded the clippers were given the rank of *captain*. Copilots became *first officers*.

It wouldn't do for Pan American pilots to look like the scruffy, leather-jacketed, silk-scarved airmail pilots of the domestic airlines. Instead, they wore naval-style double-breasted uniforms with officer's caps. When they boarded their flying boats, they *marched* up the ramp, two abreast, led, of course, by the captain.

Trippe understood pilots, having been one himself. He knew they were prima donnas who loved the pomp and perquisites of command. The captains of the great oceangoing, four-motored behemoths like the *China Clipper* needed a suitably grand title. So he gave them one: *Master of Ocean Flying Boats*.

Like commanders of ships at sea, the Masters of Ocean Flying Boats were a law unto themselves. While under way they exercised absolute authority over their aircraft and all its occupants. And with such authority went, inevitably, arrogance. And idiosyncrasy.

Some were classic martinets. Captain R.O.D. Sullivan was an early flying boat captain, a bully who managed his crews and his airplanes with the tact of a pile driver. He was also a flamboyant pilot. Sullivan liked to make low, curving approaches in the big Boeing flying boats, flaring, rolling the wings level, and alighting on the water all at the same time. Copilots were reluctant to challenge the bellicose Sullivan.

No one challenged him one evening coming into Lisbon. There was a light rain and low visibility. Sullivan swooped low over the darkened Tagus River, turning onto his final approach. The *Yankee*

Clipper caught a wingtip, cartwheeled, hit broadside, and broke up. Within minutes, she was at the bottom of the river. Twenty-four of the thirty-nine passengers died, including singing star Tamara Drasin. Another singer, Jane Froman, was paralyzed for life.

At the inquiry, Captain Sullivan denied that he was to blame for the crash, insisting that the Boeing's nose had veered downward, out of control, prior to the crash. The accident board disagreed. Sullivan's career with Pan American was terminated.

Captain Leo Terletsky was a different sort. Terletsky was a European, a White Russian of considerable charm—on the ground. In the air he was insufferable. Unlike Sullivan, he was *scared to death* of flying. His anxiety caused him to shout at copilots, issue orders and immediately countermand them. He infected his crews with his own anxiety. A number of copilots refused to fly with him.

One day in 1938, Terletsky was flying the Martin M-130 *Hawaii Clipper* from Guam to Manila. Somewhere in mid-Pacific, in an area of towering cumulus buildups and torrential squalls, the flying boat vanished from the sky. No trace was ever found of the *Hawaii Clipper*.

The press speculated about Japanese sabotage. The disappearance of Terletsky and the *Hawaii Clipper* came only a year after Amelia Earhart vanished in the same part of the world. It made for an appealing mystery.

To the Pan American pilots, though, the real villain wasn't the Japanese. It was the Pacific and its vast, brooding, hidden storms. They had reported seeing anvil-topped cumulonimbus clouds rising to above sixty thousand feet—higher than anything they had previously thought possible. To blunder into such a storm with a flying boat would be catastrophic. And it would be just like Leo Terletsky to do it.

Some of the flying boat captains were outrageous characters. Captain Steve Bancroft was a practical joker who had a fetish for snakes. He collected them—boas, pythons—on his trips to South America and brought them back in his baggage. Bancroft enjoyed standing at the customs counter and watching a new inspector search his baggage for contraband.

The effect was always the same. The agent would rummage through the bag. Then he would bound into the air as if he'd been shot from a catapult. *"Aiiiyeee! It's a—it's a goddam—"*

"Snake," Bancroft would explain. "My new constrictor. Do you like him?"

It didn't take long for the customs agents to learn about Bancroft. On one trip an agent told Bancroft that if he had any snakes in his bag today, he would find himself in jail.

"Horseshit," said Bancroft.

"All right, smart-ass, what's in your bag?"

"Horseshit," said Bancroft.

"Okay." The agent was prepared for any kind of serpent. He held a machete in his hand. "Empty the suitcase on the counter."

"The whole thing?"

"The whole thing."

So Bancroft dumped the entire contents of his suitcase on the counter. The suitcase was filled with manure.

"See?" said Bancroft. "Just like I said." Horseshit.

Ed Schultz was a boat captain who was very attached to his dog, a Great Dane. He missed the dog on the long flying boat trips. When Schultz reached his hotel room in Rio, he would have a few drinks and think about his dog. After a while he couldn't stand it any longer. He would telephone his wife in Miami.

"Put Ralph on," he would tell her.

Schultz's wife would put Ralph, the Great Dane, on the phone.

Captain Schultz would bark into the phone. The Great Dane would bark back. They would go on like that for twenty or more minutes, Schultz and Ralph, barking back and forth on the telephone between Miami and Rio.

Captain Bob Ford was in Auckland with the *Pacific Clipper*, a Boeing B-314, the day the Japanese bombed Pearl Harbor. Ford wondered how he was going to get back home now that a war had begun. The Pacific Ocean was a battleground. And then Ford made a command decision: He would take the *Pacific Clipper* home the long way—around the world in the *other* direction.

For nearly a month, Ford and his crew were out of contact. For all the world knew, they had dropped off the edge of the earth. In radio silence they flew across the Indian Ocean, the Middle East, the continent of Africa, and the South Atlantic and up the coasts of South and North America. On the morning of January 6, 1942, the startled duty officer in New York heard the radio transmission: "*Pacific Clipper*, inbound from Auckland, New Zealand, Captain Ford reporting. Due arrive Pan American Marine Terminal La Guardia seven minutes."

Bob Ford had made it home. He had also made history. He and his crew had just completed the first round-the-world flight with a commercial airplane.

Because Trippe was a pilot, he respected the airman's skills. But it was not in his peculiar chemistry to actually *fraternize* with them. Never would Trippe, the aloof tycoon, considering loosening his tie and walking into a crew room to join a flying-with-the-hands bull session.

More often than not, Trippe was at odds with his pilots. To Trippe, pilots were pampered specialists who complained too much about work rules and pay and benefits. In the thirties he had to endure the specter of a union on his property—ALPA, the Air Line Pilots Association. As ALPA members, pilots were no longer hired and fired at the company's whim. Their salaries and working rules were negotiated for them by their union. Their place on the company roster was fixed by a seniority list. Their grievances were adjudicated by union and company mediators.

Gradually Trippe distanced himself from the crew room and the cockpit and the seaplane ramp. He became more the aloof executive. To oversee Pan American's flight operations, he hired a small, gnomelike Dutchman named Andre Priester.

As chief engineer, Priester was given autonomy over all Pan Am's flying hardware. During the next three decades he stamped the airline with his own ethic of hard-nosed, conservative, meticulously planned operations. It was Priester who laid down the specifications for each of Pan Am's new flying boats. Priester plotted new routes and wrote operations manuals and calculated aircraft performance. Priester invented Pan Am's operational philosophy.

Whereas Trippe was seldom seen by the rank and file, Priester was omnipresent. He popped up everywhere, snooping, inspecting, running a finger over surfaces, asking questions. His English was still not good. "Vat are you dooink?" he would ask a loitering mechanic. If the man said he was taking a break, Priester would say, "It iss not your chob to take breaks. Work or you vill be fired." He forbade drinking or smoking on Pan American flying boats, even for passengers. He would fire a pilot for smoking in public, or a mechanic for having a dirty toolbox.

Once he boarded a flying boat that had just docked. He ordered a steward to pick up the abandoned newspapers. The steward said it wasn't his job to clean airplanes. "Dat's right," the Dutchman said. "You haffen't got a chob."

In his office Priester kept a photograph of every pilot in Pan Am's employ. Whenever an incident occurred, he could match a man's face to the problem. He sent Christmas cards to every airman, usually with a subtle message about engineering efficiency or a new year's operating goal for the airline. One pilot, Horace Brock, remembered "rather obscurely on the card one year could be found two little numbers, perhaps .87 in one corner and .55 in another. For those with aeronautical training the meaning would eventually sink in: One number referred to propeller efficiency, and the other to specific fuel consumption, efficiencies not yet attainable."

Pilots, being pilots, resisted Priester's autocratic ways. They mimicked his Dutch accent: "Ve *vant* to fly ze airplanes in a zafe manner." They stuck up cartoons of the diminutive, baldheaded Dutchman.

The pilots feared Priester. They resented his uncompromising perfectionist attitude. But in their secret hearts they took pride in what he made them accomplish.

The first Skygod, master of all the Masters of Ocean Flying Boats, was a slender, ungodlike man named Edwin Musick.

People seldom noticed when Ed Musick walked into a room. He was a man of unimposing countenance, over forty, completely lacking any of Lindbergh's youthful charisma. He had thinning black hair and a permanent five-o'clock shadow. Musick spoke only occasionally, and when he did it was with a frugal use of words. Ed Musick was a pilot, which suited him fine. It was all he had ever aspired to be. It was only when he entered the cockpit that Ed Musick seemed to grow in stature. His brown eyes would come alive, flicking over every instrument and control in the compartment. He would settle himself into the left seat and then, with thumb and forefinger, he would straighten the creases in his trousers. With a handkerchief he would clean the glass face of each instrument. He would adjust and readjust his seat, making sure his hands reached the controls at just the right angle.

This ritual would go on for a while. Not until everything was adjusted to his satisfaction would Musick order, in his soft voice, "Start number one."

The line pilots called him "meticulous Musick." Musick was one of them. They held him in a special esteem because he was not flashy, not interested in personal publicity, not ambitious for a job in upper management. He was the most professional pilot any of them had ever met.

Ed Musick was Pan American's chief pilot. In 1935, Musick received the most important assignment of his life: He would fly the world's most advanced airplane, the *China Clipper*, from San Francisco all the way to the Far East.

By the end of the *China Clipper*'s epic voyage, Ed Musick was the most famous airline pilot in the world. His life had changed forever. His face appeared on the cover of *Time*. He was presented with the Harmon Trophy, an award for aviation achievement shared only by Lindbergh and Wiley Post. His comments were sought by reporters on every subject, aeronautical or otherwise.

Musick's shyness and laconic commentary, however, were the bane of Pan Am's publicity department. During the proving flight of the Sikorsky S-42B to Hawaii, the press director pleaded for newsworthy reports. Would Ed, *please*, transmit something—anything—that was publishable?

Musick balked. "I'm a pilot, not a newspaperman. I wouldn't know what to send."

"Send something about the sunset over the Pacific."

Okay, Musick said. He would send something. From out over the ocean he radioed to the anxious world a message: "Sunset, 0639 GMT."

Ed Musick was a man who almost never used profanity, but this was a special case. When he gazed down for the first time at Pago Pago, he used the most common expletive in aviation: *Oh, shit*. They expected him to land a twenty-ton flying boat in this teacup of a harbor. Whose stupid goddam idea was this?

It was a bad place for a flying boat. The green Samoan hills swelled to fifteen hundred feet at each end of the harbor. The wind off the ocean piled up the waves in a white froth at the mouth of the bay. To land in Pago Pago harbor, Musick would have to descend along the slope of the encircling hills, using full landing flaps to keep his speed down, then break his descent at the last instant and slap the big Sikorsky flying boat down on the water before he ran out of harbor. If he glided too far, he would crash into the breakers at the mouth of the bay.

Pan American was surveying the new route from San Francisco to Auckland, New Zealand. Everyone knew it was a dangerous mission. Musick, typically, reasoned that as chief pilot it should be his assignment to fly the trip.

Their S-42B, the *Samoan Clipper*, had to be specially outfitted for the trip. Its cabin was stripped of all its seats, fixtures, and passenger accommodations. Extra fuel tanks and a new fuel-jettisoning system were installed. Because of the ever-present reek of gasoline in the cabin, the crew called her the "flying gas tank."

Musick landed the big boat in Pago Pago harbor. The next day he took off again for Auckland. Twice more he came to Pago Pago, liking the little island no more than the first time he saw it.

On the morning of January 11, 1938, he lumbered once again across the confined harbor, barely clearing the breakers at the mouth of the bay, and headed for New Zealand. Two hours and forty minutes later he radioed that he had an oil leak in number four engine and that he intended to jettison his huge load of fuel. He wanted the flying boat down to its minimum landing weight so it could safely alight back in the teacup-sized Pago Pago harbor.

He never made it. As Musick jettisoned the high-octane fuel, vapor gathered in the wing of the big Sikorsky boat—then ignited. The *Samoan Clipper* exploded like an incendiary bomb. It fell to the sea in a ball of flame.

The news flashed around the system. At Pacific island bases and in cockpits and in crew lounges, pilots shook their heads and spoke in hushed tones. The great Musick was dead.

Musick may have been gone, but thirty years later the Skygods were still around. The new-hire pilots would catch glimpses of them. The ancient airmen, living artifacts from another age, could be observed striding down the hallway to attend to their worldly business in the crew scheduling or personnel departments. Their heels clacked like hammers on the marble floor. Their penetrating gazes fixed like laser beams on the earthlings they encountered on their daily rounds.

Even their uniforms were distinctive. The gold on their cap visors and the four stripes on their uniform sleeves had a weathered, salt-sprayed dullness. The white caps rode atop their graying manes with a windward tilt. In their double-breasted, gold-encrusted Pan Am uniforms, they looked like ancient mariners.

Their trademark was the Look. Skygods squinted at the world over the tops of half-frame spectacles, down the lengths of their leathery noses. Wearing the Look, they would lock their imperious gaze on whatever subspecies happened to warrant their attention.

From a distance, the new hires watched in awe. Like everyone else, they knew these ancients had practically *invented* aviation. Back in the boat days, these heroes had braved a thousand storms, alighted on mountainous seascapes, flown over the vastness of great oceans.

And the Skygod ethic, the new pilots were learning, wasn't found just in the cockpit. It began at the top, in the corporate sanctum of the chief executive. Juan Trippe was the Supreme Skygod.

CHAPTER FOUR

JETS

Always bear in mind that airplanes get bigger. Don't make a decision now that doesn't allow you to increase the capacity of your airplane. Don't limit yourself. Get the most out of your airplane.

—CHARLES A. LINDBERGH

While Juan Trippe was still dispatching trimotor mail planes to Cuba, his thoughts had turned to flying boats. And when his great flying boats were still crossing the oceans, he was thinking about jets. That was Trippe's innate gift. The Supreme Skygod could read the future as if it were tomorrow's appointment book.

But they always fought him. The Primitives—myopic bureaucrats and bankers and slow-witted industry moguls—came out from under their rocks to oppose him. In 1935 they fought him over the *China Clipper* and the new Pacific service. In 1939 they fought him over Pan American's monopoly on the North Atlantic route. At the end of World War II they opposed his proposal for a single flag-carrying American overseas airline.

Now it was 1955, and the Primitives were fighting him again. This time it was the jets.

Few airline chiefs in the early 1950s believed they could make money with the newly invented, fuel-guzzling, screamingly noisy jet-engined airliner. At a quarter of the cost, nearly half the speed, and twice the range, propeller-driven transports like the Douglas DC-6 and DC-7 and the Lockheed Constellation made far more sense than dangerous vehicles like the jet.

Several authoritative studies, including one by the Rand Corporation, declared that the jet did not—and for many years would not—possess the range to cross the ocean nonstop. Nor could its seats be sold at reasonable fares to guarantee a profit for the operator. Further, to carry both a payload *and* the great store of fuel required to fly any distance, the jet would require impossibly long runways both to take off and to land.

C. R. Smith, the boss of American Airlines, stood up at an industry meeting and said, "We are all of us still intrigued by the glamour of the jet airplane, but neither we nor you, the consumer, can now afford it." The price of a jetliner—not yet built—was estimated to be $4 million per airplane. "We can't go backward to the jet," Smith declared. There were amens from his audience.

The logical next step, according to Smith and his disciples, was the turboprop. The turboprop was a jet engine with the compressor shaft connected to a conventional propeller. Airliners built around the turboprop made more sense. They were cheaper to build than a jet. They were cheaper to operate. Best of all, at least for wary passengers, they looked and felt like conventional propeller-driven airliners powered by conventional engines.

Claptrap, snorted Juan Trippe. Smith was leading the chorus of the Primitives.

To Trippe, the jet was imminently logical *and* inevitable. Never mind the whining about development expense and cost per copy and revenue-passenger-mile cost and noise and range and economy. Those problems would be solved. They always were.

Speed, for its own sake, was not the most important factor. Flying the Atlantic in half the time of its propeller-driven predecessors meant the jet could transport many more passengers in the same time frame. To Juan Trippe, jets meant faster travel, lower fares, more passengers, expanding airlines—and thus *profit*.

Why did the Primitives never understand that?

Charles Lindbergh was Trippe's advance scout. Even before the war was over, while he was still working for Pratt & Whitney, Lindbergh had entered collapsing Germany to sniff out secret new developments. He was looking primarily for jets, and he found them. He discovered advanced jet engine production. He found the startlingly advanced twin-engine Messerschmitt ME 262, the world's first operational jet fighter. He came upon a swept-wing aircraft, evidence that the Germans were already exploring the realms of transonic and supersonic flight. He even found Germany's leading builder of exotic aircraft, Willy Messerschmitt, living in a cow barn next to his house in Munich.

Charles Lindbergh had an association with Pan Am that went back almost as far as Juan Trippe's. Lindbergh was the captain on the inaugural flight of the *American Clipper*, Pan Am's first great Sikorsky flying boat. It was Lindbergh who surveyed the airmail routes across Latin America.

When Trippe was thinking about the Pacific, he dispatched Lindbergh, with his young wife, Anne, flying as radio operator and navigator. In their Lockheed Sirius floatplane, they flew the Arctic route to Asia, all the way to China. Two years later they flew the same floatplane to Europe. They explored the coasts of North America, Greenland, and Scandinavia, criss-crossed Europe as far as Moscow, then went down the west coast of Africa. From the Gambia River in West Africa, they crossed the South Atlantic, nonstop, to Natal. They flew up the Amazon to Manaus, over the jungle to Trinidad—and home. Their journey took five and a half months.

Lindbergh reported back to Trippe. The best flying boat route to Europe was via Bermuda and the Azores. Just like the North Pacific, the northern route over Greenland and Iceland would be ice-locked and murderous in the winter.

Lindbergh was already thinking that the big, romantic flying boats themselves were the real problem. Flying boats required safe harbors, free of ice and flotsam and heavy seas, wherever they alighted. They needed docks and jetties and boarding launches to handle passengers. Salt water ate like acid through their vital components. They were fascinating anachronisms. It was just a matter of time, Lindbergh said, before they were replaced by long-range land planes.

In the thirties, following the kidnapping of his son and the subsequent lengthy trial, Lindbergh became a recluse. He moved his family to Europe and immersed himself in scientific studies. As the world veered toward war, Lindbergh became an outspoken critic of American intervention. He made an enemy of FDR, so much so that when the United States finally entered the war, Lindbergh was barred from returning to active duty.

As a civilian "consultant" for United Aircraft Corporation, citizen Lindbergh went to the South Pacific. He flew fifty combat missions, quite illegally, in P-38s and F4U Corsairs. He shot down one Japanese Zero and came close to being shot down himself.

During Lindbergh's feud with Roosevelt, Trippe stayed out of the way. When the war was over, Trippe welcomed Lindbergh back. They never discussed Lindbergh's politics or his trouble with FDR. Lindbergh resumed his duties as Pan Am's technical consultant.

When the world's first jetliner, the British-built Comet, was about to fly, Trippe again sent Lindbergh. Lindbergh reported that the Comet was a highly advanced airplane, but it would not have the range to make it nonstop across the Atlantic. But even with one or two refueling stops, the sleek jet would beat Pan American's plodding Stratocruisers—four-engine transports derived from the wartime Boeing B-29 bomber—across the ocean by several hours.

Trippe ordered three Comets. They were Pan Am's first order for foreign-built airplanes since 1927, when Juan Trippe bought mail planes from Anthony Fokker.

And he went shopping for an American jet.

There were, as usual, three possibilities: Boeing, Douglas, and Lockheed. Lockheed was already committed to the production of its highly touted Electra propjet. The Electra was intended to replace the conventionally powered domestic airliners of the fifties, like the DC-6 and the Constellation. The Electra would not be a transocean vehicle. Smith of American and Rickenbacker of Eastern were scrapping over who would get the propjet first. Lockheed had a hot item in the Electra and made it well known that it was not interested in building a long-range commercial jet.

Boeing was at work on a prototype four-engine jet it was calling the Dash Eighty. If successful, it would become an Air Force tanker. Powered by the new J-57 engines, the Dash Eighty could cruise in the upper thirty thousands at over five hundred miles per hour. It seemed possible that an enhanced derivative of the Dash Eighty might even become a true intercontinental airliner. If so, passengers would be flying from America to Europe in less time than they now spent traveling from Chicago to Los Angeles.

Trippe dispatched Lindbergh to the Boeing plant in Seattle. The Lone Eagle flew with legendary test pilot Tex Johnston, asked several pointed questions, then reported back to Trippe.

This is the way to go, Lindbergh said. The Boeing jet represented the future. It had some big problems, the biggest being that it did not yet possess the range to fly the Atlantic—Pan Am's ocean. But that would be overcome. Pan Am shouldn't waste time with interim airplanes like Lockheed's propjet Electra.

In Santa Monica, Douglas's assembly line was already at near-maximum capacity filling orders for the venerable DC-6 and DC-7. But Donald Douglas was also sniffing the kerosene in the air. Belatedly he had jumped into the competition for an Air Force all-jet tanker aircraft. It had suddenly dawned on Douglas that the winner of the competition for a *military* jet transport would have an automatic, government-funded edge in the development of a commercial jetliner. The incredible expenses of design, testing, and tooling would already be born by the nation's taxpayers. So now Douglas was in the game with his own prototype jetliner. It was called the DC-8.

It was a situation made to order for a manipulator like Juan Trippe. He had not one but two builders competing to construct the airplane he wanted. He could play one against the other. But Trippe's problem was to get them to build *his* airplane. He needed a jet that could fly the Atlantic.

The Boeing and the Douglas versions had virtually the same specifications. Boeing's 707 prototype measured only 132 inches in width, which permitted only five-abreast seating, the same as the Stratocruiser. It would accommodate no more than a hundred passengers. The Douglas airplane carried the same load. Neither had transoceanic range.

The trouble was the engines. The state-of-the-art power plant—and the only engine available—was the Pratt & Whitney J-57, which was being used on the B-52 bomber. At about ten thousand pounds of thrust, the J-57 was a third more powerful than any other engine in the world—but still too puny to power a transoceanic jetliner.

And then news of a secret project was leaked: An advanced version of the J-57, designated the J-75, was being developed for a new generation of supersonic fighters. The J-75 was said to be half again as powerful as the J-57. Only about two hundred people outside Pratt & Whitney and the military knew about the J-75. One of them was Juan Trippe.

At age sixty-seven, Fred Rentschler was damn tired of picking up the phone and finding Juan Trippe on the line.

"Mr. Trippe calling," he would hear. It went on like that every day. And it was always the same subject: the goddam J-75.

Rentschler headed Pratt & Whitney, a subsidiary of the conglomerate United Aircraft, of which Rentschler was also the CEO. Like Donald Douglas and Juan Trippe, Fred Rentschler had begun his career in the infancy of aviation. Pratt & Whitney was his personal fiefdom, and in more than thirty years there he had built the world's most successful aircraft engines.

Back in 1929, Rentschler had taken a long shot and bought fifty thousand shares of stock in an airline called Pan American. It was the first new capital Juan Trippe had been able to raise for his airline. For years after, Rentschler sat on Pan Am's board of directors. He had seen Juan Trippe in action.

Trippe was asking the impossible. First, he wanted the J-75 released from the secret list, which Rentschler knew was probably feasible, if not popular. Then Trippe wanted to buy a batch of the engines—never mind that they hadn't even been built or tested yet—to install in jetliners that also weren't built. What's more, Rentschler knew for a fact that neither Boeing nor Douglas was willing to redesign its proposed jetliner around an experimental engine.

All this Rentschler told Trippe. Again.

One of Juan Trippe's most exasperating qualities was that he never seemed to hear what he didn't want to hear. So he never had to take no for an answer.

"We have to have an airplane that will do the Atlantic nonstop," Trippe repeated, as if he hadn't heard.

Rentschler told him again: Full-scale production of the J-75 was out of the question. There was still too much to be learned about the high-temperature metals that went into the new engine.

"But look at what a wonderful job the J-57s are doing for the Air Force."

"This is a bigger animal," said Rentschler. "We haven't flown it yet."

Trippe signed off sweetly, showing no sign of accepting Rentschler's refusal.

The next day when Trippe called, Rentschler agreed to a "final" meeting in the Cloud Club atop the Chrysler Building.

At the meeting, Rentschler went through the whole litany once again. The Boeing and Douglas designs were etched in concrete. They were to be built around the J-57, which he was in the business of selling. If Trippe wanted jetliners in the next decade, he would have to buy them the way they were designed. Forget the J-75. That was years away, and would have no effect on the design of the first jets.

Rentschler folded his arms and leaned back in his chair. His decision, he said, was final.

Trippe was smiling his angelic smile. Had he heard? No one could tell.

"Why don't we take a two-week break," Trippe said, "and think the whole matter through?"

Rentschler and his associates looked at each other. Think *what* through? What the hell? Wasn't it clear that the decision was final?

Not to Trippe. He rose from his chair and shook everyone's hand. Nothing was ever final to Juan Trippe until he wanted it to be.

While Rentschler's team drove back to East Hartford, Trippe was on the phone to England. Rolls-Royce had an engine under development that supposedly would have transatlantic capability. Trippe let it be known that he was determined to have a jetliner with powerful enough engines to fly the Atlantic. Even if he had to buy them in England.

The word leaked back to Pratt & Whitney, just as Trippe knew it would. And panic ensued, just as he intended. It was unthinkable that the first American jet across the Atlantic would fly *with British engines.*

Rentschler and his people went into an emergency reevaluation of the J-75 program. It was, the engineers pointed out, really only an expanded model of the J-57. The temperature limits could be kept the same. It was probably not as experimental and untested as most new engines.

Trippe was relentless. At yet another meeting, he put it on the line: If Pratt & Whitney could deliver those engines, Pan Am would buy 120 of them—*with or without an airplane to hang them on*—for $250,000 apiece. It was a $40 million order, counting spare parts.

Rentschler was in a corner. If Pan Am turned to Rolls-Royce, Pratt & Whitney—and America's reputation in the power plant field— would go straight down the toilet. On the other hand, if Pratt & Whitney delivered the J-75 and then the engine experienced catastrophic failures, the company would go down anyway.

Rentschler made the decision himself. Trippe could have his engines. They would be delivered by the summer of 1959.

In Seattle, it was Bill Allen's turn. Allen was the head of the Boeing Airplane Company. Allen gazed across his desk at Trippe's smiling face. *He's bluffing*, thought Allen.

Trippe was telling him that Pan Am now owned $40 million worth of experimental engines. *Without airplanes*. Just the damn engines, which had never even been tested, let alone installed and flown on a real airplane.

Now all Trippe wanted him to do was redesign the entire Boeing 707. That's all. Never mind that the prototype was already built. Make it longer and wider. Redesign the wings and reconfigure it for a third again as much power. Give it half again as much range. That was all he wanted.

This was not the first time Juan Trippe and Bill Allen had sat down like this. The two corporate chieftains had done this many times over the years, bluffing, trying to read each other's hand.

Sometimes Trippe and Allen bantered on the golf course in Greenwich, with no notes ever taken by a stenographer. They took fishing trips together in the Northwest, and again no record of their conversations ever reached paper. Trippe, the Great Dissembler, would tease Allen, the Montana lawyer, with his vague proposals.

"Would you build it if I bought it?" Trippe would ask.

"Would you buy it if I built it?" Allen would counter.

Eventually Allen tired of such recordless discussions. He learned to call Trippe back when he reached his office and go through their previous agenda—recording it all on tape.

Pan Am was Boeing's prime commercial customer. Back in 1939 the great flying boat the B-314 had been developed at Pan Am's behest. Only fourteen were built, and Boeing lost money on the project. Pan Am and TWA had been the only customers for the prewar B-307 Stratoliner, and again Boeing lost money. And Pan Am had been the main customer for the postwar B-377 Stratocruiser, a derivative of the B-29 bomber. Boeing's losses on that airplane were offset by Air Force orders for a tanker derivative.

Boeing had lost money on almost all of its deals with Pan Am. But by giving Pan Am the lead in new airline technology, Boeing had been able to drag the rest of the industry along. New orders flowed from other airline customers who were compelled to follow Pan Am's lead. Thus was Boeing ultimately able to rise from its well of red ink.

All this was in Bill Allen's mind now as he watched Trippe across his desk in Seattle.

Bill Allen was a conservative lawyer-businessman, responsible to his directors and shareholders. He was nearly the same age as Trippe. In appearance and demeanor, Bill Allen was a model of 1950s, Eisenhower-era probity—three-piece suits, receding hairline, an unshakable faith in American capitalism. It was said that Bill Allen placed his trust in only two professions: lawyers and engineers. He had little use for bankers.

Allen's forebears were Irish and Scottish. Throughout his life, Allen's two halves always seemed to be in conflict, the Irish side willing to take risks, the Scottish half balking at the outflow of corporate money.

Now his two halves were wrestling again. He thought it would be an unconscionable expense—and risk—to scrap the 707 prototype and redesign the jet on Trippe's terms. But Boeing couldn't afford to lose Pan Am's business.

Allen tried to read Juan Trippe's smiling face. *Was Trippe bluffing?*

Yes, decided Allen. *He's bluffing.* "We're sorry," Allen told Trippe. "Pan Am can have the 707 just the way it is. You'll have to take it or leave it."

Trippe left it. His next stop was Santa Monica. He put the same pressure on Donald Douglas. If Douglas didn't build the airplane Trippe wanted, someone else would. "Even if I have to go abroad," Trippe warned.

Donald Douglas was a pragmatic, Brooklyn-born Scot. He wanted to know the cost of everything. It was said that he kept an adding machine on his nightstand. He liked a sure thing, and his lineage of propeller-driven airliners—the DC-3 through the DC-7—had been very sure things. Douglas had sold more airliners than any other manufacturer in the world, and Pan American was one of his prime customers.

Douglas had balked at making the huge investment in a prototype jet as Boeing had done. He had less to lose now in a redesign of the DC-8, which so far existed only on paper. It *was* possible, he rationalized, to build a redesigned DC-8 around Trippe's J-75 engines. And if he wanted Pan American's business, that's what he would have to do.

Douglas caved in. He and Trippe shook hands. A *big* DC-8 would be built around Trippe's engines. Pan Am would buy twenty-four Douglas jets.

On his way out, Trippe had one more request: "Let's hold up the announcement for a while." Trippe wanted the deal kept secret. He wasn't through finagling.

He went back to Seattle. He sat down again across Bill Allen's desk, and this time he seemed to have given up on his unreasonable demand that Boeing redesign the prototype 707. Trippe told Allen that Pan American would order twenty-one of the *small* 707s, built around the undersized J-57 engines. The lawyers could go ahead and draw up the contract. Trippe and Allen shook hands on the deal. The first 707s would be delivered in the autumn of 1958.

When Trippe departed Seattle that day, Bill Allen was smiling. So were his vice presidents. So were his engineers. They were convinced that they had just captured the first customer for an American-built jet airliner. Best of all, they had outmaneuvered Juan Trippe.

Trippe had told them nothing about his deal with Donald Douglas.

Back in New York, Trippe quietly signed *both* contracts—Boeing and Douglas—on the same day. Neither manufacturer knew about the other's order from Pan Am.

A few days later, at the meeting of the International Air Transport Association on October 13, 1955, Trippe gave an introductory speech, talking vaguely about how mass travel by air would "prove to be more significant to world destiny than the atom bomb." That night he threw a party for the IATA executive committee at his Gracie Square apartment in Manhattan. Casually, moving through the crowd, all aviation industry chieftains, Trippe chatted with his guests. Oh, by the way, had they heard? Pan American had just bought . . . ummm, how many? . . . some *forty-five jet airliners.* Twenty-four of them were . . . . oh, yes, transoceanic models . . . built by Douglas, of course . . . with that new Pratt & Whitney engine. Wasn't that interesting?

The party was over.

Trippe's guests looked as if they had been gut-shot. They hit the sidewalk realizing that they had just been propelled—without being consulted—into the jet age.

It was painfully clear to them that every airline in America—*except Pan Am*—had invested heavily in the latest *propeller-driven* airliners. Pan Am had gone directly to jets. Their brand-new propeller machines had just become dinosaurs.

At Boeing the news flowed through the halls like a river of doom. The smiles were gone. From out of nowhere their archrival, Douglas, had grabbed the larger of the two orders—twenty-four versus Boeing's twenty-one. It no longer mattered that the Boeing product was sixteen months ahead of Douglas. Most important, Douglas was selling *long-range* jets to Pan Am. No other airline in the world would want the puny Boeing 707 when it could have the more powerful Douglas airplane. The DC-8, even before it was built, was putting the 707 out of business.

Historically, Boeing had always lost out to Douglas in the commercial airliner market. Since the thirties, when the DC-3 eclipsed the

Boeing product, the B-247, Douglas had managed to outsell Boeing.

Now it was happening again.

Bill Allen hated what he was about to do. He picked up the phone and called Juan Trippe.

Boeing would redesign the 707. Allen would be on the next airplane to New York to renegotiate the contract. Trippe could have his bigger airplanes. They would be super-707s, using the J-75 engine. They would be ten feet longer, would carry twenty-four more passengers, and would cross the North Atlantic nonstop.

Trippe could afford to be magnanimous. Pan Am would still take six of the smaller 707s—these were already in the works—and then seventeen of the big airplanes. The six smaller airplanes could be used to begin Pan Am's jet service, then be relegated to the Latin American operation later. He offered Allen a bonus of a quarter million dollars for each airplane that was delivered three months in advance of the contract date.

In his office in the Chrysler Building, Juan Trippe leaned back and savored the sweet taste of victory. He had just won the biggest gamble of his life.

CHAPTER FIVE

THE EMPIRE

Idlewild Airport, New York, October 26, 1958

The runway lights sped past in a blur, reflecting on the rain-slickened runway. Captain Sam Miller, Pan Am's chief pilot, watched the airspeed increase. *A hundred knots. A hundred and twenty . . .*

Miller nudged the yoke back. *Clipper America* tilted her nose upward and climbed into the overcast night sky.

It was the most-attended departure since the inaugural flight of the *China Clipper.* The press, television, radio, the public, the wellwishers, and the envious all turned out. It was the first transatlantic flight of a jetliner by an American airline.

Technically, jet transatlantic operations had been initiated by a BOAC Comet 4 three weeks earlier. But the Comet, as everyone knew, was not a transatlantic airliner and was merely filling in until BOAC received its own 707s in 1960.

Eight hours and forty-one minutes after the departure of *Clipper America,* including a fuel stop in Gander, the big jet touched down at Orly Airport in Paris.

Not everyone was overjoyed. Despite the hoopla, there were still those—Trippe's Primitives—who decried the event. Some were Pan American stockholders. The airline, they pointed out, still belonged to the stockholders, not to Mr. Trippe, who had just unilaterally placed orders for $269 million worth of hardware, most of it untested. And he had done this on a previous year's net earnings of only $10.4 million. They thought it was an act of egregious irresponsibility—a wild gamble—on the part of the chairman.

Trippe held his course. His confidence in the new jets—and in his own judgment—was total. The jets, he insisted, "were not a risk either from the money side or the flying side."

As it turned out, he was right. During the first quarter of the next year, Pan Am's 707s and DC-8s carried 33,400 passengers with a 90.8 percent seat occupancy—an all-time record. During the next five years, overseas traffic doubled. Pan Am's operating revenues swelled to over half a billion dollars.

Pan American World Airways would enter the jet age with a decade's lead on its competitors. And with this victory behind him, the Supreme Skygod was emboldened to gamble again.

With his fleet of jetliners taking to the skies, Juan Trippe's thoughts turned to more earthly forms of glory. He was thinking about a new headquarters for his burgeoning empire. Somewhere there ought to be a fitting monument to America's Imperial Airline. And, of course, to Juan Trippe.

But where?

Over the years there had been talk about Pan Am's leaving New York. Such suggestions always came from some brash new staffer who pointed to the advantages of operating in labor-friendlier and tax-freer regions of the country. Older executives, more interested in maintaining the connection between their heads and shoulders, instinctively headed for cover when the subject came up. They knew that Trippe treated all such cockamamie proposals with a meat cleaver.

New York was Skygod country. Let the others go to the provinces, figured Trippe. It was okay for an airline like American, which was run by the folksy Texan C. R. Smith, to move to Dallas. And it probably made sense for a blue-collar domestic like United to base itself in Chicago. And even though TWA had international routes, the airline was still, in Trippe's view, a Midwest company perfectly suited to a flatland hamlet like Kansas City.

Pan American World Airways was quite another matter. It was unthinkable that the Imperial Airline's headquarters would grace the skyline of any metropolis but New York. And that was the end of that.

The problem was, Pan Am had occupied the same offices in the

Chrysler Building for nearly thirty years and had outgrown them. The lease was due to expire in the early 1960s, and Trippe didn't want to renew it. But no other suitable home in New York had been found.

At the end of the fifties, a promoter named Erwin Wolfson was touting a spectacular new business complex for Manhattan. Wolfson's structure would be the largest corporate office building ever built. In his proposal, the ultramodern building would rise from the foot of Park Avenue, straddling the railroad tracks just to the south of Grand Central Terminal.

Wolfson needed a single tenant, a corporation of great size and image, to underwrite the project by leasing a number of floors. Already he had been turned down by several megacorporations, including General Motors and IBM. When Wolfson heard that Pan Am might be looking for a new home, he tried to arrange an appointment with Juan Trippe.

It was well known that of all the species of businessperson that Trippe disliked, real estate promoters ranked near the top. Trippe refused to see Wolfson. Wolfson tried every connection he had.

"Can you get me in to see Trippe?" he asked a vice president.

"Trippe?" said the executive. "Hell, I've been trying for six months to see him myself."

This went on for some weeks. And then the promoter persuaded a New York banker named Henry Brunie, who was closely acquainted with Trippe, to write a letter detailing the proposed new building. Trippe read the letter. Then he read it again. He called Brunie to ask several questions about the new building. But he flatly refused to talk to a promoter like Wolfson.

Wolfson was a man as persistent as Trippe was obstinate. He asked Brunie to approach Trippe once again and ask him to relent. They could be of service to each other. But it was essential that they meet face to face.

By then Trippe's interest had been stirred. He finally agreed to meet Wolfson. But the meeting had to be absolutely secret, and it must be after hours, so as to appear purely social. The two men met in the Cloud Club atop the Chrysler Building, after its normal closing time. Trippe was in his old conspiratorial role. Before they discussed anything, he gave the promoter a stern warning: If any word of their meeting leaked out, the discussions would end instantly.

There were more meetings, all conducted with the secrecy of the D-Day invasion. Wolfson's files on the Pan Am subject were labeled "Project X." Pan American was "Prince Albert." Trippe himself took the code name "Traveler."

All the while a grandiose image was forming in Trippe's imagination. He visualized a magnificent edifice—*his* building—festooned with the Pan American logo, thrusting upward in the heart of New York City. It would be wonderful! It would be an inescapable daily irritant in the eyes of the Primitives.

As the details were hammered out, it became clear that Trippe, who had shown little previous interest in architecture, was determined to put his stamp on the new building. The basic design pleased him, but he wanted the axis of the building rotated ninety degrees. The rooftop would have to be designed as a landing site for helicopters. And, by the way, he wanted the round Pan Am logo and the name Pan Am displayed in letters thirty feet high on all four sides of the building.

At this the architects and promoters lowered their notepads. They stared at each other. *Thirty feet high?* Well, now, let's wait a minute. There was already going to be quite enough flak from New York preservationists about the building's antitraditional shape. Then to turn a Manhattan skyscraper into a billboard . . . perhaps we should think that one over. . . .

That wasn't all. Trippe announced that he intended to pay a third less rent than the going rate in New York. And, oh, yes, he wanted an equity stake in the building.

What the hell? The promoters put down their pads and took another look at the angelically smiling, soft-spoken airline executive. They were beginning to get the picture. This guy Trippe was trying to set the deal up so that he would eventually own the whole damn package.

The Great Dissembler, the first airline tycoon, had metamorphosed into a hard-bargaining real estate tycoon. Pan Am's lease document filled a hundred pages. At a cost of $1 million Trippe captured a 10 percent equity in the project, with an option to increase the holding, a stake that would reap enormous dividends for Pan Am in the future. Pan Am would occupy nine full floors as well as a huge sales office on the sidewalk level. The lease was to run for thirty years with renewal options for ten-year periods. The total rental amounted to $115.5 million. It was the largest commercial lease ever signed for a Manhattan building.

On the matter of the PAN AM sign and logo, Trippe relented—but only a little. Instead of letters thirty feet high, he would settle for fifteen.

Over the next three years Manhattanites watched the building rise on their island. The chief architectural consultants were the great Walter Gropius of Bauhaus fame and Pietro Belluschi of M.I.T. When the Pan Am Building was dedicated in March 1963, Governor Nelson Rockefeller felt inspired to call it "a symbol of the genius and creativity of the free enterprise system."

Old-line New Yorkers had other names for it: "arrogant, oversize intruder," "Gropius fiasco," a "monument to greed and irresponsibility."

Trippe loved it. It was the sound of the Primitives gnashing their teeth.

He moved into his new office on the forty-sixth floor. He indulged himself by retiring his old rolltop and acquiring a great mahogany presidential desk. He had a splendid view of the great city beneath him.

CHAPTER SIX

THE MAN FROM CAMELOT

The Primitives were at it again.

Juan Trippe glowered at the newspapers on his desk. It was the spring of 1963, and both the *Wall Street Journal* and the *New York Times* had come out against the allocation of any more development funds for the SST—America's supersonic transport. In Washington a speech had been delivered by Senator William Proxmire, congressional budget bloodhound, demanding that SST development funds be shriveled from $280 million to $80 million. To Proxmire and his disciples, the SST was a boondoggle—another fleecing of the taxpayers for the further enrichment of American big business.

Such thinking incensed Trippe. The backward-thinking, naysaying Primitives! It was just like the 707 project. Hadn't he been proved correct in his determination to commence all-jet service?

Now it was the supersonic transport.

To Juan Trippe the SST amounted to more than just another pointy-nosed airplane that flew faster than sound. This was *the sound barrier*. There was magic to the idea. Supersonic flight was the final frontier in the earth's atmosphere. After that came space travel. Never mind the arguments, the economics, the risks of such an adventure. In Juan Trippe's mind, the SST represented America's—and Pan American's—destiny.

He had thrown himself into the fray with all his old passion. He was determined that there *would*, by God, be an SST, and Pan Am would fly it. Why? Because it was what Juan Trippe wanted.

The trouble was, time was running out. The SST had become a seasonal political issue. Here was Proxmire ranting about the unfairness of it all to the poor innocent taxpayers. The planet people were howling about ghastly airport noise and sonic booms and damage to the stratosphere. The liberals were wringing their hands over the notion of the elite and privileged flying in a billion-dollar airplane at the expense of America's poor and disenfranchised. At the same time, the President, John F. Kennedy, was taking heat from the bean counters in Washington, who wanted to spend America's money on a host of new social programs as well as some expensive items of Cold War hardware.

Trippe was even getting flak from America's greatest hero.

Of all people, Charles Lindbergh, *Pan Am's technical consultant*, had gone public with his feelings about the SST. It would be a disaster, the Lone Eagle was telling anyone who would listen. "It doesn't make sense," he said. Such an airplane had to be narrow and pencil-shaped to achieve supersonic speeds. You couldn't make money with the minuscule passenger loads at such a high operating cost.

But Lindbergh's real concern wasn't so much for engineering problems. Now he was worried about the environment. In his later years, Lindbergh was becoming a technological conscientious objector. He didn't think the planet needed sonic booms reverberating across its surface. The upper atmosphere didn't need any more holes punched in it by planeloads of high rollers who wanted to do business on both sides of the ocean the same morning.

People thought the great Lindbergh might be going a bit dotty. He had been heard saying things like "If I could choose between birds and airplanes, I'd choose birds." *Birds?* Lindbergh wasn't even sure anymore that the airplane had been a very good idea. The world would probably be better off without it.

This was *Lindbergh* talking? The world's most famous aviator? Well, it *did* seem a bit queer. . . .

Trippe listened to Lindbergh's admonitions. He did what he always did when Lindbergh went out on a limb. He ignored him.

Juan Trippe was sixty-three, and there was much left to do. Before he left the stage he intended to equip Pan American for the next century.

It was time to go shopping. Trippe had already learned with the jets and the J-75 engine that to get what he wanted here in the United States, he sometimes had to start overseas.

With his technical entourage—John Borger, successor to Priester, and Scott Flower, his chief pilot in charge of technical matters—he journeyed to London. There they were driven to the British Aircraft Corporation facility, where they gazed at the mockup of the supersonic Concorde. Then in Toulouse, at Sud-Aviation, they saw the actual airframe coming to life on the assembly line. The Concorde was real. The British and French had set aside a millennium of rivalry to pioneer a bold new era in transportation.

Trippe needed no more convincing. The United States could not afford to lose its leadership in aviation. America needed an SST of its own. And standing there on the factory floor, gazing at the needle-nosed Concorde, Juan Trippe thought of a way he might make it happen.

The SST had already lived and died—on paper—several times.

In 1959, during the Eisenhower administration, Federal Aviation Administrator Pete Quesada had proposed that $2 million be allocated to the development of an SST. The technology, it was assumed, would evolve from the experimental B-70 supersonic bomber being built by the military aircraft manufacturer North American. At Lockheed's famous "skunk works," where futuristic airplanes like the P-38 and the U-2 and the F-104 had been created, preliminary sketches were already rendered for a supersonic airliner. But Quesada's proposal drowned in the muddy waters of the Defense Department and the Eisenhower cabinet.

Then came young blood. The Kennedy administration replaced Quesada with a former test pilot named Najeeb Halaby. In addition to heading the Federal Aviation Agency, Halaby would be aviation adviser to Kennedy.

Kennedy viewed aerospace competition in terms of national prestige. The massive cost of landing a man on the moon made sense to a leader like Kennedy, because it would be *an American* planting the flag. The home team would win. There was glory to be gained, and for Kennedy that was reason enough.

The British and French were collaborating on the Concorde, a supersonic airplane that embodied the prestige and aspirations and egos of a rising European community—and particularly the hopes of a Frenchman named Charles de Gaulle. To further heat up the competition, the Soviet Union was constructing its own SST, the TU-144, a Concorde look-alike.

Kennedy's problem was largely bureaucratic: how to bring all the warring parties together in a joint *commercial* effort of this size. Government agencies, by their nature, didn't care whether an airplane used only by commercial airlines ever got built. Nothing of the immensity of the SST program had ever been undertaken by a consortium of private industry and public agencies.

Who would pay for it? The manufacturers—Lockheed, Douglas, North American, Boeing—were not able to absorb the huge research and development cost. Nor were the airlines.

That left the government. But Kennedy's own administration was divided over the SST. Robert McNamara, Secretary of Defense, was opposed to any purely commercial supersonic development. Advances in aviation, he thought, ought to be spin-offs from a military program. A large segment of Congress, led by Senator Proxmire, derided the project as a bottomless hole for taxpayers' money.

In the spring of 1963, Kennedy appointed the FAA administrator, Jeeb Halaby, as the point man in the SST effort. Halaby made his rounds, trying to line up promises. One of the promises he wanted was from Juan Trippe.

Kennedy had never trusted Juan Trippe. He already knew about Trippe's interest in the Concorde. A move by Pan Am to order a *foreign* supersonic transport would be taken by the rest of the world as an indication that the American aviation industry acted without any direction or policy guidance from its own government. It would give the appearance that the President could not make a decision to build an American SST, and Pan Am, therefore, had to go overseas.

There was also a history of bad blood between the Kennedys and Juan Trippe. In the thirties the patriarch, Joseph P. Kennedy, headed the powerful Maritime Commission. Kennedy had tried to bring all American overseas commerce—not only the shipping lines but international air carriers—under the regulatory control of his commission. Pan American happened to be the only American overseas airline, and Kennedy was opposed to any such monopoly in international commerce. Trippe had fought back, using all Pan Am's political clout in Washington to effect passage of the 1938 Civil Aeronautics Act, which snatched control of the airlines away from Kennedy's commission and gave it to a separate agency.

Joe Kennedy was an important figure in the Democratic Party and had been a heavy contributor to the campaigns of Franklin Roosevelt. He was now Juan Trippe's implacable enemy. And, by extension, so was the President of the United States.

Old Joe was still around. The Kennedys, everyone said, had long memories.

On JFK's orders, Halaby called Trippe, reminding him that the President was on the verge of making a decision about the SST. Would he please defer any announcement about Pan Am's intentions?

Trippe agreed. Or, at least, Halaby *thought* he agreed.

On Monday morning, Halaby arrived in New York for a meeting. "Would you care to comment on Pan Am's Concorde order, Mr. Halaby?"

What Pan Am order? Halaby had no idea what the reporter was talking about.

The announcement had been made in Paris that morning. Pan Am was buying six Concordes. Why, the reporters wanted to know, did an American airline have to go overseas for the next generation of airliner?

In less than an hour, Halaby was standing in Trippe's anteroom on the forty-sixth floor of the newly occupied Pan Am Building. Trippe's secretary, Kathleen Clair, said Mr. Halaby had a phone call. "It's the White House."

Kennedy was on the line. His language was vivid. Why had Trippe, the sonofabitch, double-crossed them? And why hadn't Halaby made it clear to him what was at stake?

Halaby said he would get to the bottom of it.

Another phone call. "It's the Vice President," said the secretary.

Lyndon Johnson was just as mad as Kennedy. Halaby told him the same thing he'd told Kennedy.

Finally, out from his sanctum came the Imperial Skygod. Trippe was smiling.

Halaby, who had just gotten a tongue-lashing from the President of the United States, and then another from the Vice President, spoke his mind. "You've double-crossed us, Mr. Trippe."

"I didn't announce the contract," Trippe said. "It was given by the French prematurely."

"As soon as you signed the contract, there was danger of a leak. You never told us you were going through with the signing. You promised to postpone any action."

The Great Dissembler shook his head. No, that hadn't been the understanding. Halaby must have misunderstood his original promise. Anyway, didn't he see? It was the *French* who had jumped the gun.

Halaby said he wanted to use the telephone. While Trippe watched, fascinated, Halaby snatched up the phone and called the White House. Within seconds he had the President on the line. Standing there in Trippe's presence, Halaby repeated what Trippe had just told him.

The President wasn't buying it. As far as he was concerned, Trippe was up to his old stunts. He told Halaby to pass on a message: "Tell Mr. Trippe we will not forget this."

Three days later, Miss Clair set the *New York Times* and the *Wall Street Journal* on Juan Trippe's desk. He found the text of the President's speech on page five of the *Journal*. At the graduation-day ceremonies at the Air Force Academy, Kennedy had announced a "new program, in partnership with private industry, to develop at the earliest possible date the prototype of a commercially successful supersonic transport."

Trippe liked the part about "in partnership with private industry." The Primitives were beginning to get the message.

For Trippe it amounted to an interim victory. He had the Concorde order in his pocket, and he had used it to catalyze the American SST project. It was classic Trippe gamesmanship, playing one side against the other, forcing them to do what needed doing.

The only problem had been that nastiness with Kennedy. *Tell Mr. Trippe we will not forget this.* But that was politics. Politicians were transient. Over the years he had taken heat from Presidents. FDR hated his guts, but that hadn't stopped him. Truman had blocked him from establishing a single United States international airline. And even Eisenhower, a Republican, had ignored Pan Am's petitions for domestic routes. But Trippe had outlasted all of them. He would outlast this one too.

It wasn't Kennedy's message that surprised Juan Trippe; it was the messenger. Halaby had picked up the phone and called the President. Just like that. Right there in Trippe's office. This fellow Halaby had the ear of the President of the United States anytime he wanted it.

If anything impressed Juan Trippe, it was power. This young man, the self-assured emissary of the President, reeked of raw, high-octane, Washingtonian power. It was just what Pan Am had been lacking.

Already Trippe had forgotten his clash with the President of the United States. He was thinking of how he was going to hire Najeeb Halaby.

It's a joke, thought Najeeb Halaby. The word was filtering back that Juan Trippe, the chief of Pan Am, had somehow become convinced that he, Halaby, was a power broker in Washington. Trippe considered Halaby to be the wielder of enormous clout in the Democratic administration.

By 1965 it was no secret that Halaby was leaving his post as FAA administrator. Being a career public servant was not his ambition, and he had never intended to stay beyond the first four years. The joke was that by quitting, he was more of an outsider than if he had never visited Washington. Lyndon Johnson's famous vindictiveness was especially aimed at Kennedy appointees like Halaby who jumped ship. Halaby's days of influence in the White House were over.

But Trippe wanted him. And Halaby needed a job. The problem was, the job he wanted was presently filled by the Supreme Skygod himself.

In his next meeting with Trippe, Halaby asked whether, if he were to take a job with Pan American, he could expect to succeed Trippe as CEO of Pan Am.

The Great Dissembler flashed the angelic smile and sidestepped. There was no timetable for his own retirement, he said. Maybe in a year or so. Maybe not. Anyway, he owed it to his faithful lieutenant, Harold Gray, who was currently the company's president, to give him a shot at the CEO's job before he retired. But that didn't mean that Halaby, too, wouldn't be given his own chance at the top job.

In other words, maybe. Maybe not.

Halaby had already heard insiders say that Trippe would *never* retire. They would carry him out of his office in a coffin. And Gray, who was only sixty-two, would be around for a long time.

All this went through Halaby's mind during the summer of 1965. After a career in bureaucratic Washington, he wanted to try his hand running a real airline. And what more glamorous or prestigious airline was there than Pan Am?

So he signed on. He would serve as a senior vice president with a seat on the board and a place on the executive committee. His salary would amount to $87,000 per year plus an incentive compensation of $50,000 the first year, and options for 25,000 shares of stock at $71 per share.

Halaby had reason to be pleased. It seemed that he, a Californian, the son of an immigrant, and a Democrat, was gaining admission to an elite old Eastern Republican club.

He would soon realize that he hadn't even gotten in the front door.

It was easy to understand Trippe's interest in Najeeb Halaby. Halaby possessed impressive—even Skygodly—credentials. He was articulate and suavely handsome. A graduate of Stanford and Yale Law School, he had the unique qualifications of being both an attorney and a test pilot.

Since the age of sixteen, when he learned to fly, he had been smitten with the mystique of flight. While still a young lawyer at the beginning of World War II, he went to work as a test pilot for Lockheed, where he eventually performed high-altitude research with the P-38 Lightning. Commissioned as a naval officer, he flew high-speed dive tests for Navy fighters, pushing them up against the then mysterious sound barrier, where prop-driven airplanes began to act crazy and shed their parts. He tested every new airplane in the Navy's inventory, including the experimental Bell YP-59A and a captured German Messerschmitt 262.

After the war, Halaby went to work in Washington. He held posts with the State Department, including an assignment in Saudi Arabia. He served under the brilliant but quirky James Forrestal in the newly established Defense Department. He survived into the Eisenhower era, despite his political credentials, and worked for "Engine Charlie" Wilson, Ike's Secretary of Defense.

In the mid-fifties, Halaby decided he needed to make some money—always a nagging consideration for public servants—and left government to work for Laurance Rockefeller in a variety of assignments. For a while he oversaw Rockefeller's interest in Eastern Airlines, then run by the irascible Eddie Rickenbacker. He was tapped in 1955 to join a task force to investigate the civil airways and airports mess in the United States, an investigation which led eventually to the establishment of the Federal Aviation Agency.

As FAA administrator, Jeeb Halaby was highly visible. He decentralized Quesada's monolithic agency. He was immediately on the scene at aircraft accidents. He tried out skydiving to determine whether the sport needed regulation. He personally test-flew new production airplanes. He even flew the FAA's Grumman Gulfstream himself to official appointments. Jeeb Halaby, everyone said, was a rising star.

His first day at Pan Am was a disaster. Then it got worse.

Halaby was introduced to the company officers at the traditional Monday lunch in the Sky Club. Trippe presided at the head of the long table, surrounded by his court. Halaby, the newcomer, sat at the opposite end. Most of the executives had already read a leaked newspaper story about Halaby's hiring.

A piece had appeared in the business press the day before, prior to the official announcement of Halaby's appointment, stating that Halaby had been hired as a senior vice president by Pan American. The story added that Halaby was Trippe's "heir apparent."

It didn't matter whether the item was true or not. It landed like a stink bomb on the forty-sixth floor.

Now Halaby, the "heir apparent," was meeting his new colleagues. Few handshakes were proffered. Introductions were perfunctory. The glacial expressions sent an unmistakable message: *You carpetbagging, publicity-chasing sonofabitch.*

Okay, thought Halaby. It was going to take a while for the ice to melt. In the meantime, he would try to learn what his job was.

And that turned out to be his biggest problem. What *was* his job? The upper echelon of executives closed ranks around the tribal elder, Harold Gray. They seemed to have made the tacit decision to exclude the carpetbagger, Halaby, from the day-to-day operational affairs of the airline.

The same newspaper piece that leaked word of Halaby's recruitment had also reported that he would run the airline's hotel subsidiary, the Intercontinental Hotel chain. This item sent Trippe's old classmate and business associate John Gates, who *did* run the hotel chain, roaring into Trippe's office threatening to resign.

So Trippe had to do something with the new vice president. But what? None of his executives wanted him on their floor. Well, how about putting him in charge of the Guided Missiles Range Division? That was far enough away from headquarters. And how about the Business Jet Division? And the helicopter operation that Pan Am was sponsoring in metropolitan New York? *That* surely would keep the newcomer out of everyone's hair.

The result was that Halaby had no direct role in the airline operation. He bit his tongue and did his job. People would ask him what his new title was. "Vice President, Miscellaneous," he would say.

Then one day Trippe came up with a new assignment. "Would you mind going down to Washington to see about something?"

Washington? Halaby knew what that meant. Lobbying. Now he was supposed to wield his "influence" with LBJ and the Democrats. So *that* was the reason he had been hired.

CHAPTER SEVEN

NEW HIRES

new hire \'n(y)u 'hīr\ *n* **1** : bottom stratum of aeronautical hierarchy **2** : lowest form of human life (in a cockpit)

The ship sailed into the void of space. On the sound track you heard Strauss's Blue Danube. *Stars glittered in the background like jewels on black velvet.*

The interior of the vessel had typical passenger accommodations —safety harnesses and handrails and a zero-gravity lavatory. There were instructions on the door for passengers who had never used a zero-gravity lavatory. Using a toilet in space took some getting used to.

The stewardess appeared, offering cocktails. That, too, took some getting used to, talking to someone who seemed to be inverted, or sideways. In space there wasn't any up or down. The stewardess wore "grip shoes," which allowed her to walk up, down, across—it didn't matter—through the weightless cabin.

It was a two-stage journey. In this ship you flew to a huge, rotating station, deep in space. From there you made the final short hop to the moon base in a round lunar landing machine.

For the earth-to-space flight, your ship had wings, which it needed for the takeoff and landing back on the planet. But the ship's most distinguishing feature, at least if you were seeing it close up for the first time, was the emblem emblazoned on the hull. The distinctive round blue logo made this vehicle instantly recognizable. You could

*see that it was a Clipper Ship—a commercial spacegoing vessel of Pan
American World Airways. . . .*

Every new-hire Pan Am pilot went to see the movie. *2001: A Space
Odyssey* was a fantasy created by writer Arthur C. Clarke and director
Stanley Kubrick. In 1968, no one had yet flown to the moon, nor was
anyone seriously thinking about *commercial* lunar flight. But it was
assumed, even in science fiction, that if anyone were to fly a scheduled
lunar service, it would be, of course, Pan Am.

What the new hires liked so much about *2001* wasn't the film's
special effects, although they were pretty terrific for 1968. What impressed them was the depiction of the commercial flight to the moon.
It validated their reason for being where they were—flying for Pan
American World Airways.

It was the beginning of Rob Martinside's third week with Pan Am.
At eight in the morning his class trooped into the classroom on the
second floor of the big Pan Am hangar at San Francisco Airport. They
had begun to sort themselves out by background and proclivity. They
learned that each fell into one of two groups: Airplane Heads and the
Accidentals.

The Accidentals were the larger group. They were there because
of a fluke in history: the Red Menace. They were kids of the fifties
and sixties who had grown up *knowing* they would be summoned to
join the holy war against communism. In those days, you volunteered
or you were drafted. Going to college provided, at best, a deferral.

Most had signed up for military flight training as an alternative to
a foxhole or a destroyer deck. A pilot was at least an officer, not a
faceless grunt. Instead of pushing a mop or carrying a carbine, he was
trained to fly the military's most expensive machinery.

And then an astonishing thing happened. They found that they
liked flying airplanes. Even more astonishingly, it turned out that they
could actually make a career of it. Waiting out there for them was a
plethora of airline flying jobs.

So they became airline pilots. Most did it for no other reason than
that it was a hell of a good job. It was something they were already
trained to do, and it beat trying to start a career with a five-year-old
degree in history or forestry. As an airline pilot in 1965 you could

make as much as $40,000 a year, about the same as an admiral or general in the military and more than most of the vice presidents of the airlines. You had a generous retirement plan, medical insurance, free travel, job security. You got half of each month off—time enough to play golf, ski, fish, coach Little League, teach Sunday school, stay up late and drink.

Sure, they knew about seniority lists, knew they would have to start at the bottom. They wouldn't be making the big bucks for a while. But the way the airlines were growing, it wouldn't take long. . . .

For the other group—the Airplane Heads—the job meant something else. They were there to *fly airplanes.* That was their life. Benefits, pay, time off—well, that was nice, but what it meant was that you had the time and money to mess with airplanes on your days off.

Typically, the Airplane Heads were kids who grew up building balsa airplane models. They collected comic books—Smilin' Jack, Steve Canyon, Terry and the Pirates. They soloed when they were sixteen at the crop duster strip on the edge of town. They *joined* the military to get into flight training. The draft and the Red Menace had nothing to do with it. They went because that's where the hot airplanes were.

Jim Wood was one of the Airplane Heads. Wood was a tall, woolly-haired young man who laughed in a high-pitched cackle. By the time Wood finished college and entered Air Force pilot training, he had constructed, all from kitless raw materials, 232 model airplanes. He learned to fly before he had a driver's license. Along with his degree in aeronautical engineering, he possessed an encyclopedic knowledge of military airplane trivia. Wood could recite the range, top speed, weight, and engine thrust of every fighter plane in service. More than anything else, Wood had wanted to be a fighter pilot.

When he finished pilot school at the top of his class, he should have gone directly to fighter training. He had every reason to expect an assignment to F-86s or F-100s or maybe an interceptor squadron that flew F-106s or F-101s.

But an odd thing was happening in the Air Force. In the early 1960s it was run by a jowly World War II bomber pilot, General

Curtis LeMay. LeMay liked to remind unwary America that the Red Menace was still out there, more evil and cunning than ever. America's first line of defense was SAC—the Strategic Air Command, LeMay's armada of bombers poised to strike the Soviets. Because SAC's mission was so important, LeMay demanded that the top graduates of Air Force flight schools be assigned to his bomber squadrons.

That included Jim Wood. Instead of strapping into single-engine, single-piloted fighters as he had always expected when he graduated from flight training, he would be a bomber pilot.

And then when he reported for duty at the remote air base in Idaho called Mountain Home, he learned the rest of the terrible truth: *He wouldn't even be a bomber pilot.* Wood was assigned as a copilot in KC-97 tankers. KC-97s were lumbering, four-engine derivatives of the World War II B-29. They weren't even jets! They were propeller-driven gas trucks whose job was to pump kerosene to LeMay's bombers on their way to pulverize the Red Menace.

For three and a half years, Wood did this, droning around the globe in a tanker, reeking of kerosene, hating every day of it. When he drove his Aston Martin out the main gate of Mountain Home Air Force Base for the last time, he was on his way to San Francisco and his new career as a pilot with Pan American.

The trouble with the military, in Rob Martinside's opinion, was that you were supposed to perform duties besides flying. You were a personnel officer, or an ordnance officer, or a maintenance officer. You were supposed to be promoted up the hierarchical pyramid until you commanded something, a squadron or a carrier or an air base.

That was the trouble with the Navy. They were always confusing what was important—strapping into an F-8 and scorching a hole straight up into the ozone layer—with trivial jobs like personnel administration and matériel accounting. Why didn't they just leave fighter pilots alone and let them be fighter pilots?

Another thing Martinside noticed: After they promoted you out of a flying slot, they got rid of you. Martinside knew Navy commanders and captains in their early forties, already judged too old to fly, who were forced to retire. In their new civvies they hit the street, looking uncertain and out of place, searching for something to do with the rest of their lives. Some became real estate agents or insurance salesmen.

Rob Martinside fell squarely into the Airplane Head category. He grew up in middle America, in a dusty Kansas town called Coffeyville.

One afternoon when he was twelve, riding his bicycle to school, Martinside saw a low-flying, straight-winged, two-engine jet bomber pass over town. A *jet!* Martinside had never seen such a thing up close.

This one—the boy knew it was a North American B-45—was clearly in trouble. It passed over Coffeyville at about three thousand feet, descending, headed for the unused World War II air base five miles outside of town.

To hell with school, the boy decided. He pedaled off in the direction of the airfield.

He was the first one there. The jet was parked on an old concrete ramp. Two men kneeled under a wing.

"Hey, kid," said one of the pilots. He wore a khaki flight suit. His hard flying helmet, which looked like a gladiator's headgear, was positioned on the rail of the cockpit canopy. "What's this place called?"

"Coffeyville," said the kid.

"Coffeyville?" said the pilot. He looked at a navigation chart. "Shit."

"See?" said the other pilot. He pointed to the spot on the chart. "I told you."

"We lost an engine," said the first pilot. "Had to come down somewhere. This was it."

The boy didn't take his eyes off the silver-skinned jet. He walked around the airplane. He touched the aluminum skin, smelled the sensuous burnt-rubber-kerosene-hot-metal smell. He felt the heat waves still shimmering from the engine tailpipe.

And then the pilot uttered the magic words that since the dawn of flight had turned kids into bona fide Airplane Heads: *Want to see the cockpit, kid?*

Charlie Scroggin was the only one in the class who owed nothing to the Red Menace. He was neither an authentic Airplane Head nor an Accidental. Charlie had come up the hard way, as a civilian-trained pilot who bought all his licenses.

Before he flew airplanes, Charlie raised pigs. When Charlie married his wife, Sue, her family set them up with a farm. Farming in eastern Oregon meant raising pigs. It rained a lot where Charlie and Sue lived, and after a rain the earth took on a gluelike, oozy consistency that would try to suck the rubber boots off your feet. It was like walking in soft cement.

Charlie was still in his twenties, raising pigs, when he was first tantalized by the notion that there might be something else. Sue's brother, Rod, was a pilot who flew for United Airlines. Though Charlie knew nothing about airplanes or flying, he noticed that his brother-in-law seemed to have a great deal of time on his hands and lived comfortably. And he had nothing to do with farming.

All this was on Charlie's mind one day as he stood in a cold Oregon drizzle, his feet mired in the trampled earth of his farm. Around him, his pigs wallowed in the slime. Charlie thought about his brother-in-law. He tried to imagine the clean, warm environment of an airliner cockpit. He looked at his pigs.

A thought struck Charlie like a thunderclap: *I hate these fucking pigs!*

It was a pivotal moment in his life. Charlie turned his back on the animals and, being careful not to lose a boot in the goo, stalked away from the pigpen. He never looked back. He was able to borrow enough money to enroll in a commercial flying course in Eugene.

As it turned out, he had a natural talent for flying. When Charlie finished flying school and had earned his commercial, instrument, instructor's, and multiengine ratings, he stayed on as a flight instructor. At the same time he found employment with a local charter flying company. He accumulated nearly three thousand hours of flying time. And though the odds were against Charlie Scroggin, history took a turn in his favor. The airlines were hiring.

Charlie applied to several, including Pan Am. At the interview they asked him why he wanted to work for Pan Am. Charlie told them about the farm and his brother-in-law and how much he hated pigs.

The crusty old interviewers, all three of them, stared over their half-frames at the young man. He was the only nonmilitary pilot they had interviewed that day. They had never heard such a story. Then the interviewers broke up laughing.

It was the beginning of Charlie Scroggin's career as an airline pilot.

*   *   *

The entrails of a Boeing 707, in multicolored schematic detail, covered the wall of the classroom.

". . . three thousand pounds pressure comes out here and fills that accumulator over here, and then this valve lets the fluid . . ."

Rob Martinside tried to pay attention. It was the sixth day of 707 systems training. They'd had the electrical system and the fuel system, and now they were hearing the nonstop, unexpurgated saga of the Boeing hydraulic system.

The instructor was a pale, wispy-haired man named Ivan White. He had a voice like a twenty-eight-volt motor. White's monotone never varied by as much as a kilocycle as he droned through the entire journey of the airplane's hydraulic fluid from its reservoir to the engine and electric-driven pumps, to the accumulators, and onward to the brakes, flaps, landing gear, and control actuators. As he spoke, he traced the route of the hydraulic fluid on the wall chart with his collapsible pointer.

". . . and when the pressure here gets to thirty-three hundred pounds, this valve thinks it's time to open up and relieve all that load, so . . ."

Thinks? They heard a lot of that in systems training—parts of an airplane becoming sensate, valves *thinking* this and that, switches *deciding* to open and close, sensors *saying*, Hey, I'm too hot or cold. Martinside wanted to ask how a valve could think. If a valve really did think, what did it think about?

Ivan White was a nice guy, despite his terminal dullness. He had been teaching ground school too long. Perhaps as much as thirty years too long, most of his students figured. White liked to let his class know that he had begun working for Pan American as a mechanic at the old Alameda seaplane base, across San Francisco Bay, back in the *China Clipper* days. No one doubted him.

Another instructor, Fred Tubbs, was in charge of emergency equipment training. Tubbs had an intimate knowledge of *every* catastrophe that had ever visited a Pan American airplane. He not only knew the cause of each accident, from flying boats to jets, he could give an account of the extent of the mayhem, complete with vivid photographs of shredded, pulverized, and roasted human flesh. This part he liked to save until after lunch.

Tubbs had a statistician's feel for the inevitable. "Two of you," he told the class, "will be involved in the crash of a Pan Am airplane."

Even those in the back row raised their heads.

"One of you," said Tubbs, "will not survive. Would you like to know why?"

They wanted very much to know why. Every head now had a forward tilt.

And then Tubbs went into his routine about life vests, fire extinguishers, first-aid kits, smoke goggles, escape slides, oxygen bottles. He had a story to go with each item. It saved lives, he told them. It might save theirs.

For ditching and evacuation training, they went to the mock-up room where actual escape slides and an emergency raft were set up. They practiced sliding down the chutes. They set up the raft and climbed in. It didn't matter to Tubbs that no commercial jet had ever actually ditched at sea. "It's going to happen," he declared with absolute conviction. "It's just a matter of time. And you may be aboard."

This was good stuff, the students agreed. Fred Tubbs knew how to make death and mayhem great fun.

New hire.

No one could remember seeing such a creature at Pan Am, at least not since the mid-fifties, which was the last time the company had hired any new pilots. The years 1955 to 1964 had been the doldrums of the airline business, when the industry was agonizing over turboprops versus real jets and it still took twelve hours' flying time to cross the Atlantic.

And then came the jets. Waves of new pilots landed on Pan Am property like boatloads of immigrants. No one quite knew how to regard them.

They soon got used to the treatment. *New hires.* They were called that by their instructors, by the secretaries, by the food servers in the company cafeteria. The appellation was neither affectionate nor derisive. It was purely a business label. It meant that they resided on the bottom of the seniority list, made less money than the janitors, could be fired for *any* transgression, and were the lowest form of life in a cockpit.

The lucky ones, like Ron Taft and Connie Smith, had wives who earned a salary. Barbara Taft was a nurse—ex–Air Force, where Ron had met her—and her take-home at the local hospital amounted to over twice what he made at Pan Am. Jean Smith was a librarian. She earned enough to allow the Smiths to live in a real house, unlike most of the apartment-dwelling new hires.

The starting salary was a joke. No one could live in San Francisco on $500 a month, not even in the mid-sixties. Pan Am took the position that if you *really* wanted to work for the world's most experienced airline, you first had to demonstrate some humility. You had to wallow in a little squalor before you flew with the Skygods.

It was especially hard on the wives. They yearned for the good times back in the military when they were *somebody*—when they shopped in the PX and dressed up for officers' club functions and the sentries saluted *them* when they drove onto the base.

Now they were anonymous nobodies. Even other Pan Am people ignored them. A yawning social chasm lay between the wives of the old-time "real" Pan Am pilots and those of the impertinent new hires.

Since they couldn't afford to go out to lunch or to join clubs, the new-hire wives pooled baby-sitters and brought contributions to parties—half-bottles of wine and spaghetti and potato salad and rice concoctions. On bleak afternoons between paydays they talked about the future—the dreamed-about hopeful someday when they would sip margaritas on sunny verandas and move into sprawling houses with new furniture and washing machines and big automobiles.

Someday, they assured each other, they would again be *somebody*. They would be spoiled, bejeweled, fur-clad, imposing wives of *real* Pan Am pilots.

One way to supplement the anemic Pan Am paycheck was by flying in the military reserves. Chuck Kraft joined the Air Force Reserve C-124 outfit at Hamilton Air Force Base north of San Francisco. Jim Wood and Chuck James went to Reno, where the Nevada Air National Guard had F-101 fighters. Navy and Marine pilots like Rob

Martinside and Mike Denham and Cale Boggs signed up with the A-4 outfit across the bay at Alameda Naval Air Station.

Besides helping pay the rent, the reserves provided something else. For some of the new airline pilots, withdrawal from the military had not been easy. They still carried with them, like old school sweaters, the peculiar culture distinctions of their service.

Fighter pilots were the worst. Early in their careers they had been imprinted with the notion that they were the elite. Everybody else who flew airplanes did so only to support the fighter jocks.

Over entrances to ready rooms and officers' messes and latrines around the world was a ubiquitous sign: IF YOU AIN'T A FIGHTER PILOT, YOU AIN'T SHIT.

They believed it. It was a separate culture among airmen. It seeped into their pores while they underwent fighter training—and it never fully left them. The culture affected how they wore their uniforms, how they invoked their own jet-jockey lexicon, how they used their hands when they described their own audacity aloft.

It even extended to the world outside. Fighter pilots were supposed to be audacious not only in airplanes but around women, in bars, on the highway. They fancied themselves in control of all forms of locomotion—airplanes, cars, boats, motorcycles, golf carts.

This kind of arrogance hadn't changed much since World War I, when fighter pilots flew Spads and Fokkers and Nieuports. Now they tore through the air in supersonic chariots like the F-100 and the F-104 and the Navy F-8 and F-4. But the idea remained the same: *They*, the fighter pilots, were the *hunters*. Everyone else, especially the lumbering multiengine bombers and tankers and transports, was a *target*.

When they were full of themselves and feeling mean, fighter pilots liked to deride multiengine pilots. They called them bus drivers. No self-respecting, hard-charging, fast-burning fighter pilot was supposed to allow himself to mutate into a bus driver.

But times had changed. Here they were at Pan American, flying many-motored airplanes. Was that not bus driving? Well, perhaps, but . . .

The military reserves made it possible to assuage their consciences about bus driving—and other things. For some, there was still a whiff of guilt about having left the service. A war was cranking up in Southeast Asia. Their buddies who had stayed in were winning all the air medals. But being in a reserve squadron sent a clear enough signal that you were still ready and willing. If things really got hot over there, all they had to do was call up the reserves, right?

That made it a little easier to be a bus driver.

During the hiring process, each pilot applicant had been asked, "Do you want to be a flight engineer or a pilot?"

Flight engineer?

Flight engineers weren't pilots, at least by job description. They sat behind the pilots, at a separate panel. They were there to handle things like fuel management and temperature control and keep an eye on how the systems were functioning.

Rob Martinside thought they were kidding. Who would want to be a flight engineer? In the Navy the only flight engineers he knew were enlisted men. They were mechanics who wore dungarees and tattoos. Martinside was an officer and a *pilot*.

So Martinside was hired as a pilot. And then he learned that newly hired pilots earned $500 per month, which amounted to $1,000 per month *less* than the newly hired flight engineers, who were also pilots. This oddity came about because of union contracts. The engineers were represented not by the Air Line Pilots Association but by their own union, the Flight Engineers International Association.

There was more bad news. "Pilot," in the Pan Am lexicon, meant "copilot," and in the case of Pan Am new hires, it meant that you could be assigned as a navigator.

Navigator! Being a flight engineer was bad enough. But navigators, in Martinside's recollection, were failed pilots who had washed out of flight training and been recycled as stargazers.

And that astonished him all the more. Why in the age of trans-oceanic jet transports and soon-to-come SSTs did Pan Am still fly airplanes across the planet with *navigators*— guys peering through holes in the ship, gazing up at the heavens for guidance? Had the science of navigation not changed since Columbus and Magellan?

And what did all this have to do with flying? That was the part that gnawed at those like Martinside. In the Navy he had been the sole occupant of his little delta-winged jet, wholly in command. Now he was not only no longer in command, he wasn't even *second* in command. Instead of occupying a front seat, he was relegated to the back of the cockpit with his eyeball planted in the socket of a sextant.

Ground school lasted six weeks. After 707 systems came an operations specifications course, and then a class on Pan Am weight and balance procedures and dispatch problems and aircraft performance.

Finally they were ready to fly.

That was supposed to be the easy part. Flying was flying, Martinside had always believed. If you could fly, say, an A-4 off carriers as he had done, you could fly anything. It was just a matter of adjustment.

One star-filled night he found himself wallowing through the sky over Stockton, California, in the right seat of a Boeing 707. Despite his best efforts with the steering-wheel-like control yoke and the rudder pedals, he could not make the damn airplane fly straight. The beast wallowed, yawing in a sickening nose-left, right-wing-down action, then abruptly swinging back nose-right, left-wing-down. They called it a "Dutch roll"—an aerodynamic phenomenon peculiar to swept-wing transports like the 707. Forty years earlier the condition had been identified by engineers and named after an oscillating style of ice skating imported from the Netherlands.

"You stop it like this," said Forster, the instructor. He applied a rightward jab to the yoke, then returned it to neutral. The rolling ceased. "Whenever it starts, just give it one of these," Forster explained, jabbing the yoke to the left. "It's easy."

Martinside tried it. It wasn't easy. But after several tries he learned to anticipate the big jet's tendency to swing its nose like a pendulum. The trick was to anticipate the yaw, then stop it with little, short jabs, as Forster had just done.

Dave Forster was a jolly man with a huge girth who smoked filter-tip cigarettes and told dirty jokes while he flew. As a military pilot, he had commanded Air Force Two, Lyndon Johnson's vice-presidential transport. Because of his extensive experience in the military version of the 707, Pan Am had recruited him as an instructor.

Actual aircraft training could be dangerous. Simulators for Pan Am's jets were still under development. Until they arrived, it was necessary to rehearse aircraft emergencies—engine loss on takeoff, emergency descents from high altitude, two-engine-out approaches—with real airplanes. The airlines had already experienced several spectacular accidents during training flights.

They trained mostly at night, when spare aircraft were available between scheduled trips. In the traffic patterns around outlying airports like Stockton and Ontario and Mojave, the novice airline pilots wrestled with the big jets, learning the vagaries of Dutch rolls and instrument approaches and engine-out landings.

Single-engine pilots like Rob Martinside and Mike Denham had never confronted the immense yaw problem when a four-engine jet—with two engines on each wing—lost the thrust of one engine. The airplane lurched sideward, slewed by the two engines on one wing versus the single good engine on the other. The pilot had to shove his foot hard on the rudder pedal to counter the yaw and keep the jet tracking straight ahead.

Forster loved to pull back the throttle of an outboard engine—simulating an engine failure—during takeoff. "Keep 'er on the centerline," he told his students. "Don't let the sonofabitch move *one inch* off the center of the runway."

With practice, they learned. Martinside learned to anticipate the 707's instant desire to head for the sagebrush just before liftoff when Forster cut an engine. He learned to feed in rudder, just enough, to keep the jet going straight down the runway. He learned to ease smoothly back on the yoke, lift the nose off the concrete, and fly away—with however many engines Forster felt like letting him use.

Flying with one engine out became easy. Then came flying with *two* engines out. Now the yaw problem was doubled—two engines thrusting on one wing, none on the other. The airplane tried to rotate sideways about its center axis, and the pilot had to shove in nearly full rudder to keep it straight.

Forster kept cutting engines and they kept shoving rudder pedals. They went around the traffic pattern at Stockton, screeching down again and again on the eight thousand feet of cement, and taking off again. Afterward they drank beer with Forster at the English Pub in

Burlingame, and he told them war stories about flying C-135s and what it was like to haul Lyndon Johnson around.

A few minutes before eight in the morning, Rob Martinside climbed out of his faded-blue XKE and gazed across the parking lot in the direction of the Pan Am hangar. He could see parked on the ramp what he had seen every Monday morning since he began training.

The tall tail of yet another Boeing 707 towered over the vehicles and equipment. It was a new airplane, freshly delivered from the factory in Seattle, parked in front of the main hangar. A new 707 was showing up in the same place every weekend.

Pan Am's fleet of jets was growing faster than the airline could train airmen to fly them. The company was hiring pilots at the rate of two new classes a month, about twenty-five pilots per class. Martinside's seniority number, drawn by lottery among his twenty classmates, was 2323. That had made him eighth from the bottom on the entire Pan Am roster. Now, six weeks later, there were sixty-two pilots beneath him on the list. The list, it was said, would stretch to over 3500 within a year.

The training department had become a factory, pumping out a steady stream of newly qualified navigators, engineers, first officers, and captains. So urgent was Pan Am's need for bodies that some lucky new-hire classes were moving directly from their initial training into the first officer's seat without serving, as Martinside and his classmates had done, an apprenticeship as flight engineer or navigator.

Across the street a new building was under construction. It would be devoted exclusively to training. The three-story cube housed tiers of briefing rooms and cockpit mock-ups and contained several sixty-foot bays for the new 707 simulators. These were hydraulic-powered, three-axis replicated cockpits that provided the sound and sight and feel of actual flight. In these simulators students could be drilled on standard operating procedures, and they could practice the dangerous engine-out work that Dave Forster was conducting every night over the blackened hills at Stockton.

At the bases in New York, Miami, and Berlin, the same thing was happening. "Old hires" of ten and twenty years seniority who had thought they would be career copilots were being propelled through captain training and taking command of brand-new 707s.

Toting his canvas carry-on bag filled with blue-bound Pan Am aircraft manuals, Martinside walked across the parking lot to the main hangar. His eyes stayed fixed on the new 707, and he felt a private jubilation. Maybe he *was* still a lowly new hire. But just look at those new airplanes, the new building, all those new pilots. There was no doubt about it—this airline, Pan American World Airways, by God, it was taking off! Why, in no time they would stop calling him a *new hire* . . . he'd be halfway up the list . . . a first officer, sure, maybe even . . . why not? . . . maybe even a *captain*.

CHAPTER EIGHT

THE EVERYMAN AIRPLANE

Puget Sound, August 1965

To Bill Allen, it was *déjà vu*. Here he was being needled again by Juan Trippe. It was just like a decade ago when Trippe was after him to build the 707. Not Boeing's 707. *Trippe's 707.*

So he had built it—Trippe's way. And as Trippe never tired of reminding him, Boeing and Pan Am—and eventually the entire industry—had reaped enormous profit. The 707 was the most successful jet in the world.

Now Trippe wanted to do it again.

It was a fine summer day. Puget Sound lay as placid as a mill pond, and in the backdrop swelled the magnificent Olympic Range. Their boat was named the *Wild Goose* and belonged to actor John Wayne. They talked about salmon and the startlingly beautiful weather of the sound, and about golf, which they frequently played together. Inevitably, Trippe and Allen had gotten around to talking airplanes, which, after all, was the purpose of the outing.

That was how the two old titans of aviation made deals. Trippe would tease and prod and try to read Allen. Allen played the same game, fencing with Trippe, trying to read the Great Dissembler's true intentions. It was how they had come to terms on the 707. Now they were doing it again.

Would you build it if I bought it?

Would you buy it if I built it?

Although both Trippe and Allen were still ardent believers in the SST, both realized that the supersonic transport was way behind schedule. Given the political storm swelling around it, the futuristic jet might *never* fly, at least during the few years Allen and Trippe had remaining at their desks.

They had to build something else.

What Trippe had in mind was a stopgap airplane—something to fill the void between the first generation of jets, the 707 and DC-8, and the yet-to-be-built SST. They needed an airplane to satisfy the growing demand for passenger seats that he and Allen themselves had created with the Boeing 707. The first jets had made world travel available to Everyman, not just the rich and elite. Now they had to build an airplane to satisfy that new yearning to travel—an Everyman airplane.

William M. Allen had just turned sixty-six; he was less than a year older than Trippe. He was a large, robust man with Western tastes and attitudes. Over the years his face had thinned and his hair had whitened, but he had lost none of his Montana lawyer's commonsense approach to business. The way he ran Boeing mirrored his own un-pretentious lifestyle. He maintained his offices not at the company's main facilities at Boeing Field, just south of Seattle, but downtown, on the third floor of an aging office complex with a railroad track running down one side. Boeing provided its officers neither limousines nor executive jets. Allen believed that people who built airliners ought to ride in them.

The truth was, Bill Allen wanted the new airplane as much as Trippe. It would be the perfect swan song if he could step down knowing that he had launched the world's mightiest ship of the sky. It would secure Boeing's future well into the next century.

Or it could ruin Boeing.

Bill Allen's willingness to take monumental risks with his company did not, in his reckoning, equate with recklessness. Nor did he think that Trippe could be accused of rolling the dice with his airline. It was something more calculated than that. Like most of the pioneers of aviation, he and Trippe had gotten ahead by a peculiar amalgam of financial savvy, vision, and guts.

By the time the fishing trip was over, Allen and Trippe had moved from "If you build it, I'll buy it" to a verbal commitment for a preliminary design.

It wasn't quite a deal. Not yet. But that evening when they stepped onto the dock from the *Wild Goose,* both men could feel the familiar old juices flowing.

One more time.

Just how big the new airliner—the 747—could be depended on the size of its engines. And therein lay the problem: There were no engines.

Trippe wanted to use the GE engine that was being developed for the Air Force's mammoth new Lockheed C-5A. But that was a military power plant, designed specifically for a slower-cruising airplane and without particular regard for the niceties of smokeless exhaust and noise abatement. Yes, said Gerard Neumann of GE, eventually GE's engine could be tweaked to provide the numbers Trippe and Allen wanted. But not now. The C-5A contract had absolute priority. No commercial engines until the military commitment had been satisfied.

Meanwhile, Rolls-Royce of Britain, which had the most experience thus far in jet propulsion, let it be known that it was willing and eager to produce power plants for the new jet. Pan Am's engineer, John Borger, was impressed with the proposals from Rolls, but he had nagging doubts about the hard-pressed company's ability to deliver.

More *déjà vu.* It was coming down all over again to the American engine maker Pratt & Whitney, the historical third member of the Boeing–Pan Am–P&W triumvirate. These were the same players as in the 707 story of a decade before. Trippe and Allen were still in the ring. Fred Rentschler, guiding spirit of Pratt & Whitney, had died almost at the same time his controversial J-75 engines began propelling Pan Am 707s at the beginning of the sixties. Jack Horner now headed United Aircraft, Pratt & Whitney's parent conglomerate, and he was selling the 41,000-pound-thrust engine P&W had produced for the C-5A competition.

Pan Am's engineers, led by Borger, met steadily throughout 1965 with Boeing's team. They swapped specifications, submitted drawings, looked at mock-ups. The project was still a closely held secret, one that Trippe shared with only a handful of his top associates.

In Trippe's original vision, the 747 was to be a double-decker.

That had been the configuration of Pan Am's popular old Boeing Stratocruiser, the transport version of the B-29 bomber, and it epitomized Trippe's idea of an Everyman airplane. It was an airborne ocean liner. But gradually, through the nudging of Borger and Boeing's payload engineer, Milt Heinemann, he came around to the idea of a widebodied fuselage, nearly round, with a two-aisled, nine-abreast seating configuration. In this way they could cram more passengers into the same cabin area with the same degree of comfort. In addition, there was a greater capacity in the belly for cargo—a factor almost as critical to the equation as the passenger load. It was becoming clear to Trippe that in the future, air cargo would be nearly as profitable as the carriage of passengers, and a more consistent source of revenue.

How much would it cost? No one really knew. The latest version of the 707, called the B-Advanced model, of which Pan Am would soon own sixty, cost about $7 million per copy. By rough guess, at two and a half times the 707's size, the 747 should go for $17 to $20 million. Trippe was promising Allen that Pan Am would take twenty-five, plus spare parts, which amounted to an outlay of over half a billion dollars.

Half a billion? It was a staggering sum. It amounted to the biggest commercial purchase in history. And it would be for a newly developed, untested airplane—one for which they didn't even have engines.

Financially, Boeing would be in as much peril as Pan Am. For a project the size of the 747, Boeing would have to build a whole new plant somewhere beyond its present facility. A production line of unprecedented dimensions and logistical complexity would have to be established. In order for Boeing just to recover the preproduction costs, it would have to sell at least fifty airplanes. Pan American was the launch customer. If the Pan Am deal did not generate at least as many orders from other customers, Boeing was doomed. And Bill Allen knew it would be his own fault.

So Allen required from Trippe a rigid payment schedule: a 2.5 percent deposit upon signing the contract, then half the entire amount paid in quarterly installments, due six months before delivery of the first 747. That meant Trippe would be anteing up a quarter billion dollars before he had even flown his first 747.

Trippe's own experience told him that new airplanes *never* lived up to their initial specifications. There were always glitches. Back in

1935 the *China Clipper*'s original payload capacity and range were insufficient until her engines were upgraded to more powerful versions. The first B-314 flying boats proved to be dangerously unstable on the water until Boeing provided a hull modification and added two more vertical fins to the tail. Even the successful 707 fell short of Trippe's expectations until Pratt & Whitney provided the JT-3D fan-jet engine that made the airplane a true intercontinental airliner.

Nor did new airplanes ever cost what they were supposed to. There were always modifications that *someone* had to pay for. Trippe knew that airframe manufacturers liked to blame a new airplane's shortcomings on the engines. So as part of his arrangement with Allen, Trippe insisted that Boeing take full responsibility for the performance of the 747. Whether the engine lived up to its expectations or not, it would be Boeing's problem.

By late 1965, the initial specifications were in ink. The 747 would have a gross weight of 550,000 pounds. A passenger capacity of 350 to 400. Range of 5,100 miles. Initial cruise altitude of 35,000 feet. A maximum speed of 0.9 Mach, or 90 percent of the speed of sound.

Trippe and Allen signed a letter of intent in December, three days before Christmas. To inside observers, the most striking aspect of the deal was the players themselves. Neither Trippe nor Allen seemed daunted by the scale of their enterprise. They were true believers. They were behaving like two old partygoers, intoxicated by the glitz and sheen of one last great gala.

A few brave souls had the temerity to question the deal. What if the 747 turned out to be a half-billion-dollar white elephant?

Trippe scoffed at the notion. Look at the facts, he said. Pan Am was the strongest airline in the world. Its operating revenues now approached a billion dollars per annum. And just look at the rate of traffic growth within the industry. Fifteen percent a year since the jets came on line. Twenty-five percent internationally. Wasn't there already a shortage of available seats across the Atlantic? The enormous revenue generated by a fleet of 747s, crammed with passengers, would repay the half-billion-dollar debt and thrust Pan Am into an era of unimagined prosperity. Pan Am would be ready for the stars.

Trippe, the airline tycoon who had just spent $500 million on new airplanes, was not one to lose his head over small amounts. One morning a couple of weeks later, Trippe was having breakfast in a hotel coffee shop with Sam Pryor, a Pan Am vice president. The bill came to $4.20.

As usual, Trippe studied the itemized bill carefully. Then he divided it in half. He let Pryor take care of the tip.

Groans came from the engineering offices at Boeing. Angry aero-engineers crumpled up drawings and hurled them into trash baskets. *Why the hell didn't Pan Am make up its mind?*

The biggest problem they had in designing the world's biggest airliner was turning out not to be technical. It was human, and its name was Juan Trippe. Almost daily, the chairman of Pan Am was thinking of changes. Now he wanted more seats. He wanted the thing to carry as many as 490 economy-class passengers, or 375 mixed economy- and first-class passengers. That meant lengthening the fuselage, widening it, moving the cockpit to the upper deck. And that meant more weight. Now Trippe was talking about a 710,000-pound airliner—an increase of 160,000 pounds.

Nothing in aeronautical science came without a price. An increase in an airplane's weight meant a corresponding decrease in its performance. Like an overstuffed bird, the 747 would suffer reduced operating range and maximum altitude because of its greater weight.

Juan Trippe had a traditional fix for the weight-versus-performance problem. It was the same fix he had used in 1923 when he doubled the passenger capacity of his Aeromarine biplanes, and had applied to every Pan Am airliner since: *You squeeze more power from the engines.*

The JT-9D fan-jet developed for the 747 by Pratt & Whitney produced 41,000 pounds of thrust, which translated to about 87,000 horsepower. It had more power than any other airplane engine ever built. One JT-9D produced more thrust than all four engines of the first Boeing 707s.

Trippe wanted more. Instead of 41,000 pounds of thrust, why not boost it to 50,000? That would compensate for the added weight of the airplane.

Bill Gwinn, who now headed Pratt & Whitney, looked as if he

were being strangled. *Hell, we don't even know if we can get 41,000 pounds*, he thought. Gwinn knew that you had to boost the maximum thrust of a new engine in small increments—after it had been tested many thousands of hours. This one had no history. Who knew what it would be capable of?

Trippe had heard all this before, of course, and seemed not to care. It was his experience that the first models of new airliners were obsolete as soon as they entered service. After the original versions flew, there was an inevitable stretching and enhancing and boosting to make the airplane perform the way it was supposed to. Pan Am's new airliner would not be just a prototype for the *real* 747s to come along later—for other customers.

When he viewed a plywood mock-up of the 747 in March 1966, Trippe gazed for a long time at the spacious compartment on the second deck, behind the cockpit. He remembered the opulent accommodations of the double-decker B-314 flying boats and the stately Boeing Stratocruisers. They had sleeping berths and lounging cabins and dining rooms. Stewards in starched uniforms served dinner with real china and silver service. They were ocean liners of the skies.

Trippe had an idea. "Why can't we have a cocktail lounge up there?"

The Boeing people exchanged pained looks.

"And a spiral staircase," Trippe added.

More pained looks. Some were on the face of Pan Am engineer John Borger. Trippe's ideas meant *more* weight, and even greater cost per airplane.

Trippe wasn't finished. "Maybe we ought to have a few staterooms on the second deck."

By the spring of 1966 the final contract was being drafted by the lawyers of Boeing and Pan Am. And then disaster struck.

On March 30, Juan Trippe was sitting in an audience of businessmen—members of the President's Business Advisory Council—listening to Lyndon Baines Johnson tell them that these were difficult times. They must all, executives of industry and government alike, join together in this mutual sacrifice.

Trippe's crisis alarm went off: *What mutual sacrifice?*

These were difficult times, Johnson was saying in his Texas hill country twang. The country must come first. The United States was in real danger of a runaway inflation. The immediate—and *temporary*—cure, Johnson wanted them know, was a "voluntary pullback in your plans to expand industries, construct new plants, broaden your capital outlays."

Pullback? Trippe caught the glance of Bill Allen, seated across the room. How could they pull back now? The pact between Pan Am and Boeing would be the largest commercial deal in America's history. Now Johnson wanted to pull the rug out from under both companies.

Trippe knew that Allen had already set in motion Boeing's plans to construct a mammoth assembly site for the 747 in a forest near the company airfield at Everett, Washington. A thirty-five-mile railroad spur would connect the site to the Boeing field. The new plant alone represented an expenditure of $250 million.

What the President was not saying, of course, was that this was 1966 and his administration was bankrolling a war. Billions of borrowed U.S. dollars were being sown into the mud of Southeast Asia. And to keep America's economy from self-immolating, LBJ wanted the business community to cool it.

Most of the businessmen just stared at the President in stony silence. They were realists. Lyndon Johnson was a notoriously manipulative President who could—and would—cut off the oxygen of any corporation that did not play according to his rules.

Before his audience became too restive, Johnson abruptly adjourned the meeting. The businessmen gathered their briefcases and stalked for the door. Johnson nodded sourly as each took his leave.

Juan Trippe did not leave. He could sense the curtain descending on his last and grandest dream. Trippe hung back, looking for an opportunity to approach the President, whose lanky frame was now surrounded by other agitated businessmen.

Trippe maneuvered himself to the head of the line. For all his famous vagueness and rambling, Juan Trippe, in a crisis, could transform himself into an impassioned salesman. For the next fifteen minutes he delivered the sales pitch of his life.

The 747, he told a skeptical Johnson, would vastly increase the Air Force's emergency troop-carrying capacity. Its foreign sales would contribute mightily to correcting America's balance-of-trade problem.

Construction of the 747 would keep thousands of workers employed. The jumbo jet's technological sophistication would place the United States light-years ahead of its envious European competitors. And anyway, by the time the assembly line was in full production the economic cycle would have swung and the expenditure for new fleets of airplanes would be just what the economy needed.

Trippe only hinted at the most pertinent detail: All this would occur in 1968, an election year.

Johnson rubbed his eyes. He had ingested too many facts in too short a time. "Does anyone else know about this?"

"Only Bill Allen at Boeing," said Trippe, disingenuously, "and now you."

"Be here tomorrow morning at ten," the President said. "My car will be waiting."

The next morning Trippe was taken to a meeting with Robert McNamara, Johnson's Secretary of Defense. Johnson called McNamara "the man with the stickum on his hair." In the post-Kennedy era, McNamara had become, in effect, the assistant President.

McNamara wanted to know why Trippe didn't use a civilian version of the Lockheed C-5A that was being developed for the Air Force. The C-5A was a mammoth cargo airplane that looked like a horizontal office building with fins. Why couldn't that be the next-generation airliner?

Trippe told McNamara that Pan Am had already looked at the C-5A. The big jet was just fine for the Air Force. It was built like a locomotive. But as a commercial airliner it would be a disaster. No one could afford to operate such a craft, because it was slow, consumed inordinate quantities of fuel, and would never meet the stringent passenger safety standards imposed by the Federal Aviation Agency. Any airline would go broke trying to fly the C-5A.

McNamara was not pleased. "You're telling me that I've just wasted five hundred million dollars of the taxpayers' money?"

No, Trippe assured him. The Air Force *needed* an airplane like the C-5A. But the airlines had a different mission. What they needed was the 747.

McNamara's analytical brain processed the information. After he'd thought for a minute, he picked up the phone and called the President. Then he dragged Trippe off to the White House.

In front of LBJ, Trippe delivered his pitch again, tailoring it to the President's concerns, which were more political than technical: How many jobs would the 747 create? In what states? Who were the subcontractors? Where were they located?

After half an hour, Johnson had heard enough. He told McNamara, "Get somebody down here from Boeing."

Trippe walked out of the White House with a smile on his face. The 747 had been spared from Lyndon Johnson's austerity program. The Everyman airplane was back on track.

The Imperial Skygod took his customary place at the head of the long table. Assembled in the walnut-paneled boardroom on the forty-sixth floor of the Pan Am Building were his directors. It was the afternoon of April 12, 1966, and they had been summoned to Trippe's court to vote their approval of his ocean liner of the skies.

There were some heavyweights on the board: General Alfred Gruenther, former Supreme Allied Commander in Europe, who had always championed American leadership in the skies and who could be counted on to support Trippe's new airplane; Dave Ingalls, an old Trippe friend from the Yale days and a Pan Am insider; old Mark McKee, former president of the Wisconsin and Michigan Steamship Company and a Pan Am board member since the thirties. McKee now usually dozed off during board meetings and awakened to vote with the majority. Charles Lindbergh was a member, and everyone knew he favored the Everyman airplane as a sensible alternative to the planet-polluting SST.

There were the inside directors, all company officers like Harold Gray and Sam Pryor, who already knew about the superjet project and would be expected—*required*—to vote with their chairman.

Trippe reeled off his numbers. Traffic was projected to increase by at least 15 percent a year into the next decade. Each 747 would replace two and a half 707s and would operate at 30 percent less seat-mile cost. The 747 would slice twenty-five minutes off each Atlantic crossing.

And, oh, yes, Trippe added, the administration of President Johnson had given its blessing to the Boeing–Pan American 747 contract.

That was the clincher. The board of directors asked a few questions, made comments, then did its duty. The board members granted their official approval to the project that Trippe had already undertaken. Trippe had authorization to buy twenty-five 747s, as well as an option for ten more. It meant that Pan Am's indebtedness for the 747s and for the previously ordered 707s now amounted to nearly a billion dollars.

There was no argument. There were no dissenting votes. The Imperial Skygod had decided. So it would be.

CHAPTER NINE

ON THE LINE

Jim Wood was the first of his class to complete first officer training. For his initial line trip he was scheduled to fly with one of the ancients, a senior captain named Lou Cogliani. The trip was to Honolulu and back.

Wood showed up an hour and a half early. His shoes were spit-shined. The three gold stripes on each sleeve glowed like neon. He was prepared to learn about flying from the old master.

"Sir," he said, extending his hand, "I'm Jim Wood, your first officer."

Captain Lou Cogliani, Master of Ocean Flying Boats, peered at the young man over the tops of his half-frames. It was the Look. He ignored Wood's hand. "How long you been flying, kid?"

"Ten years, including the Air Force and—"

"Never mind that shit. How long you been with Pan Am?"

"I'm new, sir. Just out of training."

Cogliani leaned over the operations counter. "Goddammit, Evans," he barked at the clerk. "What's going on here? I told 'em I didn't want any fuckin' new hires in my cockpit."

"I don't make the schedule, Lou. There's the phone. Call the chief pilot if you want."

Cogliani glowered at the phone. Then he shuffled through the paperwork for the flight to Honolulu. He ignored his new copilot.

They took off. Cogliani still had not spoken to Wood, except to demand that he read the checklist.

Wood watched how the old master flew the 707. Captain Cogliani, he noticed, flew an airplane the way a bear handled a beach ball. He gripped the yoke with both hands. The veins stood out on his tensed forearms. He yanked, jerked, shoved, manhandled the protesting 707 all the way to 35,000 feet.

Wood glanced back at the flight engineer. The engineer nodded and rolled his eyes.

Wood was confused. *Cogliani was a Skygod*—a Master of Ocean Flying Boats. He was one of those legends that Wood most of all wanted to be like someday. He was supposed to be a hero. Something was wrong, thought Jim Wood. The Skygod was an asshole.

Approaching Honolulu, Cogliani commenced his descent from altitude too late, ignoring Wood's reminder about their rapidly diminishing distance from the airport. Too high for the approach, Cogliani had to fly a circle to lose altitude. Then he overshot the localizer, the final approach course. Honolulu Approach Control vectored them back onto an approach course straight into the runway.

At fifteen hundred feet above the field, the captain had still not called for the landing gear down. Wood kept his silence.

A thousand feet. Still no gear. Jim Wood bit his lip and said nothing.

At six hundred feet, Wood could stand no more. "Do you want the landing gear down, captain?"

Cogliani glowered at him. "Landing gear? Goddammit, I'll *tell* you when I want the gear down." Two and one-half seconds later, with a great deal of authority, he told him. "Gear down!"

No one, not even a new hire like Jim Wood, would dare suggest that the captain—a Master of Ocean Flying Boats—might actually have *forgotten* to lower his landing gear. Instead, Wood did something even more foolish.

He laughed.

Three days later, in the chief pilot's office, Wood received his first lesson in Skygod protocol. The chief—the craggy-faced man who had welcomed Wood's class to Pan American—regarded the young man over the tops of his own half-frames.

"Do you want to keep your job, son?"

"Yes, sir."

"Then get this. You will sit there and raise and lower the captain's landing gear—on command—and keep your impertinent, newly hired mouth shut. Clear?"

"Yes, sir."

"Good. Get the hell out of here."

Lou Cogliani wasn't unique. From around the world, new hires brought back stories about flying with the Skygods.

Martinside flew with a captain named Will Fenton. Fenton was a man of fearsome visage who had a shaved head and wore a goatee. When he smiled, Will Fenton looked like evil incarnate. By company rule, pilots could not wear beards. Fenton, a Skygod, considered himself exempt from such rules.

They were flight-planned from San Francisco to Honolulu at 35,000 feet. Standing at the operations counter, Fenton scratched out the flight level on the flight plan and wrote in 24,000 feet. He scratched out ".82" in the column for Mach number and wrote in ".86." Increasing the Mach number—an expression of the airplane's speed in percentage of the speed of sound—translated to an increased cruise speed over the ocean of twenty knots. Fenton threw the flight plan back over the counter. "Refile us for the lower altitude and higher speed," he said to the dispatcher.

The dispatcher gazed at Fenton warily through his horn-rimmed glasses. "May I ask why, captain?"

"One simple reason," said Fenton. He leaned over the counter as if to share a secret. "It's faster."

The dispatcher looked disgusted. "But it wastes fuel. Flying at that Mach number at twenty-four thousand will cost"—he ran his finger down a chart—"nearly twelve thousand more pounds of fuel."

"Good," said Fenton. "Put on twelve thousand more. I'm in a hurry."

And so it happened. The Skygod had decreed. The dispatcher called for an additional twelve thousand pounds of fuel to be loaded on the 707. To the delight of its 125 passengers, Pan Am Flight 906, commanded by Captain Fenton, touched down that night in Honolulu twenty-five minutes ahead of its scheduled arrival.

Will Fenton had a date, and he hated to be late.

One of the toughest things about flying with old Bob Farnham was keeping him awake. Another was keeping him reminded of details like where they were going and what day it was.

Farnham was a Skygod, at least by seniority if not by ilk. He had been around since the early boat days. The copilots liked flying with the old gentleman, because he exhibited none of the Skygodly bellicosity and bluster. He had fluffy red-gray hair and looked like Santa Claus. Unlike some of his boat captain colleagues who had been timewarped into the jet age, Farnham could be a very competent aviator —when he remembered to be.

One evening Captain Farnham arrived at the airport, about to depart on a week-long trip to Europe. He was running late, fifteen minutes past his check-in time. He drove his Cadillac—the Skygods' chariot of choice—directly to the operations office. He parked in the drop-off space in front of the office and ran inside with his suitcase. He left the motor running on the Cadillac. He intended to check in, say hello to his crew, then go park the car.

He forgot.

Captain Farnham chatted with his first officer. He perused the seven-and-a-half-hour flight plan to Paris. With the first officer and navigator he made his way to the gate where the 707 was receiving its passengers. He took off for Paris.

The motor of the Cadillac continued to run.

For a week, Farnham flew around the globe. He flew to Paris, and later to Tehran, and then to Beirut, and on the last night of the trip to London. For not one instant were his thoughts troubled by the faraway labored chugging of the parked Cadillac.

Meanwhile, some junior pilots removed Farnham's car to the parking lot. On the day he was scheduled to return, they put the Cadillac back in its space at the operations office. They left the motor running.

Captain Farnham did not notice that there was a bigger-than-usual crowd at the operations office that day. He said good-bye to his crew.

Suitcase in hand, he strolled out to the curb where crew members normally boarded the bus to the parking lot.

There was his car. The motor was still running.

For a moment, the old captain stared at his automobile. His eyes narrowed as disconnected thoughts sought union in his brain. *Didn't I . . . how could it . . . but there's my car . . .*

The moment passed. He shrugged his shoulders—*Oh, well, screw it*—got in his car, and drove away.

One night Martinside was in the cockpit of a 707, preparing for departure. The purser came into the cockpit and handed the crew a business card. "Some guy wants to know if he could visit the cockpit."

The card read:

GENERAL CHARLES A. LINDBERGH
DIRECTOR, PAN AMERICAN WORLD AIRWAYS

"Please ask him to come up," said the captain, Bob Pfaff.

Pfaff turned to Martinside. "Before he gets here, let me tell you a story."

Pfaff said that when he was a kid, seven years old, Lindbergh came to his hometown. It was after his famous flight in 1927, and Lindbergh was making his triumphal tour of the United States. There was a parade, and everyone turned out. Pfaff was a kid with an unruly mop of hair never touched by a comb. But on this day, before the Lindbergh parade, his parents had found him in the bathroom smearing *soap* in his hair. He was plastering it down in a gooey, slicked-back mess.

What in the hell was he doing? his father wanted to know.

"I want to look good for Lindbergh," said the kid.

That had been important to him. "Lindbergh was my hero," recalled Captain Pfaff, in the cockpit of his jetliner. "That's why I rubbed that damn soap in my hair. I wanted to look good for Lindbergh."

There was a knock on the cockpit door, and in came Lindbergh. He smiled his kindly smile. The still-youthful face and the ice-blue eyes and the voice were friendly. But he was businesslike and reserved. There was a *void* there. Lindbergh had spent a lifetime being hounded by fans, reporters, cranks. He was a man who didn't let people get close.

The pilots introduced themselves. "Please make yourself at home, general," Captain Pfaff said.

Lindbergh slid his long legs around the jump seat and sat facing the flight engineer. He looked around the cockpit. He gazed at the instrument panel, then back at the engineer's panel. "Are you fellows still having problems with the CSDs disconnecting?"

The flight engineer looked surprised. "No, sir," he said. "They've gotten better. We hardly ever have one disconnect anymore."

"Good," said Lindbergh. "We researched that problem and decided to try increasing the radius of that shear fitting in the drive unit. That seems to have fixed it."

The crew members looked at each other. Lindbergh had been a technical consultant to Pan Am for forty years. He was obviously still very much involved in maintenance and engineering matters.

Lindbergh talked about JT-3 engine oil consumption. "Amazing, isn't it? All four of these jet engines consume less oil than just one of the old recips." He talked about how to handle the manual mode of the cabin pressurization system: "You'll probably never have to use it, since we made the system completely automatic." About the new navigation devices, he told them, "We knew about the Doppler effect back in the twenties, but it took this long to figure out how to use it."

Lindbergh, it turned out, knew as much about such things as most line pilots.

Then he talked about the new 747. His face brightened. "You fellows are going to love that airplane."

"Have you flown it?"

"Last week," said Lindbergh. "Out in Seattle. They let me try it out. It's a marvelous airplane."

And then the pilots noticed that their visitor had changed. *The void was gone.* Since he had come to the cockpit, chatting with the crew, Lindbergh the public figure had vanished. He was Lindbergh the pilot.

Martinside could tell by Bob Pfaff's voice and expression that the captain was living out a fantasy. It was Pfaff's childhood dream come true. Here was *Lindbergh*—in *his* cockpit—calling him *captain*.

The cockpit was silent for a minute. Martinside reminded himself that he *must* ask Lindbergh for his autograph. It would be a keepsake. He wondered why Pfaff didn't tell the story about when he was seven years old and Lindbergh came to town. Normally you couldn't shut Bob Pfaff up. He loved to tell stories. And, anyway, Lindbergh might find it funny.

But Pfaff didn't tell his story. For once, the captain was keeping his mouth shut.

After a while, Lindbergh thanked the pilots and shook their hands. He said he had work to do back in the cabin.

When Lindbergh was gone, Martinside said, "Why didn't you tell him the story about the soap in your hair?"

"I don't know," said Pfaff. "You saw how comfortable he seemed to be with us. Like he could relax for a minute and just talk airplanes without people worshiping him. I didn't want to spoil it for him."

And then Martinside remembered the autograph. *I didn't get Lindbergh's autograph.* Why not?

It came to him. For the same reason Pfaff hadn't told the story. They were both like the soap-haired boy in 1927. They were kids who wanted to look good for Lindbergh.

One dawn. Rob Martinside was flying with Captain Farnham eastbound over the Atlantic. The sun pushed through the horizon like fiery lava. Squinting against the slanting rays of dawn, Martinside pulled out one of the square plastic sunshades and affixed it to the windshield bracket. It helped cut the glare.

The fierce morning sun should have awakened the captain. But nothing ever woke up Bob Farnham. He lay sprawled in his cockpit seat. His mouth was open. He was sound asleep. He wore a tattered black sweater. His shoes were removed and his slippered feet perched on the foot rests at the bottom of the instrument panel.

Beneath the left wing, Martinside could see the outline of southern England. In a few more minutes they would be starting down toward their destination, Amsterdam.

"Think we ought to wake him up?"

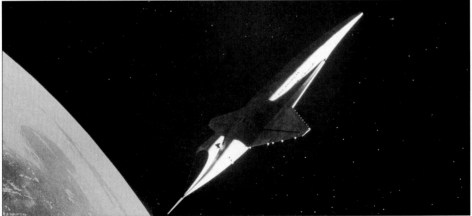

The Boeing 314, the greatest flying boat of them all, was built to Pan Am specifications. The legacy of the Skygods began with Pan American's ocean-faring clippers.

"Congratulations, gentlemen. You're going to be SST captains." Newly hired pilots in the 1960s were assured that Pan American would be the first American airline to fly supersonic transports.

Not even the sky was the limit. In the 1968 movie 2001: A Space Odyssey, *passengers journeyed to the moon aboard a Pan Am vessel. Pan American was already accepting reservations for its first commercial lunar service.*

The Pan Am building was Juan Trippe's monument to his own imperial vision. When it was finished in 1963, it was the largest commercial office building in the world.

Pan Am's Internal German Service. For forty years Pan American maintained an aerial lifeline to Berlin, stranded behind the Iron Curtain.

With the futuristic Boeing 707, Pan Am gained a decade's lead on its competitors and soared to record earnings.

Boeing 707 simulator. Until realistic cockpit simulators were introduced in the late sixties, Pan Am pilots took all their training in actual airplanes, often in hazardous circumstances.

An occasion for smiles. Trippe yields power to his chosen successors, Gray (left) and Halaby (right). But behind the smile, Harold Gray concealed the secret of his fatal illness. As Pan Am's chairman, he would last eighteen months.

"If I build it, would you buy it?" Boeing's Bill Allen and Pan Am's Juan Trippe were the titans of the airline industry. Nearing the end of their careers, they wanted to make history one more time.

The 747 was Boeing's—and Pan Am's—greatest gamble. The arrival of the 747 coincided with the beginning of Pan Am's decline.

Boeing wasn't accustomed to having the chairman of a customer airline actually want to fly his new airplane. But Jeeb Halaby, here in the left seat of a new 747, was an old navy test pilot.

From the battlefield to the beach. GIs flew directly from Vietnam, aboard Pan Am jets, to Honolulu for a week's respite from war.

Pan Am's multinational flight attendants wearing the uniforms designed for them by the wife of Chairman Seawell.

The Cold War Gladiator. A former air force general, Pan Am's chairman William T. Seawell raised the meaning of "Skygod" to new heights.

Pan Am's navigation school. New-hire pilots in the sixties began their careers as navigators or flight engineers. Even in transonic jet airplanes, over-ocean navigation techniques were little changed from the days of sailing ships.

C. Edward Acker. The king of the hipshots, Acker made deals that kept Pan Am alive— while he dismembered it.

Fated to be Pan Am's last CEO, Tom Plaskett took up the struggle to save the airline despite daunting problems—including an unthinkable disaster.

"Those are my goddamned cigars." National Airlines boss George T. Baker was a legendary tough guy who loved nothing so much as a good fight.

Hired as a pilot and then furloughed, Marty Shugrue put away his uniform and ascended the corporate pyramid all the way to the vice-chairmanship.

Bob Gould was a pilots'-union official who leaped the fence to management and, as a senior vice-president, put his own stamp on Pan Am operations.

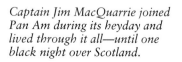

Captain Jim MacQuarrie joined Pan Am during its heyday and lived through it all—until one black night over Scotland.

"Yeah," said the engineer. "We're coming up on London. He likes to give a PA announcement about where we are, the weather, and all that bullshit."

Martinside was the relief copilot. On long-range trips a relief pilot was assigned to the crew so the captain and first officer could each go back in the cabin and take a rest break. Farnham managed to sleep the whole time.

Martinside nudged Farnham. The old captain came to life, opening his eyes one at a time. He scratched himself and looked around and then asked the same question every captain asks when he reassumes command of his cockpit: "Where are we?"

Martinside told him.

"Yeah, okay. Go back and get Bob. Take the rest of the day off."

"Yes, sir."

In the forward cabin, Martinside woke up Bob Mahanor, the first officer. Then he had a coffee and chatted with Inge, a pretty, dark-haired stewardess from Hamburg.

Over the cabin speakers they heard the captain's announcement. "Good morning, folks," came Farnham's croaky voice. "We're at . . . ummm . . . thirty-seven thousand feet. Beneath the aircraft is . . . aahh . . . the English Channel, and off to the right you can see . . . uuhhh . . . the shoreline of Belgium and the Netherlands. And over there, let's see, just passing off the right wing is . . . ah . . . the city of Amsterdam—" The voice cracked. *"Oh, shit, we're supposed to land there!"*

The arrival of newly hired young pilots on Pan Am property, beginning in 1964, was a cause for celebration by the stewardesses. (Not until the next decade would "stewardess" be replaced by "flight attendant.") They had seen no new male crew members since the late fifties.

Pan Am boasted an international, multilingual cabin service. Stewardesses were recruited for their looks and for their language skills. A significant number came from Europe—Sweden, France, England, Germany—and from Japan. Most were single.

The stewardesses called the short-haired, fresh-faced new-hire pilots "babygators." The babygators loved it. These were the 1960s, and between the newly liberated working girls in the cabin and the crew-cut, hot-blooded babygators, airborne romances blossomed like wildflowers.

Which made it hard on young marriages. Divorce was already an epidemic among veteran Pan Am airmen, as it was at most major airlines. No one could say exactly why—the long trips away from home, the proximity of young, available women, or just some rampant hormone in the pilot chemistry—but airline pilots divorced at about twice the national rate. Now it was cutting a swath through the new hires, obliterating marriages that had survived the hardships of remote military posts, long separations, and war.

Within the first year there were half a dozen divorces in Martinside's group. One of them was Martinside's.

It happened on a flight to Guam.

"What's her name?" asked Martinside.

"Jill Southall," said the engineer. "Don't even think about it."

"Why?"

"You want your ass fired? She's married to Frank Southall. He's a check captain and happens to be the meanest sonofabitch in the Pacific. I know two new hires already who got the boot because of him."

"Oh."

Check captains were Skygods of the ultimate magnitude. Their job was to police the way pilots were flying Pan Am's airplanes. They were the enforcers—and the terminators. Some of the check pilots were patient instructors and excellent airmen in their own right. Some, like Captain Frank Southall, were just plain mean.

All this Martinside already knew.

But she *was* lovely. She had red hair and an English accent and a mocking laugh. The signals sent by the flashing green eyes and the touch of her fingers on his sleeve were unmistakable.

Most of the new-hire pilots, like Martinside, had migrated from college to the military to the airlines. In their brief adulthood, they had never been exposed to the plenitude of comely young women they found at Pan Am. For many it was too much to resist. And so it was with Martinside.

He had already told himself to be sensible. To be prudent and disciplined. It was, after all, his career.

Then one night in Guam he dismissed prudence and discipline. He picked up the phone in his room. "It's Rob, Jill. Want to meet for a drink?"

That was all. One drink. Then the walk on the beach. Then the moonlight swim, even though there was no moon. And then back to his room because they were wet and sandy and, anyway, they needed a drink, even though it turned out he had nothing to drink. But it didn't matter.

Jill and Rob became an item.

In the subsequent weeks of their romance, Jill proved to be masterful at scheduling. As a junior pilot, Martinside had little control over his itinerary. But when he again landed in Guam, there was Jill. When he flew to Tokyo, Jill was one of the stewardesses assigned to the flight. Wherever he flew, it seemed, there was Jill. She arranged it.

It was wonderful. And it was dangerous. They could sense disaster trailing them like a shadow, lurking outside the door, peering through curtained windows. It was like making love at the edge of an abyss.

One day Jill made a mistake. She checked Martinside's schedule, and then, as usual, adjusted her own. But for once she neglected to check whether her husband had changed his schedule.

He had.

They were caught. There was an ugly scene in the hallway of the Royal Hawaiian Hotel in Honolulu between the Skygod and the new hire. The result was as predictable as the sun rising over Diamond Head.

The message was waiting for Martinside when he returned to San Francisco:

TO: THIRD OFFICER R. D. MARTINSIDE, SAN FRANCISCO BASE
FROM: CHIEF PILOT, PACIFIC

    YOU ARE SCHEDULED FOR A PROBATIONARY PILOT RETENTION HEARING IN THE OFFICE OF THE CHIEF PILOT AT 1300, 4 MARCH. YOU ARE ENTITLED TO REPRESENTATION BY ALPA.

Retention hearing. Like all probationary pilots, Martinside knew what that meant. It was airline code. It meant *fire his ass.*

He wore his blue suit, the same one he'd worn to the initial hiring interview. He had a fresh haircut. In a manila envelope tucked under his arm he carried copies of his initial aircraft training grades, which were excellent, and copies of two letters of commendation from captains he had flown with. It wouldn't hurt, he figured. Balance the bad with some good.

Even though probationary pilots had no contractual rights, they could be accompanied by a representative from ALPA, the pilots' union. Martinside declined. He thought his chances were better going it alone.

He showed up at five minutes before one o'clock. The outer office was swarming with company officials and uniformed pilots. Harried secretaries were simultaneously answering telephones and talking to the men leaning over their desks.

He worked his way to the desk of a matronly secretary. "Miss Becklund," he said, "I'm Robin Martinside—"

"Who?" Miss Becklund looked exasperated. She had worked around pilots for thirty years.

"Martinside. I'm here for a—"

"You picked a bad day for it."

"I didn't really pick it, Miss Becklund. I'm supposed to have a retention—"

"Look, young man, you'll have to come back another time. Haven't you heard? We've just lost an airplane."

Martinside walked back out of the office. His manila envelope was still tucked under his arm.

The news filtered down to the crew lounge. Pilots stood in clusters talking about the crash.

"What was it?"

"A 707 freighter, on descent into Manila. Disappeared off radar. They think it hit the mountain range east of the airport."

"Who was the captain?"

"Lou Cogliani."

Cogliani. No comment, just a silent nod. It wasn't the right time to make judgments. But each pilot guessed in his heart what had happened out there in the Pacific. And he worried that it could happen again.

It did. There were more accidents. And there was a series of near-accidents, most involving veteran captains of boat days vintage. An ominous trend was developing that no one was yet willing to examine. But a suspicion was taking root among the junior pilots that *something* was inherently flawed with the way Pan Am was flying airplanes. And it began somewhere in the inner soul of the company culture—with the Skygods.

One embarrassing incident involved Check Captain Frank Southall, who, on a gloriously clear day in Montreal, landed a Pan Am 707 at the wrong airport. Southall was relieved of his check duties and soon slipped off into retirement.

Not long after, when Rob Martinside went into the office to inquire about his "retention hearing," he was told to forget it. The matter had been dropped.

CHAPTER TEN

SUCCESSION

The old man rose early that morning. At the street level his driver was waiting in the Chrysler. It was a Tuesday, and traffic was heavy. Looking down Park Avenue, he could see the great canyon blocked by the towering slab with the fifteen-foot-high letters—PAN AM. It was still the world's largest commercial office building. The old man knew it continued to irritate the Primitives, and that thought gave him pleasure.

The driver deposited him at the usual place at the curb. His private elevator whisked him to the forty-sixth floor. He shuffled down the hall, smiling cordially to the minions whose names he couldn't remember.

It was the day of the annual stockholders' meeting, Juan Trippe's fortieth such occasion. The meeting was to be in the Windsor Ballroom of the Commodore Hotel, across the street. Trippe had forgotten when the meeting was supposed to convene. He called his vice president for public relations, Willis Player. "What time is the meeting?"

"Two-fifteen," said Player. Trippe acknowledged, and then promptly forgot. He returned to his task, working on the statement he would make to the stockholders.

At one-thirty, Player came by. It was time to go, he told Trippe. Trippe gathered his papers, and, Player leading, they took the elevator downstairs, descended by escalator into the Grand Central lobby, and went through the underground corridor to the Commodore.

Eight hundred stockholders were assembled in the ballroom. Uniformed Pan Am stewardesses were serving refreshments and distributing annual reports. Chairman Trippe called the meeting to order. In his high-pitched Eastern Establishment monotone he rambled along, reciting the mountain of statistics about the airline's economic performance.

Nineteen sixty-seven had been another spectacular year—when examined by itself. Pan Am had earned $65.7 million on revenues of $950 million. But that represented a 21.5 percent drop from the previous year. And the first quarter of 1968 showed that the slump was continuing—revenues up 15.6 percent against increased operating expenses of 22.6 percent, a loss of 4 cents a share versus last year's profit of 15 cents.

The numbers were buried in Trippe's forty-five-minute-long report. Few of the stockholders paid much attention. Several fell sound asleep.

The reason for the decline was obvious, but not easily explained: The phenomenal growth of passenger traffic during the first two-thirds of the decade was reversing itself. Pan Am's fleet of jets was flying around half empty. Worse, American overseas travelers were flying in larger numbers—over half of them—aboard foreign flag carriers.

Among the bored Pan Am stockholders there were no cries of alarm. No questions were raised. The numbers and their ominous trend caused them no concern. What the hell, Pan Am was still making money, wasn't it? They had come to vote on the directors, not to be bored with accounting data.

The chairman droned toward the end of his report. It was midafternoon and the audience was glassy-eyed. Several dozed in their chairs. Trippe told them that after the stockholders' meeting was adjourned, the new board of directors would meet.

And then he dropped the bomb.

"It is my intention to retire," Trippe said.

An electric current passed through the audience. *What did he say?*

"At the meeting of the board," the old man announced, "I plan to nominate President Harold Gray to succeed me as chairman and chief executive officer of our company."

Trippe is stepping down? Business reporters scurried for telephones. This was hot stuff. After forty-one years, the last airline tycoon was packing it in.

It took a moment to sink in. Someone began clapping. The rest of the stunned audience, unsure of the correct response, hesitantly joined in. The applause swelled and filled the ballroom.

Like all publicly held corporations, Pan American was supposed to be answerable to its stockholders and board of directors. And so it was, but Pan Am's directors also understood that Pan Am was, in effect, Juan Trippe's airline—his personal fiefdom.

Since July 1964, when Trippe arranged to have himself promoted to the newly created rank of chairman of the board, his control of Pan American had been total. Now he reigned over his conglomerate— airline, missile range, business jets, hotels, office building—in imperial isolation. Pan Am's corporate hierarchy was arranged along feudal lines with Trippe, the Supreme Skygod, at the head of the court. Beneath him his senior executives were moved like chess pieces, promoted and demoted at Trippe's whim, often without warning. Although he left the day-to-day management of the airline to his company officers, it was Trippe alone who steered Pan Am's course into the future. Trippe himself, often without any other consultation, made sweeping commitments to the boldest of new ventures.

By long tradition, the directors of Pan American World Airways were men of Trippe's choosing. They represented a cross section of the American Establishment, chosen less for business acumen than for their public stature. There were no mavericks among them, no dissenters, no shrill voices demanding explanations. They included Arthur Watson of IBM; Cyrus Vance, who would become Secretary of State; bankers James Rockefeller and Robert Lehman; Donald David, who had been dean of the Harvard Business School; Norman Chandler, chairman of the Los Angeles Times Mirror Company; Robert B. Anderson, former Secretary of the Treasury; and Charles Lindbergh, who was, perhaps, most unlike the others.

The board of directors met in the walnut-paneled boardroom on the forty-ninth floor an hour after the stockholders' meeting. Like the stockholders, none of the directors expressed concern that the traffic statistics were on a downward slope. No one was alarmed that the 707s were flying across the oceans less than half full. On this historic day no one wanted to suggest the awful possibility that Pan Am might be heading into stormy seas. Not one of the eminent persons on the board of directors interrupted the proceedings to clear his throat and pose the awkward question: *Excuse me, gentlemen, but if we can't fill our 707s, how are we going to make money with a fleet of 747s, each of which carries two and a half times as many passengers as the 707?*

The directors were there to do what Pan Am's boards traditionally did: vote their approval of Juan Trippe's decisions. On this auspicious day, the business of Trippe's retirement and the succession overshadowed any discussion about the company's performance. Trippe was stepping down. The company was doing business as usual. The giant new 747—Trippe's Everyman airplane—was coming next year. All in all, it was an occasion for smiles.

It was a ritualistic passing of the torch. Trippe, still the chairman, asked seventy-six-year-old Robert Lehman, investment banker and longtime Establishment figure, to take over as temporary chairman. Trippe then formally nominated Harold Gray and Najeeb Halaby for the posts of chairman and president.

Each director cast his vote. It was unanimous, in favor.

And then Charles Lindbergh nominated Trippe for the post of chairman emeritus. Again, a unanimous vote.

None of the directors was surprised by Trippe's choice of Gray to succeed him, because Trippe had called each of them the week before. They were comfortable with Gray, although no one had ever thought of him as some bright new vision for Pan Am's future. Gray was a solid manager, an insider who understood Pan Am's cabalistic company culture.

When Harold Gray came to Pan American at the age of twenty-three, the tenth pilot in its history to be hired, everyone knew he was different. He was not at all like the seat-of-the-pants, fly-for-the-hell-of-it pilots of his time. Gray was a cerebral aviator, one of the few of his generation with a degree in aeronautical engineering. At Pan American he became known as a flying theoretician. He was an oddball with a slide rule.

It was Gray who figured out the most economical power settings for the Ford trimotors. Gray put the first instrument flying methods to the test at Pan American. It was Gray who oversaw the extensive testing and modification of the troubled Boeing B-314 flying boats.

Harold Gray was a Skygod from the same mold as Ed Musick. When the great Musick's S-42B erupted in a ball of flame off Pago Pago in 1938, Gray quietly took his place. The first pilot to pass all the tests and ascend to the rank of Master of Ocean Flying Boats was, of course, Harold Gray.

Gray was just the sort of thinker/pilot/manager Priester had in mind for Pan American. In 1937 he tapped Gray to command the S-42B *Clipper II,* the first Atlantic survey flight to Europe. Gray was captain of the inaugural Atlantic crossing of the *Yankee Clipper,* the Boeing B-314 flying boat. At the age of thirty-two, he was chief pilot of the Atlantic Division (in those days Pan Am had Atlantic, Pacific-Alaska, and Latin American divisions). Then he became a vice president of the Pacific-Alaska Division, where he was the first manager to operate the division without government subsidy and still make money. When he became vice president of the prestigious Atlantic Division, he also made that operation profitable. When the east-west departments were combined into the Overseas Division, Gray was put in charge.

In 1964, when Juan Trippe decided to elevate his own rank to that of chairman of the board and chief executive officer, he named Harold Gray as president.

Among the old hands from the boat days, Gray commanded intense loyalty. He was seen as a decent man, perhaps one plateau removed from the deviousness that characterized Pan American's top management.

A streak of Boy Scout ran through Harold Gray. Throughout his career he held to the belief that the pure, unvarnished numbers—speed, capacity, profit, loss—would speak for themselves. Gray despised the political games Pan Am played in Washington—the incessant lobbying, the mansion Pan Am kept in the capital just for entertaining, the stroking of pet politicians like Senator Owen Brewster of Maine and Congresswoman Claire Booth Luce, wife of Trippe's fellow Yaleman Henry Luce. Such things shouldn't be necessary, Gray thought. If the airline was run efficiently and safely enough, everyone would know. The world, of its own accord, would beat a path to Pan Am's door.

Which was why, of course, a man like Harold Gray had no use

for a man like Najeeb Halaby. Halaby was not one of the old boat hands. Halaby hadn't worked his way up in the airline business as Gray had. He was a Washington glamour boy whose only role was to do what Gray most despised—to *lobby.*

To Juan Trippe, such naiveté was worrisome. Many thought that it explained his choice of Najeeb Halaby as Gray's backup man. It would be a typical Trippe solution—combining Gray's clear-headed operational sense with Halaby's political savvy. It ought to be the perfect match.

Not all the board members were as sanguine about Trippe's choice of a successor for Gray. Some of the directors, privately, had raised objections. *Halaby?*

"What does he know about running an airline?"

"Jeeb? Well, now, Jeeb's a nice fellow and all that, but . . ."

"I *love* Jeeb Halaby. Terrific guy. But he's hardly qualified to . . ."

They knew better than to bring it up with Trippe. One of them went to Gray with his concerns. Gray had never concealed his own misgivings about Halaby.

But now Gray only shrugged. "What difference does it make?" he said. "There isn't anybody else."

And in a sense, there wasn't. Trippe had approached the matter of succession as he had done everything else at Pan Am—with a calculated vagueness. Those few executives he had recruited with the apparent intent of grooming them for the succession inevitably gained the impression that the old man would *never* retire. And even if he did, he would somehow continue to rule Pan Am from the wings. Maybe even from the grave. Pan Am would *always* be Trippe's airline.

For years it looked like John Leslie, a brilliant young engineer who had joined Pan Am in the thirties, would be Trippe's heir. Trippe had made Leslie a vice president and, in 1950, a director. But then Leslie had been crippled with polio. After a long absence he managed to come back to work, but for the rest of his life he was bound to a wheelchair.

Another candidate was Roger Lewis, who had come on board in 1955 from his job as assistant secretary of the Air Force. Lewis had distinguished himself as a talented manager and seemed to be the heir apparent. But like the others, he had doubts about Trippe's ever turning over command of his empire. And along the way, Lewis had acquired doubts about Pan Am's long-term chances. He worried that Pan Am's constant political maneuvering in Washington had poisoned its chances for further route awards. He saw the domestic airlines eventually overrunning Pan Am's position as the premier international carrier. When the offer came to assume the top post at General Dynamics, an aircraft manufacturing conglomerate, Roger Lewis jumped ship.

There had been no one else, no one but the old Master of Ocean Flying Boats, Harold Gray. Onto his shoulders, almost by default, would slip the mantle of Supreme Skygod. And after him, Najeeb Halaby.

They took the official photograph of the three of them. In the picture, they were all smiling. It was a portrait of unity, the torch being passed from Trippe's strong hand to the firm grips of his successors. Gray, the faithful lieutenant, sat at his customary place on Trippe's right. Halaby, the novitiate, was on the left. The polished table and the mahogany paneling in the backdrop reinforced the photograph's message of stability and permanence. There was a model of the mighty new 747 nearby.

For those who expressed nervousness about Najeeb Halaby, the company line now was that Halaby was there to learn. He had plenty of time. "Don't worry about Jeeb," the insiders were saying. "Harold is only sixty-two. He'll be the chairman for at least five years before Jeeb takes over."

Five years. That was the envelope. It allowed everyone to feel less worried about the succession. A lot could happen in five years.

But there was more in the photograph they took that day. When examined up close, the picture revealed dark shadows ringing Harold Gray's eyes. Beneath the affable smile and outward show of exuberance, Gray was concealing a deadly secret. He had been diagnosed with a virulent form of cancer. He was undergoing cobalt treatments and was frequently in severe pain. The fate of Pan American World Airways was in the hands of a dying man.

Juan Trippe walked down the hallway with his old colleague. Trippe ushered Harold Gray into the big office at the southwest corner. He told Gray to take over the office, desk and all. Don't bother moving new stuff in, he told him. In any case, Trippe said, he would be moving into a smaller office down the hall. He would be in next morning.

Trippe said good-bye to Kathleen Clair, his secretary of the past eighteen years. She had tears in her eyes. As he shuffled down the hall he acknowledged with a nod and a smile the well-wishing staffers standing outside their offices.

His driver was waiting at the street below. Spring sunshine slanted down the walled avenues. It was May 7, 1968. The long death of Pan American World Airways had begun.

PART II

DESCENT

CHAPTER ELEVEN

CRASH

Every night for a month after the accident, Jim Wood dreamed about Lou Cogliani. It was a recurring dream, and it was very real.

You're too low, said Jim Wood. *You've descended too soon.*

Captain Cogliani didn't hear. He continued descending.

Lou Cogliani didn't like crew members riding in the jump seat behind him. He always said that he didn't want people looking over his shoulder. But in his dream, Wood rode the jump seat of the Boeing 707 freighter, *Clipper Rising Sun*, directly behind the captain. He watched the approach into Manila, and he was powerless to interfere.

They were making a VOR/DME nonprecision approach to the Manila airport. The thirty-mile descent path to the runway was divided into segments, like stair steps. Each segment was flown at a prescribed altitude that allowed the airplane to clear the mountainous terrain beneath. The descent from one stair step to the next was determined by the DME—the distance-measuring equipment—which told the crew exactly how many miles they were from the airport.

It was a dark, moonless night. Squalls from an offshore typhoon buffeted the jet, and intermittent rain hammered on the aluminum skin.

The 707 passed through three thousand feet. Outside the cockpit windows, there was only darkness.

You're supposed to be at thirty-one hundred feet, Lou. No lower.

Cogliani was at twenty-nine hundred feet. He continued descending. Twenty-eight hundred feet. Twenty-seven . . .

103

In the right seat, the first officer, Tom Rehman, was busy. He had his head down, studying the approach plate, trying to read the tiny print that identified the distance and altitude for each segment of the approach. At the same time he was answering questions from Manila Control. He seemed confused. "You're supposed to be at . . . uh, let's see . . . twenty-five hundred feet at twenty-three miles out." And then he returned to his radio conversation with Manila Control.

They were still *thirty miles out*. And they were too low.

Lou Cogliani's attention was riveted on his instruments. Occasionally he sneaked hurried glances at the approach plate near his elbow. Wood could see that Cogliani was glancing at *the wrong segment* for the altitude he was flying. The descending 707 was one stair step lower than it was supposed to be.

Jim Wood watched helplessly. *There's a mountain out there, Lou. It's not on the approach plate. You can't see it in the darkness.*

Cogliani descended to twenty-five hundred feet.

Pull up, Lou.

Rehman's head was still down. He was trying to determine the DME mileage for the next step-down altitude in the approach. Manila Control called on the radio, asking for the airplane's position.

The mountain loomed out of the darkness like an expanding shadow. A sudden blackness filled the windscreen, and for an instant both pilots glanced up.

What's that . . . ?

Clipper Rising Sun slammed into the sloping crest of the mountain. Her 130 tons of aluminum and steel alloy tore a mile-long swath through a forest of mahogany trees.

The debris littered the forest, where it burned for over six hours. There were no survivors.

The preliminary accident investigation had already determined the probable cause of the accident, and Jim Wood was not satisfied. It was one thing to attribute the accident to a mistaken altitude, or a procedural error. What bothered Wood was that it seemed so inevitable.

One night over beers in Sausalito, he told Rob Martinside about the dream.

"Why didn't somebody—the first officer, the engineer—tell him he was at the wrong altitude?"

"Because he was a Skygod," said Martinside. "You don't tell Skygods they're wrong."

"I do."

"Yeah, I remember. You almost got fired."

"But I was right."

"So what?"

"So it will happen again."

And so it did.

Papeete, Tahiti, July 22, 1973

A moonless South Pacific night.

The heavily laden Pan Am 707 lumbered toward the runway for takeoff. In addition to her sixty-nine passengers and ten crew members, she carried the great store of jet fuel needed for the flight back to Honolulu. The rotating beacon on the belly of the jet cast a red hue on the tropical grass by the taxiway.

The usual crowd—relatives, fellow tourists, airline employees—waited in the open lounge, watching the jetliner depart. The Papeete airport had an informal, open-air ambiance. It was like something from a Somerset Maugham story. Travelers hated leaving Tahiti. In a short time the place grew on them, and they wanted to stay.

In the cockpit of the 707, Captain Bob Evarts responded to the checklist. Evarts was a senior captain, now in his last year of a career that had begun in the flying boat days. His first officer, Clyde Havens, was the same age—fifty-nine. His career had been nearly as long as Evarts's, but Havens had never been a captain. Years ago he had failed the upgrade training for the left seat and was relegated to the status of permanent copilot. "Clyde's okay," captains said about Haven. "He's just a little slow. You have to watch Clyde."

Following the instructions from the tower, they taxied onto the active runway. Beyond the twin rows of white runway lights that stretched for nearly two miles in front of them was the end of the runway. Then an inky blackness. There was no horizon. The sea and the sky melded together in a featureless black void.

"Clipper eight-oh-two," said the Papeete control tower operator, "the wind is two-four-zero at eight knots. You're cleared for takeoff."

Havens acknowledged the clearance. The jet began its takeoff roll.

From the airport terminal they watched the 707 trundle down the runway. The noise of the four fan-jets swelled in a crescendo. The jetliner gathered speed, rushing to the distant end of the runway. It lifted, and climbed into the blackness beyond the shore. From the terminal there was no way to tell if the jet was climbing, descending, or turning. The lights of the departing 707 twinkled in the black void beyond the shore.

And then, an orange flash.

Seconds later, nothing. The lights were gone. Clipper 802 had vanished from sight.

In the terminal, disbelief.

"What happened?"

"Where did it go?"

"Do you think . . . ?"

Airmen hate mysteries. For every accident, they want to know the *probable cause*.

No probable cause was determined for the loss of Flight 802. Most of the wreckage of the Boeing 707, including the vital flight data recorder and cockpit voice recorder—crashproof "black boxes" that capsulized the jet's last flight—sank to the floor of the Pacific. It was never recovered.

Investigators combed the scant evidence, looking for clues. In the maintenance history of the airplane was a recent wing flap discrepancy. Had the flaps retracted asymmetrically? If so, might it have caused an uncontrollable roll, making the jet plummet downward to the ocean? Another discrepancy involved the windshield heat. Could a windshield have shattered, distracting or blinding or incapacitating the pilots?

Maybe. Or was it something else? Something nonmechanical? One inescapable statistic about aviation accidents was that most were caused by human factors. Since the first flight of the Wright brothers, aviation was a plethora of mistakes waiting to be made—landing short of the runway, forgetting to lower the landing gear or the wing flaps, running out of fuel, misjudging things like altitude, airspeed, distance.

Such lapses were always branded with the most searing of aviation indictments: *pilot error.*

By a great extrapolation of logic, investigators could conclude that *every* accident was somehow the result of human error. *Someone* should have caught the discrepancy, the circumstances, the procedural omission that permitted an accident to occur. In the final analysis of aviation mishaps, it always came down to the pilots. Pilots were almost always in the loop of blame, because they had the last vote in every impending calamity.

But that view was simplistic. In the accident equation, it still missed the all-important *Why?*

A more significant fact was that most fatal airline accidents—more than two-thirds—happened during the takeoff or landing phase. And a disturbingly high proportion of those accidents occurred at night, or in low visibility, and at airports that lacked an ILS—an instrument landing system, an electronic approach path transmitter that guided airplanes precisely down a glide path to the touchdown point on the runway.

Which described the world of Pan American.

Pan Am's planet-wide route system covered the typhoon-scoured atolls of the Pacific, the equatorial republics of South America, the backwaters of Central Africa. Pan Am had the highest exposure to primitive airports of any major airline in the western world. Unlike the domestic carriers that operated exclusively in the comfortable, radar-controlled airway system of the United States, Pan Am's jets made daily—and nightly—arrivals into the world's most backward facilities.

So what happened in Tahiti? No one would ever know for sure. Rob Martinside blamed the "black hole" syndrome. Since aviators first flew at night, there had been a problem with spatial disorientation in the blackness. For the first few seconds after liftoff, as pilots made the transition from gazing outside at runway lights to looking inside at their instruments, they didn't always believe what they saw. It was particularly difficult over an empty, horizonless ocean. A common accident off aircraft carriers was the phenomenon of airmen launching into the black night off the bow of the ship, then inexplicably flying into the water. The cause was visual disorientation—the pilot's flawed senses overruling what he read on his instruments.

But such speculation was blasphemy in Skygod country, particularly when spoken by new-hire know-nothings. You didn't second-guess the actions of a lost crew, particularly when there was no hard evidence in the form of a cockpit voice recorder or flight data recorder. Every trace of evidence from Flight 802, black boxes included, lay eighteen thousand feet beneath the waves.

The older Pan Am pilots closed ranks around their peers. Give the deceased the benefit of the doubt. Maybe it *was* a split flap, or a windshield problem. Better to accept such an explanation than to impugn the reputation of a Pan Am captain.

"Bullshit," said Jim Wood, who saw no reason to be charitable. He had seen the Skygods in action. It angered him that no one wanted to confront the *real* problem.

"How many airliners have had accidents because of a split flap— day *or* night? Virtually none. Or a shattered windshield?"

None.

Wood had his own theory: "It was dark. They took off in a 707 that was heavily loaded and didn't climb fast. They got disoriented and let it fly into the water."

It was a private theory. He had the good sense to keep it to himself.

Pago Pago, Samoa, July 22, 1973

Another Pacific island. Another dark night, with rain and gusty winds, and yet another instrument approach to a runway without an electronic glide slope. A Pan Am 707 plowed through the jungle short of the runway, then burned. Ninety-one people perished.

By now it was clear to everyone, even the Skygods. The crash of Flight 806 on the island of Pago Pago brought to ten the number of Pan American 707s destroyed. Pan Am was littering the islands of the Pacific with the hulks of Boeing jetliners. The chairman of the board ordered a special task force to be put together, called the Operations Review Group. The group was to study the reasons for Pan Am's recent abysmal safety record and to recommend methods to prevent another crash.

The group's sixty-nine-page report was completed on April 23, 1974. It was too late.

Tokyo, April 22, 1974

Captain Al Neubaur yawned. In nearly thirty years of international flying, he had never adjusted to the nine-hour time change between the Far East and California. Back in Palo Alto it was nearly dinnertime. Here in Tokyo it was morning, and Neubaur wished he were going to bed, not departing on a flight.

Neubaur glanced at the wall clock in the lobby of the Keio Plaza Hotel. Ten to six. Ten more minutes before he and the rest of the crew would be picked up for the long drive out to Haneda Airport. The flight to Guam departed at nine in the morning. Outside, a damp winter grayness lay over Tokyo. Neubaur would be glad to leave. He had been away from home for four days, and he had four to go. At least in Guam the sun would be out.

Five of his six flight attendants were already downstairs, chatting in the lobby. The first officer and the flight engineer, in their gold-striped uniforms, sat in the lounge reading newspapers.

"Telephone for Captain Neubaur," said the uniformed page boy.

Damn, thought the captain. A schedule change, probably. Another night in Tokyo.

It was the Pan Am station manager at Haneda Airport. Neubaur's face hardened. "You want *me* to tell them?"

Neubaur motioned for his crew to follow him to an empty corner of the lobby. He repeated what the station manager had told him.

There was a stunned silence.

Then a stewardess, a pretty, blond woman in her early thirties, went crazy. *"You're killing us!"* she shrieked. She flailed at the captain with her fists. *"You goddam pilots!"*

Neubaur tried to hold her arms. Astonished hotel guests stared at the bizarre scene. The hysterical woman was beating at the captain's chest.

The other crew members managed to calm the stewardess. She collapsed into a lounge chair, sobbing.

One of the flight attendants, a steward, glowered at Neubaur. "Those were her roommates on that flight."

Incredibly, *another* Pan Am 707 was down.

The circumstances were depressingly familiar. Another moonless night. Another Pacific island. A nonprecision approach to yet another primitive airport.

Again, no survivors.

This time it was on the island of Bali, in the Indonesian Archipelago. The wreckage was strewn over a remote mountainside twenty-five miles north of the airport.

Flight 812, inbound from Hong Kong, had begun its approach in darkness toward the Bali airport using the NDB—the nondirectional radio beacon. Like most Pacific island airports, Bali lacked an instrument landing system.

An NDB approach was a primitive procedure, by jet age standards, more suitable for bush pilots and gun runners than for commercial airliners. Nonetheless, in the developing countries of the world—Pan Am's working world—NDBs were still in wide use. Instead of making a straight-in approach on an electronic glide path, as they would do at most United States airports, pilots at Bali had to fly over the archaic NDB radio beacon, fly out over the blackened ocean for several miles while they descended, then turn back and fly to the airport.

Pilots tracked their course by watching a quivering pointer needle on the radio compass. The trick was to fly directly over the station, which the pilot recognized by a "swing" of the needle, from the top to the bottom of the compass. Then he turned to fly outbound before turning back to the airport.

They called it a "teardrop" procedure, because the pattern—the outbound leg, a reversal of course, then inbound to the same place—had a teardrop shape. Pilots hated the procedure, because it was difficult and imprecise and things could go wrong.

On the night of April 22, something went wrong. Flight 812 went down somewhere on the island of Bali.

The investigating team spent two sweaty, insect-infested weeks in the mountainous jungle. When at last the flight data recorder and the cockpit voice recorders were uncovered, one vital clue emerged.

The pilots had not flown over the station before beginning the outbound turn for the teardrop approach. They had turned too soon.

Again, the agonizing question: *Why?*

Snippets of crew conversation from the recovered cockpit voice recorder provided clues. While still inbound to the station, the pilots of Flight 812 mentioned that they observed the needle of number one radio swinging. The 707 was equipped with two direction-finding radios, and the number two needle remained steady, still pointing straight ahead. This was confusing, one radio indicating they had passed the station, the other indicating they had not.

The crew made a fateful decision. They concluded that the swinging needle was the correct one and that they had passed over the station.

In their next radio communication, they reported to Bali Control that they were turning outbound on a 263-degree track and descending to a lower altitude. Bali Control, which had no radar and no way of knowing where Clipper 812 actually was, acknowledged the report.

Flight 812 was still thirty miles to the north of the airport, descending in darkness toward the crest of a 7,500-foot mountain.

When Bali Tower had heard nothing from the Pan Am jet for several minutes, the tower controller radioed: "Clipper eight-one-two, Bali Tower."

No answer.

"Clipper eight-one-two, Bali Tower, how do you read?"

Clipper 812 did not read. What had once been a gleaming aluminum jetliner was now a litter of pulverized and burning wreckage scattered a hundred meters below the summit of the mountain.

The Bali calamity brought Pan Am's 707 losses to eleven. Pan Am had crashed more Boeing jets than any other carrier in the world. And not just 707s. A three-engine 727 was lost during a night approach to Berlin. One of the new 747s struck the approach lights and incurred heavy damage during a miscalculated takeoff in San Francisco. Another 747 was lost to a new and still unrecognized threat—Arab terrorists, who hijacked the jumbo jet in Amsterdam, then had it flown to Cairo, where they blew it up.

Something had to be done. Before the smoke subsided from the burning wreckage on Mount Patas in Bali, the probe of Pan American's flight operations had begun.

Inspectors from the Federal Aviation Administration climbed aboard Pan Am Clippers all over the world. FAA men rode in cockpits, pored through maintenance records, asked questions, observed check rides and training flights.

The inspection went on for six weeks. The FAA's findings confirmed the dismal facts that the internal Operations Review Group had already determined: *Pan Am was crashing airplanes at three times the average rate of the United States airlines.* Worse, Pan Am's accident rate was on the rise, a reverse of the steadily decreasing industry-wide accident experience with jet airliners.

The report was scathing. Pan Am's accidents in the Pacific, declared the FAA, involved "substandard airmen." Training was inadequate, said the inspectors, and there was a lack of standardization among crews. The FAA's list went on to cover a host of operational items, matters of training manuals, route qualification, radio communications, and availability of spare parts.

But at the heart of Pan Am's troubles, according to the FAA, were *human factors.* That was the trendy new term psychologists were using in accident reports. It meant *people who screw up.* When applied to airline cockpits, it had the same taint as *pilot error.*

With the exception of a crash caused by a cargo fire, and excluding the unknown circumstances of the Tahiti crash, *every recent Pan Am accident could be attributed to some form of pilot error.*

The indictment landed in Skygod country like a canister of tear gas.

Substandard airmen? Wait a minute, you bureaucratic piss ants . . . this is Pan American, the world's most experienced airline. . . . We were the first fly jets, the first to . . .

That was then, said the Feds. This is now. Clean up your act, or you will be the world's most *grounded* airline.

Heads, of course, would have to roll. And so they did, particularly in the San Francisco base, where the Skygod umbrella had long ago been raised over the heads of the venerable Masters of Ocean Flying

Boats. Since the boat days the most senior pilots of Pan Am had made San Francisco *their* base, the Pacific *their* ocean.

The vice president of flight operations and the airline's de facto chief pilot, Don Kinkel, was replaced. Before his rise to senior management, Kinkel had been the chief pilot of the Pacific operation. His lieutenant, Ira Anderson, the new San Francisco chief pilot and former head of training in the Pacific, received his walking papers directly behind Kinkel. Down through each succeeding level of management, in quick succession, the airmen in charge of training, checking, and administration were dismissed.

Jim Waugh, a 747 captain with an unblemished record in the training department, was made a vice president and placed in charge of Pan Am flight operations. Walt Mullikin, a bright and tough-minded manager, became the new chief pilot of the Pacific operation. Ned Brown, a Miami captain with a reputation for hard-nosed efficiency, took over the Atlantic. A separate department was established to oversee all matters of flight safety, headed by Fran Wallace, a highly regarded senior captain from the flying boat era.

Pilots' training and performance histories were reviewed. A list of over a hundred senior pilots with spotty records was compiled. Quietly, with much dignity, the old pelicans received a gentle but emphatic shove into retirement.

But the most profound change was still coming. It was an invisible transformation, and it had more to do with philosophy than with procedure. Pan Am was forced to peer into its own soul and answer previously unasked questions. Instead of *What's wrong with the way we fly airplanes?* the question became *What's wrong with the way we manage our cockpits?*

A new term was coming into play: *crew concept.* The idea was that crews were supposed to function as management teams, not autocracies with a supreme captain and two or three lackeys. It meant the captain was still the captain, but he no longer had the divine license to crash his airplane without the consent of his crew. Copilots and flight engineers—*lowly new hires*—were now empowered to speak up. Their opinions actually counted for something.

Disagree? With the captain? In the enclaves of the Skygods, it amounted to anarchy. Hadn't the Masters of Ocean Flying Boats labored for thirty years to preserve the cult of the Skygod? The barbarians were storming the gates.

But history was running against the ancient Skygods. Though Pan American technology had led the world into the jet age, Pan Am's cockpits had not emerged from the flying boat days. A new era, like it or not, was upon them. The Skygods were about to become as extinct as pterodactyls.

It was painful at first, but time was already solving part of the problem. Most of the hard-bitten Skygods—relics of the boat days—were at retirement age. Many had already been swept out in the purge by the Operations Review Group. Their younger counterparts, the more recently promoted captains, were quicker to embrace the new crew concept, because they had endured the tyranny of the Masters of Ocean Flying Boats for their entire copiloting careers.

The cockpit transformation came down to two separate problems. The first was to de-autocratize the cockpit—to dismantle the Skygod ethic. Pan Am captains would have to learn the subtle differences between commanding and managing. Junior pilots must learn to participate in the decision-making process.

This was revolutionary. Pan Am *copilots* actually having an opinion . . .

The other problem was standardization. There wasn't any. With each captain he flew with, a copilot had to learn a new set of procedures.

Pilots from the unregulated, make-the-rules-as-you-go-along flying boat days were inherently nonstandard. They were, by God, *supposed* to be different. Flying was a game for individuals—chest-thumping, throttle-pushing, flint-eyed Masters of Ocean Flying Boats—not compliant drones.

The newer breed of airmen had grown up in a different environment. High-tech airplanes demanded a collaborative effort from their crews. Uniqueness in a pilot was okay, but it ought to be manifested by *excellence,* by a mastery of technical skill, rather than by eccentricity.

The Pacific Division, home of the Skygods, had the most idiosyncratic captains. Each had a personal fetish.

"Forget that damn checklist, son," a captain told Rob Martinside.

"You're not flying for Pan American today. You're flying for me."

One of Lou Cogliani's idiosyncrasies was that he wanted his airplane flown everywhere, over the ocean or on airways, *one hundred feet off the assigned altitude.* "It's smoother," he explained. "No one else is flying at that altitude, stirring up the air."

Crew members would nod at each other and wink. *Stirring up the air?* That would be like throwing a pebble in San Francisco Bay and making waves in Honolulu. But they knew better than to get into an argument about applied physics with Cogliani. "Sure, captain, that's a great idea. . . ."

Hud Gibson, a portly and mean-spirited captain, was conservation-minded. He ordered his crews to turn off every nonessential radio, light, instrument, and navigation device. "It saves electricity," he said, sitting in his blacked-out and nearly radioless cockpit.

Some captains scheduled themselves exclusively on the round-the-world route, a week-long journey that took them completely around the planet. But they would do it in only one direction—east-bound—because they flew in the northern hemisphere and the annoying rays of the sun always beat on the right side of the cockpit, the first officer's side.

Other captains didn't bother with such complications. They taped navigation charts over the windscreen and all the windows on their side. The sun—and everything else—was blocked from view. They flew around the earth in sublime, shady comfort.

"But you can't see outside, captain," said a foolish copilot.

"I don't need to, son. I'm the captain."

The magic word *standardization* brought eventual relief. It meant that everybody operated the airplane the same way. Total strangers—captains and first officers—could check in for a flight, enter the cockpit, and work in total harmony. They could fly the airplane around the world—and each would know what the other would do. Gone were the surprises.

It would take time to change an ethic so deeply embedded in the airline's skin, but there was no choice. It had to work.

And work it did. The nightmare was over.

From 1974, following the Bali accident, *not another Pan Am 707 was lost in a crash.*

The 747, which was emerging as the new flagship, established itself as the safest airliner ever operated by Pan Am. Not a single life would ever be lost in a flying accident with a Pan Am 747.*

Pan American went on to establish a safety record that was the envy of the industry.

---

* In neither of two fatal 747 disasters—the bombing of Flight 103 in 1988 and the ground collision with a KLM 747 at Tenerife in 1977—was the 747 or the Pan Am crew held to blame.

CHAPTER TWELVE

VIETNAM

Ton Son Nhut Air Base, Saigon, May 1968

What the hell are we doing here?

That was what Rob Martinside wondered, standing there beneath the broad wing of the jetliner. He squinted in the bright sun. Across the sprawling ramp he could count six more tall tails bearing the blue Pan Am emblem. There were others—World Airways, TWA, Flying Tigers—but most of the commercial aircraft hauling troops and matériel into Vietnam belonged to Pan American World Airways.

The troops went to war in the upholstered comfort of a Pan Am jetliner. Even as they stepped out into the searing heat of Saigon, they could hear the din of war—artillery firing over on the Mekong shore, the afterburners of the F-4s thundering down the same runway Pan Am had just landed on, the load masters yelling at the grunts who were sliding cargo pallets out the cargo door of the 707.

So far no Pan Am airplane had been hit by ground fire in Vietnam. But on the home front, Pan Am was taking heavy flak. The airline's role in the Vietnam airlift was attracting the wrath of the war-haters, who considered Pan Am to be as criminally culpable as the Dow Chemical Company, Bob McNamara, and the CIA. Rocks smashed through the windows of Pan Am ticket offices in sporadic demonstrations around the country.

The war had become an awkward subject with the Pan Am new hires. None thought of himself as a military service evader. Most had already been in the military, and some had even served in Vietnam in the pre-buildup days. When Martinside and his classmates joined Pan

Am, Vietnam had not yet escalated to a full-fledged war. But that was before the Tonkin Gulf affair in 1964, the putative raid by North Vietnamese gunboats on American warships. Then came the Lyndon Johnson blow-'em-back-to-the-stone-age bombing campaign, followed by a steady increase in American troop strength. Martinside and his classmates still had friends flying missions in Southeast Asia.

Now, a strange irony. Intentionally or not, they had been spared from the war. But here they were anyway.

Pan Am jets hauled toilet paper and canned food and ammunition and spare tires and clothing. They hauled troops in, and they hauled them out.

At the far end of the ramp a load of soldiers was waiting to be hauled out. They were in no hurry. They lay in aluminum coffins, sixteen to a pallet, waiting to be loaded in cargo bays of the jetliners —the same jetliners that hauled in the foodstuffs and toilet paper and ammunition and spare tires. A forklift could slide an entire pallet of coffins into the cargo bay of a jet freighter.

Martinside tried not to think of the coffins as he performed his checks for the flight back to Guam. There another crew would continue the flight to Honolulu. Their passengers were soldiers—live ones—bound for a week of R&R, rest and recreation, in Honolulu.

They took off for Guam. After a layover, Martinside and his crew continued on to Honolulu, where they would pick up a new load for the flight back to Vietnam.

That was the part Martinside hated. Taking them back.

Pan Am had a contract to fly rest and recreation flights, airlifting GIs out of the battlefield for a week's leave in Hong Kong, Taipei, Sydney, Tokyo, or Honolulu. The married soldiers usually chose Honolulu, because their wives could fly on discounted tickets to join them.

What troubled Martinside wasn't the coffins. The war was over for them. What he didn't like was the endless stream of live bodies being pumped into the maw of Vietnam.

He was doing the pumping.

The soldiers were mostly kids from down-home America—the farms, the dusty little towns, the urban barrios. He saw them strolling the sidewalks of Waikiki, hand in hand with their sunburned, teenaged, usually pregnant, scared-to-death wives, trying to condense a lifetime into seven days.

The hard part—the time that Martinside came to hate—was the departure. It was early, just before sunrise. The wives, as usual, came to the airport to say good-bye to their soldier husbands. Their lifetime-in-a-week was over.

The front of the 707, the cockpit, pointed directly into the departure lounge. For the pilots there was no way to avoid it. As they sat there performing their preflight, waiting to be pushed back from the gate, they had to look through the window of the lounge, directly into the tear-streaked, swollen faces of the young wives. The women stared back at them.

Martinside had never seen such grief. They were weeping, not in the way people commonly cry in departure lounges, but in an ancient, intuitive way women have always wept when their men went off to battle. Each of the women looked as if she had just seen her husband for the last time.

A heavy silence hung over the cockpit. None of the pilots felt like talking. They all wanted to leave Honolulu. Martinside was thinking about the pallets—*sixteen coffins to a pallet*—that would fill their cargo bays on the trip home.

"We're cleared to push, captain," said the voice on the ground interphone.

"Good," said the captain. "Let's get the hell out of here."

Darkness had fallen over South Vietnam.

"Clipper eleven-oh-one," said the Saigon approach controller, "you're advised to fly a high approach."

"Clipper eleven-oh-one, understand," acknowledged Martinside, the first officer. A high approach into Saigon was standard practice, especially at night. It just meant that you descended to the runway at a very steep angle to increase the vertical distance between you and any unfriendlies outside the airport perimeter.

They were still twenty-five miles out when they saw the flashes.

"What's going on down there, approach?" Martinside asked.

"Uh, we think it's incoming fire, Clipper. Don't know yet. We're checking."

They could see Ton Son Nhut from the cockpit now. Orange belches of flame were erupting along the northern airport boundary. Then they saw a brilliant flash *inside* the perimeter, near the operations complex.

"Did you see that?" said Al.

"Uh huh," said Martinside.

More flashes on the airport. Downtown Saigon began to light up with scattered explosions. It looked like a major fireworks display.

A silhouetted object swept past the nose of the 707, trailing a torch of flame.

"What the hell was that?"

"I don't know," said Martinside. "A fighter, I think."

"Uh, Clipper eleven-oh-one," said the controller, his voice an octave higher than before, "be advised they're launching F-4s from Ton Son Nhut and also from Bien Hoa. We're not controlling them."

"Shit!" said Al. "Turn on the landing lights."

"Lights on," replied Martinside, reaching for the switches. The jetliner would be illuminated like a lighthouse. What was the biggest risk? he wondered. Being rammed by a friendly fighter, or being hit by ground fire?

They could see parachute flares descending on the airport. The landscape around the Ton Son Nhut airport was lit bright as day.

"Clipper eleven-oh-one, this is Pan Op. Do you read?" It was the Pan Am operations office at Ton Son Nhut on the company frequency.

"Go ahead, Pan Op."

"Message for you. Divert, Red Brick instructions. I Repeat. Divert, Red Brick instructions. Is that clear?"

"Roger, Pan Op. Understand Red Brick. We're diverting. Can you tell us what's going on?"

"Negative. We don't know. We're getting the hell out of here and heading for the shelter. See you later."

"Red Brick" was company code. It meant an emergency was in progress at the destination airport, and the inbound aircraft was instructed to divert to another airport. In this case, they were supposed to go to Hong Kong.

Climbing into the night sky over South Vietnam, Martinside looked back over his shoulder in the direction of Saigon. It looked like the city was in flames. Orange spurts of fire were blossoming across the blackened countryside.

When the radio chatter had subsided and a new flight plan was filed to Hong Kong, they talked about what had happened.

"I must have missed something in the briefing package," said Al. "Was there anything about expected fighting around Saigon?"

"Nope," said Martinside, leafing through the sheaf of papers. "All it says here is that this is a Chinese holiday. Things are supposed to be quiet. Something called Tet."

CHAPTER THIRTEEN

THE BOY SCOUT

He was a man of a hundred and ten percent integrity—as a
man who trusts a slide rule ought to be.

—AN ASSOCIATE OF HAROLD GRAY, 1968

People who had known Harold Gray for years thought of him as a
cold man, almost as cold as Trippe. But Gray possessed a different
chemistry. He lacked Juan Trippe's facility to charm, to slither and
dissemble. Where Trippe thought in terms of influence and political
gain, Gray scorned such tactics, preferring to concentrate instead on
product. He was a pragmatist. White was white, black was black.
Anybody with any sense ought to know the difference. "All we have
to do is be good, and people will recognize it," he liked to say.

Harold Gray lived by the numbers. Every problem, he thought,
ought to be reducible to hard numbers, and then it could be solved.
Gray's slide rule was his talisman at staff meetings. Boil the problem
down to numbers, put it on the slide rule, let the facts speak for
themselves.

As the new chairman of the board, Gray inherited the problem of
the 747. The Everyman airplane was behind schedule for delivery—it
was supposed to be on line by early 1970—and already the deadline
was coming up for options on eight more. The biggest problem was
in the engines. A newer, more powerful version of the JT-9 engine had

to be produced by Pratt & Whitney in order for the 747 to meet the specifications agreed to by Trippe and Allen.

But who should pay for the redesign? Throughout the summer of 1968, Boeing, Pan Am, and Pratt & Whitney engaged in a running fight over who would pick up the tab. Not until late summer 1968 was a compromise hammered out.

In the meantime, Gray pondered the matter of the options on more 747s. The $175 million for the eight additional jumbos was just for starters. Pan Am's terminal at Kennedy would have to be rebuilt into a modern edifice capable of handling the fleet of jumbo jets. That would cost $126 million. And there was the matter of a new maintenance facility, also at Kennedy Airport. Another $98 million.

It was a monstrous outlay—the greatest in airline history. But Gray had run the numbers across his slide rule, and they made sense to him. As a formality, he sought the concurrence of his executives, including the new president, Jeeb Halaby, who had headed a committee to study the feasibility of increasing the order. Halaby concurred.

Chairman Gray put his pen to contracts for eight more 747s, making a total of thirty-three, and for a glittery new Worldport at Kennedy and a sprawling new maintenance facility. When he was finished, Pan Am's indebtedness for its new jumbo jets and facilities had swollen to over a billion dollars.

Meanwhile the annual report statistics were coming in for 1968, and they were not good. Earnings were down by nearly 19 percent. From its 1966 peak of $39 a share, Pan Am stock was selling in the middle twenties.

An odd malaise seemed to be settling over the Imperial Airline. No one could put his finger on it, but there it was. Everyone from top to bottom in the airline knew it, from Harold Gray all the way down to Marty Shugrue.

Riding sideways in his engineer's seat, Marty Shugrue sometimes wondered why he had gotten out of the Navy.

In the Navy he had flown S2Fs off aircraft carriers. He had flown them in the left seat, facing forward, in command, not riding sideways as he was now. There he had been *in charge*. That was what Shugrue had liked about the Navy. At a very young age they made you responsible for airplanes, weapons, personnel. You got to run the show.

When he left the Navy, Shugrue had tried private industry. He took a job with the Hamilton Standard Company, an aircraft components manufacturer, in Hartford, Connecticut. It was an office job and had nothing to do with flying. He was in charge of nothing. He lasted eighty-nine days before he quit to work for an airline.

For Shugrue, being an airline pilot took some rationalization. Everything in a pilot's career—promotion, furlough, pay, vacation—was dispensed by seniority. You took a number when you were hired, and there you stayed, relative to your fellow pilots, for the rest of your career. It wasn't like the military, which was a pyramidal hierarchy where you could pass your peers—or be passed—depending on how well you played the game. In the airline it didn't matter how well you played. There was no passing. There were no merit promotions in the cockpit.

And that was okay with Marty Shugrue so long as he made a steady ascent on the seniority ladder. That would occur naturally, he figured, as long as the airline was making money, growing, adding pilots to its roster.

But lately he was having doubts. There were a lot of things Shugrue didn't understand about Pan American. When you didn't understand something at Pan Am, it was said that you just didn't have the Big Picture.

One thing he didn't understand, for example, was Rock Sound. Here he was on a Sunday morning, riding sideways in his flight engineer's seat, flying down to Rock Sound on the island of Eleuthera in the Caribbean. Pan Am maintained a regular 707 service to Rock Sound. The flight was almost always empty. Nobody wanted to go there.

Why were they flying to Rock Sound?

And then one day during the transit in Rock Sound, Shugrue suddenly understood. They boarded two passengers who had a home on Eleuthera. Their names were on the manifest: Mr. and Mrs. Juan T. Trippe.

Pan Am was providing what amounted to a private 707 to carry the boss back and forth to Eleuthera. On most days the flight's only purpose was to deliver Trippe's *Wall Street Journal*.

Ooookay . . . that cleared up a tiny piece of the Big Picture. But what about all the other profitless flights? Pan Am was flying empty airplanes to places like Pago Pago, Rabat, Monrovia, Lagos. Pan Am had just announced that it would offer nonstop 707 service to Moscow. *Moscow?* In the Soviet Union? Who in 1968, other than the odd tourist and a few spies, would pay to travel to Moscow?

Whenever Shugrue asked someone who was supposed to know—someone who had the Big Picture—he would get a shrug. Nobody could say. It was just the way it was. Because we're Pan Am. Pan Am is supposed to fly to exotic places.

That was the kind of thing that bothered Shugrue about Pan Am. How could it make money flying empty airplanes to exotic places?

New hires, he was informed, weren't supposed to trouble themselves with such matters. It was over their heads. Don't worry about it, kid. You just don't have the Big Picture.

And then came something that was even harder to understand. It was the F word.

Shugrue stood in front of the bulletin board. The board was covered with several printed pages containing pilots' names and seniority numbers. It was the furlough notice. Shugrue found his name two-thirds of the way down the list. With the furlough notice was a message from Jeeb Halaby to the effect that he was sorry it had to happen, but everyone should understand that it was only temporary. As soon as Pan Am completed its period of retrenchment, all furloughed airmen would be recalled and the hiring would resume.

The F word.

Furlough was the flip side of the new-hire process. You began your career at the bottom of the seniority list. That was okay as long as your airline was growing. That's why it hired you, and that's why you came aboard. But when the airline stopped growing and began contracting, the process reversed itself. It furloughed you, which was to say it threw your expendable, newly hired carcass back on the street whence it had come. In reverse order of seniority. Last in, first out.

Shugrue was angry, just like the others. No one was taking it well. Pilots were clustered around the board, jaws clenching, fingers jabbing at the glass-covered board.

"The bastards! They knew all along. They damn well knew they were going to furlough us when they hired us."

"Nobody else is furloughing. Why Pan Am?"

"I knew I should have taken the job with Braniff."

"What are you going to do?"

"No idea. Look for a job, I guess."

They were right about one thing. Pan Am *had* known it would have too many pilots, even while it was still hiring. The airline had been developing new technology that would eliminate the need for navigators altogether. The Doppler system was an on-board electronic device that could be operated by the captain and first officer. No longer was it necessary for an airborne navigator to plant his eyeball in the socket of an octant, Magellan-like, to plot the jetliner's progress over the ocean. The Doppler system would eliminate the need for several hundred pilot-navigators.

And it would get worse. It didn't take much calculating to figure what would happen when the 747, with two and a half times the seat capacity of the 707, came on line. Fewer airplanes, fewer pilots.

More of the F word.

Shugrue wondered what he would do. He knew how to land aboard an aircraft carrier. That didn't count for much outside the naval service. He possessed a degree in economics from Providence College. That carried little weight in the real world.

The truth was, he *liked* the airline business. And he particularly liked Pan American. He still thought it was a classy airline, despite its Skygods and its recent propensity for losing money. He would like to help straighten it out.

And then someone told him that Pan Am was recruiting management trainees. They would be junior managers sent around the airline system as troubleshooters. Furloughed pilots would be given first consideration.

Hell, thought Shugrue, why not?

The next week, when he learned he had been hired, he packed away his Pan Am pilot's uniform. He showed up for work as a junior management trainee. And that's where Marty Shugrue stayed. He never wore the uniform again.

In San Francisco, Rob Martinside and Jim Wood stood looking at the furlough notice. Their names were not on it. But the reduction in numbers meant that they had descended uncomfortably close to the bottom of the roster.

"I guess this means we won't make captain this year," said Martinside.

"It means we're lucky to have a job," said Wood.

The furlough notice gave everyone an uneasy feeling. Something was slipping away. Hadn't they been told they would be SST pilots? Pan Am had been aimed at the stars. Now it was coming back to earth. Something was going wrong.

The SST was in trouble, too. The project had fallen into the grasp of Congress, which was being lobbied heavily by both sides. Boeing, which had won the contract for the prototype, was pushing for further allocations. Organized labor, in the person of crusty old George Meany, was using its huge influence. Washington State's two powerful senators, Scoop Jackson and Warren Magnuson, were twisting their colleagues' arms.

But the timing of the SST was all wrong. It was a season of protest in the United States. Not only were Americans resisting the war in Southeast Asia, they were disenchanted with government in general. They were angry with government's use of technology in making weapons and launching space vehicles—and constructing unwanted supersonic transports.

The SST finally died at the hands of a mob. A coalition of groups as diverse as the Sierra Club, Zero Population Growth, Friends of the Earth, and the United States Senate put the futuristic airplane to death in November 1970. In a vote of fifty-two to forty-one, the Senate voted against the expenditure of another $290 million on the SST. In the spring of 1971, both houses of Congress voted to terminate the project.

In Seattle, the immediate result was a layoff of five thousand workers. The SST mockup, which had cost $12 million, was sold for $43,000 to a promoter, who moved it to a roadside park near Disney World.

At Pan Am, among the not yet furloughed airmen, there was a dismal shrug of the shoulders. The loss of the SST was mostly symbolic. Everyone knew the day was past when Pan American could afford to be the torchbearer for new aviation technology.

But for the new hires, it was the death of a promise made on the first day of their careers: *Congratulations, gentlemen. You're going to be SST pilots. . . .*

CHAPTER FOURTEEN

BESIEGED

We have an unround situation.

—EVERETTE WEBB, *Boeing 747 project engineer*

Well, maybe they wouldn't be SST pilots. But Pan Am had the Everyman airplane, and it was almost ready to fly.

On a cold January day in 1970, Pat Nixon followed the example of First Ladies since Herbert Hoover's wife launched Pan Am's first S-40 flying boat, back in 1931. "I christen thee *Clipper Young America*," she said, then yanked the handle of a device that sprayed streams of red, white, and blue fluid over the nose of the new jumbo jet at Dulles Airport in Washington, D.C.

The 747's first commercial flight was scheduled six days later. It was a bitterly cold and bleak night in New York. No movable jetways had yet been constructed at Kennedy Airport for the boarding of jumbo jets. The passengers climbed the exposed boarding stairs, shivering, clutching their collars against the lashing winter wind.

Bob Weeks, New York chief pilot, was the captain for the inaugural flight. Weeks and his crew started the engines and taxied toward the runway. While they were still out on the windswept taxiway, the flight engineer, watching the engine gauges on his panel, saw the exhaust temperature of one engine shooting off the scale. The blustering wind off the mudflats of Jamaica Bay was raising hell with the sensitive JT-9D engines. It was blowing into the tailpipes, from back to front,

129

restricting the flow of compressed air and exhaust gas through the big engine. The new JT-9Ds were surging and exceeding their temperature limits.

The flight engineer shut down the engine. Minutes later, another engine stalled. It was no use. Back to the terminal limped *Clipper Young America*, her engines stalling and overtemping. The inaugural flight was postponed.

A reserve airplane, *Clipper Constitution*, was summoned. Seven hours behind schedule, the first 324 passengers of the jumbo jet era finally took off for London.

Clipper Young America's engine troubles were the precursor of a bigger problem. During the 747's flight testing, the Pratt & Whitney JT-9D had revealed a nasty trait. It was prone to stalling. In a jet engine, this meant an interruption in the flow of air from the front, the compressor section, to the aft, which was the turbine section. Sometimes the stall was silent. The only indication was a sudden rise of the exhaust gas temperature gauge toward the red-marked danger zone. On other occasions, usually in flight, it stalled thunderously— *kabloom!*—rattling the entire airframe and belching a twenty-foot sheet of flame. The phenomenon was known to make experienced passengers faint and grizzled flight engineers soil their underwear.

The engine troubles had already sparked an ugly fight between Boeing, Pratt & Whitney, and Pan Am. Who was going to take the hit for the delays caused by the misbehaving engines? Pan Am threatened to withhold payment on the first 747s and to parcel out the rest as "progress payments" until the problems were worked out. Boeing had already gone out on a limb with the 747 and could not afford such an arrangement. The Boeing engineers blamed Pratt & Whitney. Pratt & Whitney blamed Boeing. The specter of millions of dollars of lost revenue and the subsequent lawsuits hung over the offices of all three corporations.

The problem seemed to be that the engine case was subject to bending. The beer-barrel-shaped JT-9D engine weighed nearly ten thousand pounds and had a massive forty-six-blade fan section in front, eight feet in diameter. Nothing that size had been mounted to a commercial airplane before. More than 70 percent of the JT-9D's power came from the fan section. Under high-power situations, the normally round engine casing took an "unround" shape, distorting all the clearances and making the engine unstable. "Ovalizing," the Boeing engineers called it. It was a perplexing problem. Pratt & Whitney's engineers went into an all-out emergency program to fix the engines.

In the original deal between Trippe and Allen, Pan Am was supposed to have its 747s in service twelve months before its competitors, primarily TWA. Now that lead, for which Pan Am had already paid millions of dollars in deposits, was evaporating. Here were Pan Am's new 747s fresh off the assembly line—without engines. They filled up the Boeing ramp, their naked engine pylons hanging empty. The engineless jets looked like tethered pterodactyls. The Pan Am pilots were calling them 747 gliders.

Meanwhile, Pan Am was having even worse problems in Washington. Since the *China Clipper* days, Pan Am had enjoyed a virtual monopoly on its Pacific operations. But all that was about to change. For more than a decade an overseas airline decision called the transpacific route case had been debated before the Civil Aeronautics Board, the politically appointed five-member panel empowered to parcel out international route authority. Virtually every American domestic airline, cargo hauler, and nonscheduled carrier, as well as a host of regionals—twenty airlines in all—had applied for authority to fly Pan Am's Pacific routes. The transpacific case was the longest and most complicated in the history of the CAB. By 1968 the mountain of briefs and hearings had swelled to over ten thousand volumes weighing thirty tons.

The Pacific was Pan American country. Over the years, Pan Am had managed, mostly through heavy lobbying in Washington, to maintain a monopoly on the routes it had pioneered. Under the Truman, Eisenhower, and Kennedy administrations, a loose formula of *limited* competition on overseas routes was applied. Pan Am, it was understood, should have to contend with *one* other major competitor on any particular segment—TWA in the Atlantic, Northwest in the Pacific, Braniff in Latin America.

Lyndon Johnson changed all that. Under LBJ, the route award process became purely political. All members of the CAB were political appointees. Three were from the majority party, the Democrats, and two from the Republicans. The chairman was appointed each year by the President. During the transpacific route case hearings in 1968, LBJ had inserted a fellow Texan, John Crooker, a friend of Texas-based American Airlines and Braniff Airlines, into the chairmanship.

Nineteen sixty-eight was an election year. By that fall the transpacific case had metamorphosed into an ugly frenzy of political favor-buying and debt-paying. Each CAB appointee had political obligations to his own party and to his home state congressmen. Members of Congress, in turn, owed fealty to their home-based airlines, which were conspicuously heavy campaign contributors. The applicants deployed brigades of lawyers and lobbyists. Contributions flowed like honey from airline treasuries to candidates' coffers.

In the Pan Am Building, there was a wringing of hands and a feeling of moral outrage. Campaign contributions? *Buying* what they had already earned? Neither Pan American the corporation nor its officers or directors were conspicuous contributors to political campaigns. Pan American was founded in an old-fashioned, Boy Scoutish sense of its own correctness, and that attitude was now personified in the chairman himself, Harold Gray.

Pan American flying boats had surveyed the Pacific routes. Pan Am had constructed each of the island bases like stepping-stones to the Orient. In time of war, Pan Am had conveyed supplies to the Pacific beachheads. Pan Am had paid in blood for its experience. The charred shell of Ed Musick's *Samoan Clipper* still lay on the ocean floor off Pago Pago.

Now here were the Johnny-come-latelies—upstarts like Continental and American and United and Eastern—which actually thought they could just step in and begin flying those routes. It was unthinkable!

Gray, now the CEO and chief Boy Scout, was inclined to ignore the whole distasteful mess. But down the hall resided the chairman emeritus, who, though officially retired since May 1968, still came in to his office nearly every day and attended each meeting of the board of directors. Trippe had long been watching and worrying about the transpacific case. Now the old man came out of his sanctum to render counsel. It was time to twist some arms, he advised Gray.

What Trippe had in mind was, of course, what *used* to work for Pan Am in such cases: serious lobbying. And he had somebody in mind.

"Send Halaby," Trippe said. After all, that's what he had been hired for.

Times had changed. What used to work for Juan Trippe back in the prejet days didn't work anymore. The era when Trippe could pick up a phone and influence a route decision was not only over, it had left a lasting resentment against Pan Am.

The last time anyone could remember Washington actually doing something *for* Pan Am was in 1950. That was when Trippe applied for the right to buy out an American Airlines subsidiary called American Overseas Airlines, which was operating a North Atlantic service in competition with Pan Am. The CAB rejected Pan Am's merger application. But in a surprise move, the *Democratic* President, Harry Truman, reversed the CAB's decision. Trippe was allowed to buy out his competitor. It was the last major favor Pan Am would ever receive from an occupant of the White House, Democrat or Republican.

Pan Am had become a political orphan. As a New York–based, international enterprise, the airline had no partisan representation in Congress. There were too many other corporations with large New York offices for the state's congressmen to openly favor Pan Am. Pan Am was on its own.

Most of Pan Am's domestic competitors lived under an umbrella of protection from their own states' congressmen. Florida's senators argued hotly for the rights of Eastern and National airlines. Texas gave its wholehearted support to American. TWA enjoyed the backing of its senators from Missouri, and Northwest was boosted by Minnesota. California's senators usually threw their support to Continental and to United, which had established a giant maintenance base in the state. Pan Am had no such voice.

Even the contractors joined the transpacific fray. The manufacturers of airplanes, engines, and components had much to gain, because the winners—the Pacific awardees—would immediately be expanding their fleets and upgrading their capacity. It meant new orders for 707s and DC-8s.

Which was another irony. The very vehicles that now made it possible for the Pacific applicants to intrude into Pan Am skies—the long-range 707s and DC-8s—had been placed in service by Pan American.

Jeeb Halaby, now the president of Pan Am, dutifully went to Washington. He spent most of the summer of 1968 visiting congressmen and the White House. He took his place in the long queues of lobbyists waiting to make their pitch. When the CAB finally completed its deliberations and sent its recommendations to the President, the same army of lobbyists lined up at the White House.

In the waning days of his presidency, Lyndon Johnson handed down his decision. It was classic LBJ: *reward your friends, punish your enemies.* The right to serve Hawaii was granted to Braniff, American, Northwest, Continental, and Western. Flying Tiger got Pacific routes. Continental was given an extensive Pacific network. TWA received new Pacific authority and round-the-world rights.

For Pan Am it was a stunning blow. It was a personal blow to Jeeb Halaby, for it highlighted his true status—or lack of status—with Lyndon Johnson's White House. For Juan Trippe it confirmed the long-festering Democratic contempt for Pan American that had begun back in the thirties with venomous old Joe Kennedy, passed on to his son, and now swelled to its full nastiness under Lyndon Baines Johnson.

But there was still hope. The incoming President, Richard M. Nixon—*a Republican*—announced that he intended to review Johnson's decision. In the Pan Am Building there was subdued optimism. Surely Pan Am could expect better treatment from the Republicans.

Richard Nixon was true to his word. He *did* review Johnson's route decision. And he changed it. In the style that epitomized Nixon's own career, he passed out route awards to *his* friends and he meted out punishment to *his* enemies.

The most significant change was to remove Continental's windfall and grant American Airlines a plethora of South Pacific destinations. For Pan American, it made no difference. The Pacific fortress had been breached.

Halaby left Washington in disgust. "The transpacific case was the lowest point in the long history of the regulatory process," he said.

The shadows beneath Harold Gray's eyes were darkening. His face had become a reflection of the pain that infused his daily life. It was no longer a secret on the forty-sixth floor that the chairman suffered from cancer and was undergoing cobalt treatments. With a grim stoicism, Gray went about his business with needles stuck in his leg veins.

Harold Gray's declining health mirrored the Pan Am balance sheet. The first two quarters of 1969 netted a loss of $12.7 million. The loss was forecast to double before the end of the year. For the first time in thirty years the board of directors voted to omit the second-quarter dividend that Pan Am shareholders had learned to expect. Domestic airlines and start-up nonscheduled carriers were decimating Pan Am's international market share.

The prediction on which Juan Trippe rationalized his fleet of 747s—that traffic would increase by 17 percent a year—was not coming true. By 1970, international air traffic was growing hardly at all, only 1.5 percent. A recession gripped the United States economy and spread to Europe, and tourists were staying home. Businesses were cutting back on travel. The great boom in air travel that had begun when Juan Trippe introduced jets had run its course.

Gray wanted to close his eyes and get away from it all—the troubles, the pain, the frustration of trying to solve problems that didn't fit on his slide rule. But Harold Gray was a man who had lived his life bound by duty. Before he left, he wanted to turn things around. "I want to get the company profitable again," he told a vice president. "Then I'll go back to my cellar and finish my inventions."

But how could he leave? He had the same old nagging doubts about Halaby. "Jeeb isn't ready, yet," Gray was telling his closest associates. "I haven't trained him enough."

Which was true. Halaby *hadn't* learned very much about the airline, and it was mostly Gray's doing. During Halaby's apprenticeship as vice president, miscellaneous, he had been deliberately excluded from the operational affairs of the airline. Even as president, under Gray, he was an outsider. He was still snubbed by the old hands, who regarded him as a slick bureaucrat who had sneaked in the back door. Halaby's major assignment was still in Washington, as a lobbyist.

But duty-bound or not, Harold Gray could feel his life ebbing away. He was losing his fight against illness. In November 1969 the old Skygod—the first Master of Ocean Flying Boats—informed the board that he wanted to retire. He was turning over all his duties to his successor, Najeeb Halaby.

CHAPTER FIFTEEN

JUST CALL ME JEEB

It was like trying to bail out a sinking ocean liner with a sand
pail.

—NAJEEB HALABY

Jack Waddell, Boeing's chief test pilot for the 747, didn't know what
to make of this guy. Here was the CEO of Boeing's prime customer
—and he wanted to fly the 747. Not ride in it, or inspect it, or be
briefed about how it flew. He wanted to *fly* the damned thing. Himself.
The only people who got to fly the 747 were test pilots.

But this guy Halaby was a bit odd. He *was* a test pilot.

Now that Jeeb Halaby was the chairman at Pan Am, he liked to
fly himself and his entourage around the country in one of Pan Am's
two-engine Falcon business jets. But nobody at Boeing had ever seen
the CEO of one of its customer airlines come out to Seattle to personally take the yoke of a new airliner.

Off they went in the 747, Halaby in the left seat—the *captain's*
seat—Waddell in the right. Waddell talked him through the start procedure and fed him the numbers for the takeoff and climb. Halaby did
the rest. The old Navy pilot hadn't forgotten how to fly.

First they tried flying through the turbulence that surrounded
Mount Rainier, just to see how the big jet handled. Then they went
to altitude. Halaby put the 747 through steep turns, pulling it so hard

136

it buffeted. He tried flying with one engine pulled back, and then with two.

They flew back to Moses Lake, and Halaby practiced landing and taking off. He tried it first with all engines running, then with one out. When he'd finished wringing the big jet out, they returned to Boeing Field.

Climbing down the tall access ladder, Halaby wore his old test pilot grin. He'd had a grand time, he said. The 747 was a hell of a good airplane.

It was clear that Jeeb Halaby was a different kind of CEO. One thing different was that no one was afraid of him. And that was turning out to be a serious problem.

Trippe, the Imperial Skygod, had been an efficient despot. He commanded both fear and loyalty. Gray had been even more coldly efficient than Trippe. With the two old tyrants, you knew what to expect in the way of inspired leadership: *Do your job and you will share in the glory. Screw up and your head will become disunited from your body.*

After the forty-two-year reign of the Imperial Skygods, the softer vision of Halaby's Camelot seemed, at first, a refreshing change. Instead of rule by fear, with your head gracing a platter when you erred, the new regime was talking sensitivity. You were supposed to love your associates. You loved your customers. By inference, it meant you were even supposed to love the bureaucrats, bastards that they were, who were systematically dismantling your route structure.

Jeeb Halaby liked being liked. Even though he accepted the outward trappings of the Skygod cult—the pomp and glitz of running the Imperial Airline—he didn't display much of the Skygodly inner steel. Jeeb smiled a lot. He held heart-to-heart meetings with flight attendants and mechanics and passenger service agents. He traveled in economy class in order to hear passengers' complaints.

And that was why so many of his subordinates began to hate him. It simply wasn't the way things were supposed to be. In the offices of middle and upper management, fear gave way to anarchy. Gone was the mailed fist, and gone with it the raw fear that had unified them and lent purpose to their labors. The serfs were swarming into the courtyard.

They squabbled among themselves. Departments fought with departments. Divisions fought with divisions. Vice presidents sniped at vice presidents. There was disunity in the house of Pan Am, and the rumors began leaking out to the business press.

Halaby was instituting changes at a dizzying pace, mostly on the recommendations of outside consultants. Over thirty senior executives departed Pan Am in the first two years after Halaby took the chairmanship. Halaby replaced most of them with outsiders. Most had no airline experience.

One of the trendy ideas Halaby embraced was an "office of the president." Instead of a single president acting as a chief operating officer, four separate vice presidents were supposed to act in unison, sharing power as Halaby's executive operating unit. His four "co-presidents" were James Leet, vice president for marketing; Frank Doyle, in charge of personnel and administration; Richard Knight, who was vice president for finance; and Frank Davis, whom Halaby hired away from Kaiser to run operations, engineering, and maintenance.

It didn't work. The "office of the president" amounted to management by committee. The four rivals butted heads like mountain goats.

As he watched Pan Am's losses mount, a hard reality was coming clear to Jeeb Halaby. Without domestic routes of its own, Pan Am was being eaten alive by its competitors. Pan American had no domestic routes because it was treated as an international carrier—the "chosen instrument." In exchange for that grand status—and exclusivity on its overseas routes—Pan Am was denied access to the American domestic market.

But that formula—the exclusivity of Pan Am's overseas market—was as extinct as the flying boat. It had been thrown to the winds by the CAB and the White House. The door to the international market was swung open to the domestic airlines—but it was a one-way door.

Pan Am was still denied a domestic feed to its overseas routes. There was still no nonstop service from the East Coast to Hawaii. No route between New York and Miami. Not even a hearing would be granted on Pan Am's application for coast-to-coast service.

It was the same old political problem. Every application for domestic authority by Pan Am was trounced by the powerful lobbies and political patrons of the domestic carriers. Wasn't Pan Am supposed to be purely an *international* airline? And wouldn't it be unfair to allow an international airline like Pan Am to also feed at the domestic trough?

But what about the so-called domestic airlines flying international routes? Wasn't that discriminatory, giving them Pan Am's routes but not letting Pan Am fly on theirs?

Well, perhaps. But if it was, no one in the government was feeling any remorse over it. Washington took the view that international air commerce was a separate arena, sort of a shared national treasure. It was in everybody's best interest to have competition. The more players, the better.

Halaby reached a grim conclusion. To survive, Pan Am had to gain domestic routes. Clearly, they couldn't be won in the political arena. Nor could they be bought. If Pan Am was to have domestic routes, it would have to be through a merger with a domestic airline.

It had been tried before. Proposed mergers of major airlines always aroused the regulatory watchdogs. In the sixties, Trippe and Charles Tillinghast of TWA had considered a union of their two international carriers. The CAB vetoed the marriage because, in the board's judgment, it would have made the United States dependent on a single carrier over the major international routes. The specter of a monopoly in a transportation system—railroad, shipping company, or airline—had forever been anathema in Washington.

But times were changing. The single-carrier argument had become a joke. The Johnson and Nixon handouts in the transpacific route case and the CAB's further generosity with the other overseas routes—the Caribbean, South America, the North Atlantic—had made international carriers out of almost every domestic airline—National, Eastern, Braniff, American, Continental, United—as well as a swarm of supplemental and charter airlines.

In late 1969, Halaby met with American Airlines' president, George Spater. A Pan Am–American merger made sense. American's huge domestic network made a perfect complement to Pan Am's overseas routes. But when word of the talks leaked out, American's upper management—wary of invasion by a crowd of Pan Am outsiders—killed the idea.

There were other attempts. Harding Lawrence of Braniff came up with a brash plan for taking over Pan Am—a minnow-swallows-the-whale deal. Halaby politely told him to take a hike.

In 1970 there was talk about a merger with Eastern, and then United, and even Delta. None got past the discussion stage.

In the summer of 1971, Halaby began talking with Charles Tillinghast of TWA. TWA was in the same kind of trouble as Pan Am. TWA had its own fleet of 747s, and they, too, were flying around with hundreds of empty seats. And TWA had been injured nearly as badly as Pan Am by the infiltration of the domestics onto the international routes.

The two airlines' staffs looked at the numbers. By eliminating duplicate stations, airplanes, and facilities, they figured they could save as much as $200 million a year in operating costs. Moreover, with TWA's thirty-nine domestic destinations, the merged airline would be a formidable competitor with any of its rivals, foreign or domestic. Their combined armada of 747s outclassed any airline fleet in the world.

One hidden dividend of the merger was the hotels. TWA owned the prestigious Hilton International Hotel chain. Pan Am owned Intercontinental. The joining of the two would result in the world's most superb hotel conglomerate.

Even Juan Trippe, watching from the wings, was ecstatic. For years the old Skygod had preached the need for a "community" airline—an amalgamated flag carrier composed principally of Pan Am and its most significant competitor, TWA. He had bargained with Howard Hughes, and later Tillinghast. Each time it had come to nothing. Now the old man was seeing his favorite dream about to come true.

But they hadn't reckoned on the Nixon White House.

A merged Pan Am and TWA would be a *big* airline—big enough to again raise the old bugaboo about monopoly and unfair competition. Before proceeding with a merger of such a size, an antitrust clearance would be needed from the Justice Department, headed by Attorney General and Nixon confidant John Mitchell. And before the

Justice Department acted, there would have to be a clear signal of support from the President.

Halaby and Tillinghast went to Washington to make their case. They sat down with Peter Flanigan, the White House staff officer in charge of transportation and regulatory matters. Flanigan seemed supportive of the merger and said they would have an answer from the President in sixty days.

Sixty days passed. Nothing happened.

Sixty more. What was Nixon's position on the merger?

Nobody was saying, not Flanigan, not anyone at the White House. The autumn of 1971 came and went with no decision from Washington. Halaby knew *something* was going on. But what?

He telephoned Flanigan at the White House.

"I'm sorry," said Flanigan, "but we just can't give you an answer."

"You can at least say yes, no, or maybe."

"No, it's not possible to give you that."

Halaby realized that he *had* his answer. The Nixon people were not going on record as opposing a Pan Am–TWA merger. That wasn't their style. They would stonewall the idea until it died.

And so it did. Halaby and Tillinghast told their merger staffs to put away their memoranda and charts and get back to work on something else. Each reported to his board of directors that the Pan Am–TWA merger was a dead issue.

It was about this time that Jeeb Halaby had another idea. This idea was even more controversial, at least in the Pan Am boardroom, than the merger scheme. And it met the same fate.

Why doesn't Pan Am leave New York?

While he was the FAA chief, Halaby had overseen the development of Dulles Airport in Washington, D.C. It now struck him that the modern new Dulles complex was an eminently logical headquarters for Pan American. For one thing, it was in the Virginia countryside, close enough to the capital city, but free of the urban messiness. The idea had a stars-and-stripes aura—America's premier flag carrier based in America's capital—that would translate to political profit. Besides, there was plenty of hangar and office space. It would be easy to feed connecting flights.

He should have known better. If Jeeb Halaby had been around long enough he would have realized the question would ignite a firestorm among the corporate elders. The response always went something like: *This is Pan American World Airways*. The Imperial Airline *belonged* in the Empire State. New York was where it had always been. That's where Pan Am would always be.

And that would be the end of the discussion.

But here was the chairman of the board, a Californian who abhorred the rude seaminess of New York anyway, asking the question. Why, Halaby wanted to know, did Pan Am insist on concentrating itself in such a hostile environment? New York was the toughest town in the country in which to run an airline. He pointed to the statistics —eight entrenched and venal labor unions, the highest airport facility rent in the country, concessionaires and vendors reputedly controlled by the mob, a long tradition of cost overruns and waste.

As they'd just learned, the political value of New York residency was nil. While American, Braniff, United, Continental—all Pan Am's challengers—were backed by senators and congressmen from their home turf, Pan Am's case was consistently ignored by the New York delegation.

On the forty-sixth floor, there were glacial stares. The most glacial of them all came from the chairman emeritus, who still maintained his watchful presence in the back office.

The subject was dropped. The Imperial Airline would not move to the provinces.

Along with his other problems, Halaby was having trouble with his middle managers. These were the old hands who had worked their way up from the seaplane ramps and the radio shacks and the typhoon-swept atolls of the Pacific. They called themselves the Faded Aristocracy. Now they ran things like the dispatch center, the scheduling department, the airport services offices. "We *built* this damn airline," said one member of the Faded Aristocracy, a field services director. "The Pan Am culture was in our blood."

Now Halaby was bringing in waves of consultants and new executives, downgrading the old hands, and, in many instances, farming them out. An entire contingent came from Northeast Airlines, which was acquired by Delta, including James Leet, one of the four occupants of Halaby's "office of the president"; Dan Colussy, a marketing executive; and eventually F. C. "Bud" Wiser, who had emigrated to TWA.

The Faded Aristocracy was furious. The newcomers were swarming through the halls, snooping, changing, invading every niche of the airline's headquarters. "We called it the M.B.A. syndrome," said George Denison, a senior scheduling director. "They were whiz kids with business degrees who had never worked at an airline before but knew all about it." The whiz kids arrived with trendy new ideas straight from Harvard Business School, and they wanted to try them out.

"Seventeen of these types—M.B.A.'s and Ph.D.'s—came in to help us do our jobs," remembered Archie Leonard, a director of traffic and sales. "Most of them were duly regurgitated, but they lasted long enough to screw up the operation for years."

One of the new ideas was psychologists. *Shrinks!* Someone decided that it was time Pan Am's executives "got in touch with their feelings." They needed to develop sensitivity. A psychologist was hired to sit in on top management meetings. He was supposed to offer advice about restructuring the airline. A platoon of shrinks fanned out through the executive offices to administer the new sensitivity training program.

Halaby encouraged the program. He tape-recorded messages that employees could hear by dialing a certain number: "Fellow Pan Americans, this is Jeeb Halaby on the Pan Am line. Don't look upon youth-fare passengers as problems. Look upon them as prospects and love them. We need them."

At this the old hands were aghast. It was unbelievable! Sensitivity training at the airline of the Skygods? It was like teaching table manners to a tiger shark.

In private moments in downtown bars, the Faded Aristocracy would get together and down a few martinis and reminisce about the boat days. They missed the time when their bosses were Skygods and not bleeding-heart chaplains. They remembered when a Pan American flying boat sailed into a harbor and an entire city stopped what it was doing to come watch. That was when Pan Am—the Imperial Airline

—omnipotently *took* what it wanted. If Pan American decided to fly across a stretch of ocean, it did it. Competition be damned. There was no competition.

Each of the old boat hands, given enough to drink, would grudgingly admit that he missed the old man. Trippe never cared a hoot in hell about things like sensitivity. If the old man were still there, he would know how to get Pan Am flying again.

In fact, the old man *was* still there, removed by some twenty-three floors from the action. Halaby had finally nudged Trippe off the executive committee of the board and gotten him to vacate his office on the forty-sixth floor and move downstairs. But Trippe's presence, like that of a watchful angel, still hovered over the executive floor. He was still a member of the executive committee, and he still attended every board meeting. Trippe was appalled at what was happening.

"I made a mistake in hiring Halaby," he was now telling his old confidants.

Pan Am was losing money by the planeload. The recession of 1969–71 had dried up overseas travel just as the 747s—the Everyman airplanes—flooded the market with thousands of new, and empty, seats. Now the Everyman airplane was infuriating everyone. Pan Am was, in effect, providing the test beds for the troubled Pratt & Whitney JT-9 engine. And the engines were still stalling.

It had become a daily occurrence. One of the big jets would start out on its overseas journey and then—*kabloom!*—an engine would stall. The exhaust gas temperature would soar into the red. An orange sheet of flame would erupt like hellfire from the tailpipe, panicking passengers and loosening the bowels of astonished flight engineers.

Flights were canceled. Entire planeloads of passengers were accommodated in hotels. Disgusted travelers cursed Pan Am, swearing never to fly the airline again. The delays and cancellations caused by the engine problems added yet another $2.5 million to the $10 million monthly burden of owning the Everyman airplane.

Jeeb Halaby was like a man swimming in a waterfall. In his four-year metamorphosis from Washington bureaucrat to Pan Am's vice president, miscellaneous, to chairman of the board, he had never been trained in day-to-day management of a global corporation. His pre-

occupation with the transpacific case and the unsuccessful Pan Am–
TWA merger further interfered with his on-the-job training.

As Gray's successor, he wore both hats—chairman of the board
and president. He desperately needed executive help, a strong number
two man who could attend to the daily chores of running the airline.
Even though a search had been under way since 1970 for a president
and chief operating officer, many had come to believe that Halaby
didn't really want to share power. Jeeb Halaby seemed determined to
drown all by himself.

By September 1971, the board of directors, concerned about Pan
Am's growing losses and the unfavorable reviews in publications like
Business Week and *Fortune,* had become anxious about Halaby's leadership. They instructed him to find a president, immediately, or they
would take the matter into their own hands.

A headhunter firm, Booz, Allen & Hamilton, and an outside consultant, Henry Golightly, scoured the corporate countryside for candidates. Many leading candidates, knowledgeable about the extent of
Pan Am's huge losses, politely declined to be considered.

One name, William T. Seawell, kept popping up on the headhunter
lists. Seawell had glitzy credentials: a former Air Force general, graduate of West Point and Harvard Law School, commandant of the Air
Force Academy, and senior vice president for operations at American
Airlines. He had been a World War II bomber pilot and had served
twenty-two years in the Air Force. He was currently president of Rolls-
Royce Aero, Inc., the North American subsidiary of the British power
plant builder.

Bill Seawell fit the Pan Am profile. Fifty-three years old, tall and
silver-haired, he was a Skygod in looks and temperament. Seawell
passed the committee's scrutiny.

On December 1, 1971, he went to work as Pan American's fourth
president.

The general wasted no time. He set to work paring staffs, reducing
management head count, applying his personal stamp to the office of
president. He was assertive and managerial in style. Seawell wanted it
made clear to everyone: *He* was in operational charge at Pan Am.

And at first that was okay with Halaby. He sat in on some of

Seawell's staff meetings and observed the changes from a discreet distance. He was enjoying the respite from the daily combat he had been undergoing.

For a while it looked like the two-tiered executive scheme might work. Halaby envisioned an arrangement by which Seawell performed the day-to-day grunt work of directing the airline while he, the chairman, attended to loftier matters like global strategy and next-generation fleet acquisition and government affairs. Halaby could distance himself from the internecine warfare with the Faded Aristocracy. He could be the benevolent commanding officer, a revered father figure. Seawell, the executive officer, could fight with the grunts.

But it didn't work that way. Inevitably, there was friction. Halaby noticed some of the disgruntled old guard dropping into Seawell's office. Halaby haters were becoming Seawell supporters.

There was the matter of Willis Player, the vice president for public relations. Halaby hadn't gotten along with Player. He suspected Player of conniving behind his back and of leaking some of the uncomplimentary stories to the press. Halaby had eased him out of the job.

Now Seawell wanted him back. The two executives clashed.

And then they argued about Frank Doyle, a Halaby appointee in charge of personnel industrial relations and one of the four previous occupants of the "office of the president." Seawell didn't like him. Halaby did. Seawell wanted Doyle out and someone of his own choosing in.

Reports of the disputes trickled out to the press and to the worried board of directors. On top of the reports of disharmony at Pan Am, the 1971 annual report came out. Pan Am had lost another $45.5 million, capping a three-year hemorrhage of $120.3 million. Debt soared to well over $1 billion. The $270 million revolving credit that Trippe had negotiated in 1965 for the 747 purchase had to be renegotiated by March 31, 1972.

The board of directors called for a special meeting on March 22.

Jeeb Halaby tried to read the faces at the long table. On his left sat his chief operating officer, Bill Seawell. Seawell's eyes were narrow slits. On Halaby's right, like a living artifact, sat Juan Trippe. His hands were clasped expectantly on the table before him.

A few faces were friendly. The "inside" directors were Halaby imports—Frank Doyle, Jim Leet, Bill Crilly, Frank Davis—Pan Am executives who could be expected to side with him on the board.

But on the faces of the "outside" directors there was grimness. They were corporate bluebloods like Tom Watson, Cyrus Vance, General Alfred Gruenther, Frank Stanton, Stillman Rockefeller—old guardsmen from the Trippe era. They were Establishment elitists who regarded themselves as custodians not only of Pan American but of the nation's fiduciary well-being.

One of the faces across the table belonged to the Icon, Charles Lindbergh. Still handsome in his seventy-first year, the Lone Eagle returned Halaby's gaze. Halaby wondered what Lindbergh was thinking. Was he sympathetic? Hostile? With Lindbergh you could never tell.

Jeeb Halaby cleared his throat and said his piece. It was the most crucial sales pitch of his life. "Two more years," Halaby asked. "Give me your confidence another two years to run Pan Am and complete the turnaround I sincerely believe we have started in motion." Otherwise, if the board saw fit, he would step down.

The directors glanced at each other. They weren't buying it. *Turnaround?* Here was the incontrovertible evidence of Pan Am's losses during the thirty months of Halaby's chairmanship. In their minds, too, were the recent specters of two other corporate debacles, Penn Central and Lockheed. They wanted no part of such a mess at Pan Am.

In the hard, unsmiling faces Halaby saw his answer. They didn't believe in his turnaround. All they knew was that the airline was going to hell in a handcart. Perhaps it was the economy, perhaps the 747 purchase for which Halaby hadn't been responsible, perhaps the ruinous route decisions of the CAB. The directors didn't care. They had already made up their minds about whom to blame.

The board asked Halaby and the inside directors, including Seawell, to leave while they held an executive session. Two and a half hours passed. Then they sent Cyrus Vance, a Halaby board appointee and old friend from the Washington days. "Jeeb, the board has decided it would like to accept your resignation."

Halaby trudged back to the boardroom. He acknowledged their decision. The next order of business was to elect Halaby's replacement.

Juan Trippe had someone in mind. The old tycoon unclasped his hands and declared in his Eastern, clipped accent, "I nominate William T. Seawell as chairman and chief executive officer of Pan American World Airways."

As it had done for forty-five years, the board obeyed the Imperial Skygod. There were no dissenting votes.

CHAPTER SIXTEEN

A PLACE WHERE YOU NEVER HAVE TO GROW UP

"Mama, I'm going to grow up and be an airline pilot."
"Make up your mind, son. You know you can't do both."

Jim Wood was cruising at ten thousand feet in the southern Berlin air corridor. He couldn't believe what he was hearing on the air traffic control frequency. It sounded like a chicken.

Prrrrruck-puck-puck. Prrrrruck-puck-puck-puck.

Yes, thought Wood, that's what it was. It was definitely a chicken. Why was a chicken transmitting on the radio?

Prrrrrrrrruck-puck-puck-puck.

"Chicken Man, this is Berlin Center," said the air traffic controller. "Is that you?"

Prrrrrrruck-puck-puck.

"Roger, Chicken Man. Nice to hear you back on the air."

Chicken's Man's identity was supposed to be a secret, but everyone knew that he was really a wacky Berlin-based pilot named Al Bond. Bond's talisman was a rubber plucked chicken, which he liked to carry in his flight bag with its head dangling out. He would board his airplane this way, carrying the bag with the rubber chicken, and then make a ceremony of hanging the chicken in the doorway of the cockpit. Startled passengers had been known to scream and demand to be let out of Chicken Man's airplane.

One day an inbound flight crew radioed the maintenance office: "Have someone meet the airplane. We had a bird strike on the windshield."

A collision with a bird was a serious incident. It could cause severe damage to the jetliner and sometimes even injure the crew. Maintenance personnel rushed to meet the airplane. As the 727 taxied toward the ramp, the mechanics could see that there was indeed evidence of a bird strike, and it was a bad one. The carcass was still on the windshield.

But something wasn't right. As the airplane rolled nearer they saw the corpse. It looked like . . . could it be . . . yes, that's what it was . . . a damned *chicken* hanging from the windshield wiper.

This happened on Jim Wood's third day of flying in Berlin. Everyone seemed to think it was good fun, especially Chicken Man.

As Wood stood on the ramp watching the mechanics remove the rubber bird, he saw another pair of pilots walking toward their airplane. One was wearing a red fez. The other had a cape and a Russian fur hat.

This was not the way Pan Am pilots were supposed to look. *These guys are weird*, thought Wood.

And then Wood suddenly realized a truth. He had found a home.

The Berlin base, two hundred miles behind the Iron Curtain, was an outpost. Because of its remoteness, a tradition of eccentricity had taken root there, like a strain of mutant oats. Pilots liked to say that if you weren't weird when you came to Berlin, then you had to pretend to be. The base was considered by the rest of the system to be a loony bin. The crew room in Berlin was called, aptly, the Cuckoo's Nest.

Most airline pilots, by inclination and screening, were straight arrows. They tended toward conservatism in politics, dress, social behavior. But as in any assemblage of professionals, a small number of pilots—about 10 percent by most guesses—turned out to be different.

A few, in fact, were downright weird. For such airmen employed by Pan American, the base for them was Berlin.

Berlin was a place where you never had to grow up. It was where the Peter Pans and black sheep and oddballs of the airline found refuge. It was where you transferred if you were hiding from a wife, ex-wife, creditor, or ill-humored husband.

To the dismay of their supervisors, the Berlin airmen didn't even *look* like airline pilots. They disdained traditional uniforms. They affected bizarre trappings that included berets, babushkas, capes, monocles, and, in the case of Chicken Man, a rubber fowl.

Pilots got away with such things in Berlin for one reason: They flew well. The Berlin operation consistently posted the most enviable flying safety record in the airline. Since its inception during the Berlin blockade of 1948–49, the Berlin-based pilots had flown millions of Germans in the foulest imaginable weather through the air corridors to Berlin—and never injured a passenger. Moreover, the Berlin base always boasted the best on-time schedule performance in the Pan Am system.

And so years back a tacit decision was made in Pan Am's headquarters: Okay, let them be a little weird—as long as they fly safely and on time.

As a result of the four-power pact dividing Berlin among the occupying powers—the United States, Britain, France, the Soviet Union—Pan Am had an exclusive right to serve Berlin as the single designated American carrier. Air France and British European Airways also flew the corridors to West Germany, while the Russian and East German airlines operated from Schoenfeld Airport in the Eastern Zone. Since the construction of the Berlin Wall in 1961, Berlin had been a divided city, living under the guns of the Red Army.

For the pilots, Berlin had the camaraderie of a fighter squadron, a men's social club, a fraternity house. It was an airline within an airline. The pilots flew together and skied together and drank together. They lent each other money and rotated girlfriends.

Their cohesiveness was due, in part, to the shared uniqueness of their outpost, Berlin. They were settlers in a strange land. And they knew that what they did had a purpose. Every day they saw the reasons for their presence—the Berlin Wall that split the city, MiG fighters skulking in the corridors, Red Army tanks maneuvering in the countryside. It was great fun and deadly serious all at the same time.

In San Francisco, Rob Martinside received a cablegram:

WEATHER TERRIBLE. CORRIDOR FLYING DIFFICULT. GERMANS INSUFFERABLE. RUSSIANS HOSTILE. WOMEN AGGRESSIVE. YOU'LL LOVE IT. COME ON OVER.

WOOD

There were copilot openings in the Berlin base. Like everything else in the airline profession, new assignments were filled according to seniority. The most senior pilots who bid for the new openings received the assignments. Martinside submitted his bid, and three weeks later he received notification of his transfer as a first officer to the Internal German Service, based in Berlin.

His contemporaries thought he was crazy.

Berlin? Berlin was, after all, a self-imposed demotion. A pilot's pay was based on the size of the airplane he flew. The Boeing 727, the only airliner Pan Am operated in Berlin, was a smaller and, thus, a lesser-paying machine than the intercontinental 707 Martinside had been flying.

Beyond the issue of money, it still didn't make sense.

"You're living in California. Why would you want to give this up to go to Berlin? The place is surrounded by commies."

"Are you crazy, Rob? Over there I hear you can't get football on TV. You can't get parts for a Corvette or a Harley-Davidson. You can't join a country club. You probably can't even get a decent haircut."

"Hell, I bet they don't even speak good English."

Many of the pilots commuted to Berlin. They maintained traditional homes and families in Minnesota or Pennsylvania or Oklahoma and divided their lives between there and Berlin. Some became aeronautical models of the character in the old movie *Captain's Paradise*, in which Alec Guinness played a sea captain who kept wives in separate ports.

There was, for example, the Deacon. The Deacon was a captain who kept a home and a wife and two daughters in Ponca City, where he really *was* a deacon in his church, as well as a teetotaler and a member of the school board. In Ponca City the Deacon was a paragon of morality and godliness.

Then he would go to Berlin.

As he stepped off the airplane at Tempelhof Flughafen, a metamorphosis took place. The Deacon's saintly countenance would transform into a debauched grin. Gone were all thoughts of church and family. Foremost in the Deacon's needs were tall foaming steins of Pilsner Urquel and an ample-breasted barmaid named Helga.

The Deacon spent most of his idle hours in a bar called the Hundekehle. Because of the money he had invested over the years in the Hundekehle, a bar stool was permanently reserved for him. Perched on his stool, surrounded by like-minded comrades, the Deacon would hold court. He consumed Urquel, smoked evil-smelling Polish cigarettes, and waited for Helga to get off work. Helga had moved in with the Deacon.

Every morning he reported for duty. A day of flying in Berlin meant three round trips, through the corridors to West Germany and back. They were tough days, particularly with bad weather and a hangover—standard conditions for Berlin and the Deacon. By six in the evening, he was back on his bar stool.

After two weeks of such duty, it was time for the Deacon to assume his alternate life. It was Ponca City time.

The metamorphosis reversed itself. As he stepped onto the plane, the Deacon's features began to smooth. His red-ringed eyes would clear. The saintly countenance found its way back onto his jowly face. Gone were his taste for Urquel and his lust for Helga.

He was never found out, at least in Ponca City. For years the Deacon happily maintained his dual life. Helga was eventually replaced by Renate, who was replaced by Ilse, who gave way to Soni. When the Deacon hit age sixty and retired from his airline career, two separate ceremonies marked the occasion. One was at the Pentecostal Baptist Church in Ponca City, with hymns and homemade ice cream. The other was at the Hundekehle, with Pilsner Urquel.

* * *

From the air the old airport still looked as it had in the days of the Third Reich. The terminal building, constructed in the shape of an eagle, rimmed the north quadrant of the circular airfield. The building's spread wings enfolded the sprawling ramp where Pan Am's fleet of 727s was parked in neat rows.

Back in the thirties, Tempelhof had been a circular grass airfield, designed to permit takeoffs and landings in any direction, whichever way the wind blew. Now it had parallel east-west runways, but the longest was only six thousand feet—barely adequate for modern jets. To add even more challenge to the approach, each end of the runway was obstructed with tiers of apartment buildings.

On the downwind leg for runway 27, you flew over East Berlin. From the traffic pattern you looked down on the Wall, meandering across the city like a fresh scar, dividing east from west. Though more than a quarter century had passed since the end of World War II, bombed-out buildings still jutted like broken teeth from the city landscape. Within the city, incongruously, were great forests, home to foxes and deer and wild pigs. Berlin boasted more trees per capita than any other major city in the world.

During the winter, Berliners endured weeks without a glimpse of pure sunshine. The Pan Am pilots briefly escaped the gloom when they took off in the morning's gray murk and five minutes later popped through the cloud layer into glorious sunshine. At the end of their flight, they again descended through the thickening clouds to their destination. In a typical day of flying, Pan Am pilots made three round trips from Berlin to airports in West Germany—usually Frankfurt, Hamburg, Munich, or Stuttgart. Each trip ended with an instrument approach to a fogbound or snow-enshrouded runway, often with a ceiling of no more than a hundred feet and visibility less than four hundred yards.

For most airline pilots, an approach to a fog-blanketed airport, down to a hundred feet above the ground, was not a relaxed, everyday procedure. Seldom was it necessary to fly all the way down to treetop height before seeing the runway. It was a rare enough event that when it happened, adrenaline flowed like floodwater through the cockpit.

You descended on an electronic glide path, downward through the gray swirl, toward the invisible runway somewhere ahead. You watched the altimeter needle slowly unwind to the minimum altitude

—the decision height—where you would make the call to land or to go around.

It was like flying into the pointed end of a cone. Ground and sky came together at an invisible spot where there were only two options: land or go around. At decision height—usually a hundred feet above the runway—the captain announced, "I have the runway," which meant he saw *something* out there—approach lights or threshold lights or the merciful strip of concrete itself. And he would land.

Or he saw nothing. If he was cool, his commands flowed in a level, exaggeratedly calm voice—"No contact, go-around thrust"— and at the same time he shoved the throttles full forward and rotated the nose up, up, up to fifteen degrees, and he raised the flaps, and, after the airplane was safely climbing, the landing gear. Back into the murk they would soar, engines roaring, adrenaline pumping.

For the IGS pilots, such activity was routine. It happened every day. They seldom needed to feign coolness, because they *were* cool. Adrenaline was an inert substance.

"What's the weather up ahead, captain?"

"I don't know, kid. Who cares? We're going to land anyway."

The weirdness of the Berlin pilots took different forms. Some were self-styled bohemians, like Everett Wood. He had come to Pan Am via the old American Overseas Airways, which Pan Am bought out after the war. Most of his career Woodie had spent in Berlin.

Woodie was the victim of a time warp. He was a scholar whose soul still lived in the romantic past. He knew Wagner and Chopin and Schopenhauer and Dante. He could quote entire pages of Hemingway and Remarque and Goethe. He could distinguish between vintages of *grand cru* Bordeaux, and he invariably wept at the conclusion of *Othello*.

Woodie had been married twice. Each of his brides, while adoring Woodie, had finally grown exasperated with a life of skimpiness. His last wife was a clever ex-stewardess named Barbro. One day she summed it up: "Woodie, we've been married for ten years. All we have to show for it is a bed and a refrigerator. And now the damned refrigerator doesn't work. Why don't we call it quits?"

Wood spoke both German and French fluently. He lived the life of an ascetic, owning neither a car nor a television. His inexpensive, meagerly furnished apartment lay under an elevated railway track. Its ancient exposed plumbing traversed the ceiling and ran along the walls. Woodie cared little about money, and his only unfrugal expenditures were on books and wine, both of which he consumed with relish.

Because he disdained most of the things pilots hold dear—money being foremost—he was regarded with suspicion by the Skygods. Even in Berlin, the Mecca of weirdness, Woodie was considered aberrant. Why the hell did a Pan Am captain have to ride the *subway* to the airport? It was embarrassing. Who did this guy think he was, for Christ's sake, giving passenger announcements in *German,* and sometimes even in *French?* This guy Wood was clearly some kind of a deviant.

The truth was, Berlin was a good deal. Whenever the Pan Am pilots' contract came up for renegotiation, the Berlin base always demanded—and usually received—special perquisites. They insisted on reduced duty time limits—a maximum of six flights a day—because of the stressful and "hazardous" nature of their corridor flying. They expected a pay bonus—called foreign station allowance—for the "hardship" of their overseas assignment. And, of course, they required a special tuition allowance because their children attended private, international schools.

They were the prima donnas as well as the weirdos of the airline. More so than at any other pilot base, in Berlin the pilots were a tightly knit group, capable of shutting down the operation over any infraction of their working conditions—inadequate crew meals, unfavorable currency exchange, a perceived insensitivity by management. Chief pilots in Berlin played a composite role—part manager, part baby-sitter, part grooming supervisor.

Hair was one of the burning issues of the seventies. The copilots had a lot of it, in the mod style of the times. Sideburns crept well below the earlobes—the official grooming limit. Mustaches flourished like fir forests. Cascades of hair flowed from beneath uniform caps. Even the caps themselves were an issue. The pilots didn't want to wear them because they didn't fit, with all that hair squeezed inside.

But hair was one of the chief pilot's lesser problems. That was a problem to be dealt with on the *ground*. What concerned him was when they did something unspeakably stupid in the *air*.

The woman in the copilot's seat wasn't supposed to be there. Her name was Marin. She was a twenty-year-old stewardess, and she was the latest love of Captain Ed Shaffer, a fifty-five-year-old IGS pilot going on, everybody estimated, about sixteen.

It was illegal as hell. But it was a ferry flight—meaning there were no passengers, just an empty airplane and its crew being moved back to Berlin—and who would know? Darkness had come, and there they were at the Hannover airport. All they had to do was get the empty 727 back to Berlin. Anyway, Marin *was* a pilot, more or less, having taken some flight instruction in a Cessna. Shaffer persuaded his first officer, a compliant young man named George Van Houten, to vacate his station. Into the copilot seat climbed Marin, smiling and smelling of musky perfume.

They took off, Marin at the controls. Ed was coaching her and thoroughly enjoying himself. It went fine, the jetliner wobbling only a little, Ed tutoring, Marin gripping the yoke with both hands. They leveled at 9,500 feet and flew through the central air corridor toward Berlin.

Ed talked her through the approach and landing. Again she managed just fine. The big jet's wheels bonked onto the concrete no harder than most landings at Tempelhof.

Everyone was pleased. The woman was thrilled. Shaffer's love life had soared to a new plateau. Best of all, they had gotten away with it.

Or so they thought.

As on most ferry flights, the cockpit door was left open. In this instance, the other two flight attendants, riding in the cabin, were curious that the first officer was not in his seat for the takeoff or landing. When they peeked into the cockpit they could not help but notice . . . *mein Gott* . . . *guck mal* . . . their stewardess colleague, Marin.

They thought it was quite funny, so much so that they couldn't help talking about it on the ground. No names were mentioned, but the story made the rounds from the stewardesses' lounge to a cocktail party to the commanding general of the Berlin Brigade, and even to the *Berliner Zeitung*, a local paper. Everyone laughed.

Everyone except Walt Mullikin. Mullikin was the chief pilot at the Berlin base, and it was his job to manage the weirdos. But this caper exceeded weirdness. Pan Am was being made to look bad in the German press. Messages were landing like mortar shells from Pan Am headquarters in New York:

What are those clowns doing over there? Find out who let a stewardess fly our airplane. Fire his ass.

Mullikin scanned his pilot roster. Who could it be? How many amorous, adolescent captains did he have who would do something so irresponsible and childish?

Well, he had to admit, there were a few. . . .

The trail of guilt quickly led to Ed Shaffer. Both his first officer, George Van Houten, and the flight engineer, an old veteran named Frank Nyalis, were asked for their own statements. Mullikin explained their options: Their jobs were on the line. If they were found to be lying . . .

So they told the story the way it happened. Each received a brief suspension. Ed Shaffer lost his job.*

In the Berlin base there were no strangers. Every airman was a known quantity. In such a tightly knit flying community, where each pilot knew the foibles of every other pilot, captains tended to treat copilots more as equals. The tyranny of the ocean-flying Skygods had never afflicted the Berlin base.

But Captain Art Gilson was an exception. Gilson *was* a tyrant. He was a short, shrill-voiced man who believed every copilot in Pan Am was trying to get him. And after they had gotten to know him, most were.

The crew-scheduling department in Berlin allowed copilots to bid

---

* After a two-year suspension, as part of a complex negotiation with the pilots' union, Ed Shaffer was reinstated. He finished out his career as a 747 captain.

not to fly with captains with whom they had personality conflicts. Several went on record requesting not to fly with Captain Gilson. When the no-Gilson list had grown to thirty-two copilots, the chief pilot summoned Gilson to his office. "It's easier to retrain you, Art, than to retrain thirty-two copilots. *Please* try to get along."

When copilots were bored or feeling mean, they would push Captain Gilson's buttons, just to see if they could make him crazy. It was easy.

Gilson stood only five feet four, a statistic that many believed accounted for his contrariness. He was prickly about his height. Any reference to Art's size would send him into a Napoleonic snit. They would do things like place a Berlin telephone directory—four inches thick—in Art's seat before he came in the cockpit. That *always* got Gilson going, no matter how many times he had seen it.

Sometimes, just for amusement, they would simply *suggest* that Art—a Skygod—might be screwing up.

"Art, aren't you supposed to be heading zero-four-zero degrees?" said Jim Wood one day. He and Gilson were flying toward Berlin in the southern air corridor.

"I *am* heading zero-four-zero."

"Well, not exactly," said Wood, squinting at the compass on his own instrument panel. "I show you heading about, oh, zero-five-five."

Gilson reddened. He peered at his compass. "I am *not*. I am heading zero-four-zero, just as we were assigned."

"Okay, have it your way," said Wood. And then, after a minute, "But you're still off heading."

Gilson raised himself in his seat. "Listen, mister, I don't need you to tell me how to fly this airplane." His voice rose in a crescendo that could be heard in the forward cabin. "I *know* when I'm off heading. I happen to be the captain of this aircraft, and I won't have *you* telling me—"

"Okay, Art, okay. It's no big deal," said Wood. Another minute would pass. "Just a lousy fifteen degrees or so . . . I guess that doesn't matter much."

Gilson's face would be purple. He would sputter and simmer, and that, of course, was the intended effect. For some reason, it never occurred to him that was why they did it.

But after a while, pushing Gilson's crazy buttons became boring for the Berliners. It was too easy. And then one day they discovered another irresistible aspect of Gilson's personality: Art Gilson, it turned out, was a man who *abhorred* crotch shots.

It was Beaver Man who took the credit for pushing Gilson over the edge. Beaver Man was a phantom distributor of anatomical photography. He was particularly fond of the centerfolds from the raunchiest men's magazines, which he liked to hide in the cockpits. No one knew Beaver Man's true identity, though it was generally assumed that he was a copilot. It was also suspected, because of the sheer volume of his work, that Beaver Man had several accomplices.

In the center of each pilot's control yoke was a "hubcap"—a plastic cover with the Boeing logo stamped on it. The yoke hubcaps were Beaver Man's favorite hiding place. He left cutouts—glossy, up-close, wide-open gynecological photos—beneath the covers. Eventually he managed to insert a tiny, neatly tailored cutout beneath *every* yoke cover in the Berlin-based fleet of 727s. He even rotated them on a frequent basis so that the pilots wouldn't get bored with the same old crotch shot day after day. The first time Art Gilson uncovered one of Beaver Man's photos, he went crazy. He yanked the offending picture out of its hiding place. "Filthy," he said. "Disgusting. I can't believe we have such dirty-minded people working for this airline."

One day a crotch shot appeared in Art's crew mailbox. The essential subject of the glossy photo could be viewed through the slot in the mailbox door, like a gynecological peep show.

Gilson flew into a tantrum. "Animals!" he screamed. He ripped the photo to shreds. "Filthy depraved animals!"

The next time it happened, Gilson marched upstairs to the chief pilot's office and threw the photo on the desk. He wanted the chief to see for himself the depths to which his pilots had sunk. The chief pilot studied the picture. Yes, he had to agree, it certainly was a tasteless picture. But Art really ought to slacken up a bit. He shouldn't take it so seriously.

It went on. More crotch shots appeared. Each time Gilson had another tantrum. Art Gilson was becoming a disturbed man. He was a sputtering volcano about to erupt.

One day it finally happened. Art walked into the crew room and, as usual, stooped to inspect the slot of his mailbox. There it was . . . *another* one . . . a glossy, wet, brilliantly hued crotch shot . . . *laminated* to the inside of his mailbox door . . . gazing out at him in living color.

Art went crazy. He ripped the door from its hinges. He whirled like a dervish through the Cuckoo's Nest, babbling incoherently, waving the mailbox door and the affixed crotch shot at all the astonished pilots. He charged upstairs to the chief pilot's office. "Look what they've done," he screamed. "Look what those crazy bastards have done."

They never saw Art again in the Cuckoo's Nest. They heard that he had agreed to accept an early retirement.

There were a few regrets. "We're going to miss Art," said Jim Wood. "Who are we going to pick on now?"

No one knew for sure how the chicken got in Al Bond's locker. But there it was one day, when Chicken Man came to the crew lounge and opened his locker.

The chicken had been there for some time, a couple of days, judging by the smell and the shower of feathers and chicken droppings when the bird exploded from the locker.

Chicken Man made a halfhearted attempt to capture the escaped fowl, then said to hell with it. So the pilots adopted the chicken. It roosted in the Cuckoo's Nest, flapping from locker to locker, leaving droppings on briefcases and uniform caps, filling the air with a barnyard smell.

One day the chief pilot came down to the Cuckoo's Nest. He sniffed the air and looked at the fresh droppings on the radiator. "Get rid of the goddam chicken," he said.

They did. Later, they talked about how Berlin was unique. It was the only pilot base in all of Pan Am with its own chicken in the crew room.

CHAPTER SEVENTEEN

THE COLD WAR GLADIATOR

Don't trust him, son. Look at his eyes. He's got eyes like a snake.

—MOTHER OF NAJEEB HALABY *on first meeting*
General William T. Seawell

General William T. Seawell, chairman of the board and chief executive officer of Pan American World Airways, was a casting director's dream. Tall, blue-eyed, with silver wavy hair, he looked every inch the Supreme Skygod, master of the Imperial Airline. Seawell looked so good that the Rolex Company even persuaded him to appear in its advertising, the general steely-eyed and exuding command authority, gold Rolex prominently affixed to his wrist, West Point ring on the third finger of his right hand.

The Pan Am pilots, however, weren't so sure about Seawell. They had liked his predecessor, good ol' Jeeb. Maybe Jeeb Halaby hadn't worked out as CEO. Maybe, they thought, he just inherited too big a mess to clean up in the short time he was aboard. But at least Halaby had been a pilot—one of them, who spoke their language. Halaby used to come around the pilot lounges, ride the cockpits, swap flying stories with the troops.

Jeeb was a good guy. In fact, his whole problem might have been that he was *too* good a guy. Some people suspected that Jeeb Halaby, in his inner core, might have been a little too soft for the job.

No one had ever accused Bill Seawell of softness. There was, in fact, a meanness to Seawell that revealed itself in his dealings with underlings. Seawell was charming, courteous, ingratiating—to those from whom he needed something. To those beneath him—the enlisted and lower-ranking subspecies—he was cold, even cruel. The nastiness of his temper became a thing of awe on the forty-sixth floor, peeling paint from the walls and causing battle-toughened secretaries to weep.

Seawell's tantrums came as a shock to staffers accustomed to the autocratic courtliness of Juan Trippe, the cordial coldness of Harold Gray, and the easy affability of Jeeb Halaby. It was like going to sleep with Snow White and waking up with Godzilla.

Out on the line, the pilots wondered about Seawell. They figured they *ought* to like him. After all, he was a pilot, and that should have been good. But Seawell came from SAC—the Strategic Air Command—where he had been a goddam *general*. And that was bad.

SAC was America's nuclear bomber force, prime weapon in its standoff with the Red Menace. It was virtually a separate military branch, an air force inside the Air Force, with its own labyrinthine culture and hierarchy. SAC's bases were mostly in remote places—Idaho, upper New York State, Maine, North Dakota—presumably for the shortened flying distance to the Soviets.

SAC was the Devil's Island of the Air Force. It was invariably the last choice of every newly graduated Air Force pilot, his worst dream come true. As a SAC pilot you flew great lumbering B-52 bombers in endless patterns across the globe, or else you flew great lumbering C-135 tankers, also in endless patterns across the globe, while you pumped fuel to the bombers.

Nothing that was fun ever happened in SAC. But your whole life was spent in readiness for something to happen. You were supposed to be ready at any time to rain destruction down on the Red Menace. And in the meantime you just kept flying the endless patterns and standing alert and filling out the paperwork. There was lots of that; more paperwork, in fact, than flying, because SAC was the world's biggest bureaucracy.

SAC was commanded by Cold War gladiators, generals whose

eyes glinted when they spoke of things like megatons and throw weight and preemptive strikes. It was the language of Armageddon. SAC had a tradition of tyranny unlike any other branch of the service. Generals berated colonels, who beat up on light colonels and majors, who in turn made life a living hell for the captains and lieutenants. No one knew why. That was just the way it had always been.

Any Air Force pilot who actually *wanted* to be in SAC was, by definition, a dangerous mental case. And anyone who purposely *stayed* in the outfit needed a lobotomy to prevent him from doing grievous harm to other living creatures. Almost to a man, young pilots assigned to SAC left the Air Force at the first opportunity. They left in droves, most of them joining the airlines, which thus became the recipients of millions of dollars spent training SAC pilots.

General Seawell was a SAC product. He had other credentials— the Harvard M.B.A., and the experience at American Airlines and Rolls-Royce. He had wrapped up his Air Force career as commandant of the Air Force Academy. But beneath all the veneer, Bill Seawell would forever remain what he was: a *general* of the Strategic Air Command. He was a Cold War gladiator.

A story was making the rounds of the crew rooms: One night at Kennedy Airport, Seawell worked himself into a seething rage. He was pacing the carpeted floor of the Clipper Club like a caged lion. Watching him from a discreet distance were his wife—known to Pan Am executives as Mrs. Chairman—and the airline's president, Dan Colussy.

They were flying to London that evening. Rather, they were *supposed* to fly to London that evening. But the Pan Am 747, *Clipper Westwind*, had a mechanical problem. For nearly two hours, mechanics had been trooping on and off the airplane, climbing up and down the spiral staircase to the cockpit, shaking their heads, and calling on their walkie-talkies to maintenance headquarters.

Seawell took one more glance at his gold Rolex and frowned. Enough was enough. He was taking no more of this crap. The general swiveled and marched out of the lounge and down the corridor, his heels hammering like drumbeats on the marble floor.

In the cockpit of the 747, the captain ran one hand through his mane of white hair and with the other removed his bifocals. He tossed the spectacles down on the opened maintenance log. "Hell," he said to the flight engineer. "We oughta be halfway across the Atlantic by now. How much longer, do you think?"

"No idea," said the engineer, a grizzled old-timer with a balding pate. "With a hydraulic system leak, you never know." The 747's hydraulic systems were like an arterial system. They routed hydraulic pressure to the aircraft's vital components—flight controls, landing gear, flaps, brakes.

The cockpit door burst open. Standing there in the aft cockpit, eyes burning like embers, was the airline's chief executive officer. "Why isn't this goddam airplane moving?" General Seawell demanded.

The three airmen stared at the general as if he were a visitor from Uranus.

"I beg your pardon?" said the captain.

"We've been here long enough," said Seawell. "Move this airplane."

"We have a leak in the number one hydraulic system," explained the captain. "We can't move until it's been isolated and repaired."

"I don't give a shit," said Seawell. "We paid millions of dollars for backup systems for these airplanes. Use them."

The captain was six months from retirement. He had been flying Pan Am airplanes for thirty-one years, most of that time in command, which made him a possessor of authentic Skygod credentials. He had no intention of taking abuse from someone like William T. Seawell.

"The airplane will depart," declared the captain, "when *I* am satisfied that it is airworthy. Not before."

"I happen to be the chief executive officer of this airline," said the general. "I'm telling you to get this goddam airplane out of here."

"I happen to be the captain of this airplane," said the captain. "We'll move when I'm good and ready. And you're interfering with the operation of this crew, sir. I'll ask you to leave *my* cockpit."

They locked gazes. It was a standoff of Skygods—Master of Ocean Flying Boats versus Imperial Airline chief executive.

One hour and forty-four minutes later—when the repair to the number one hydraulic system had been completed to his satisfaction —the captain ordered the doors closed and the external connections removed from *Clipper Westwind*.

Without further incident, they flew to London.

When the board of directors requested Najeeb Halaby's resignation and turned the chairmanship over to William Seawell, they had given Seawell a mandate to clean house at Pan Am. So the general started cleaning. And slashing. His mission, as he saw it, was to save Pan Am by shrinking it.

The airline *was* bloated, both in staffing levels and in route structure. Pan Am had stations staffed with managers, agents, mechanics, public relations people, that had only one flight a day transiting their station. Some of the stations, though far off the beaten path, were outfitted like extensions of government. "Pan Am didn't have just stations," reported the *Wall Street Journal*. "It had embassies."

Accounting at Pan Am was a joke. No one could say at any given time whether a particular segment of the airline was making or losing money. "They simply had no statistics," said a business reporter, "no analysis and no control. They were losing bushels of money, but didn't know where. It was like a company out of the thirties—they simply loaded all the passengers they could, added up the bills at the end of the month, and looked at the total to see where they had come out."

Another joke was the management structure. Pan Am had almost as many vice presidents as it had secretaries. *Anyone* could be a staff vice president. "Being a vice president at Pan Am was like being a Kentucky colonel," said an airline consultant. It was a token handed out, usually in lieu of a raise, for an up-and-coming manager to stick on his résumé. "There wasn't any rhyme or reason to it," said Dan Colussy, the airline president appointed by Seawell. "A guy would come in and ask to be a VP because Joe Blow down the hall was a VP. It just proliferated."

And so the heads rolled. Under Seawell the employee count shrank from 42,000 to 27,000. The platoons of vice presidents went back to being what they were—middle managers. The rank of staff vice president was eliminated completely.

The route system shrank. Pan Am dropped service to Paris, Vienna, and Moscow and ended flights between Seattle, Portland, and Honolulu. It shut down operations in Boston and closed the recently opened pilot base there as well as the new crew base in Hong Kong. Closing the bases, said the official bulletin, would save $15 million at each location.

Which was also a joke. In the hoopla of *opening* each base two years before, the company had proclaimed that it would save $15 million. "*Imagine* the money we're saving," said Joe Diedrich, a Berlin pilot. "Between opening and closing the bases, we're saving thirty mil on each one. Now that's *management*."

It sounded like a fairy tale when the story broke in the May 13 *Wall Street Journal*:

> NEW YORK—Pan American World Airways is saved. Its existence now seems assured for many years, and it may even turn a profit this year—thanks to some special circumstances.

And the circumstances *were* pretty special. In Pan Am's darkest hour, a fairy godfather had come to the rescue.

It happened like this.

In 1974, following the Yom Kippur War and the resultant oil price hikes by the Organization of Petroleum Exporting Countries, the cost of jet fuel went through the ceiling. Only about 6 percent of Pan American's total jet fuel was purchased from domestic sources. The rest was bought overseas, at OPEC-controlled prices. Pan Am's fuel bill suddenly doubled.

Because of the hugeness of the airline's losses that year, Seawell applied to the Civil Aeronautics Board for temporary subsidy. It was hoped that the Nixon administration, which had persuaded Congress to guarantee loans to Lockheed when the aircraft manufacturer had been about to go under, would do as much for another American institution, the financially troubled Pan American.

Pan American? The *financially troubled Pan American*? By now it was well known that the mention of Pan Am caused a narrowing of the eyes and furrowing of foreheads in the Nixon White House. It was a bitter irony that the Nixon Republicans were no more favorably disposed to Pan Am than the Johnson Democrats had been. Pan Am had gotten short shrift in the Nixon international route handouts, been stonewalled by Nixon's Justice Department in the merger effort with TWA, and now was being ignored in its request for subsidy.

Why?

Old-timers scratched their heads and wondered. How had Pan Am, the airline that used to be called America's Chosen Instrument, become so politically disconnected?

The explanation seemed to be that Pan Am, by its very arrogance, had poisoned the political water. Washington was awash with old Pan Am enemies—Democrats, Republicans, bureaucrats, lobbyists for competitors—who still nursed grudges about the Imperial Airline and its high-handed ways.

The Nixon White House had a more specific reason. The name Pan American had been conspicuously missing from the list of contributors to President Nixon's reelection campaign. In the post-Watergate revelations, two other airlines, Braniff and American, would be charged with making illegal contributions to the campaign. As it turned out, each of the airlines had received generous new route authority—on Pan American routes—from the Nixon administration.

Now Pan Am was requesting assistance from the White House. Months went by. The subsidy application lay moldering in a tray at the CAB like a letter from a deadbeat cousin. In August 1974, after Richard Nixon resigned and fled the White House, Pan Am submitted a second, more hopeful and urgent request.

The Ford administration was no more inclined to help Pan Am than the Nixon bunch. Forget subsidy, was the message. Pan American would have to deal with its own troubles. It should not expect help from *this* government.

That meant the *United States* government. But what about some other government?

The first winter snows had already capped the summit of Mount Demavend, towering above the city of Tehran, when Pan Am's station manager there telexed a strange message back to New York: *The officials of Iran Air have expressed an interest in helping Pan American.*

Iran Air? Iran Air was owned by the Iranian government, which was owned, for all practical purposes, by the Shah of Iran.

Seawell would take help from wherever he could get it. He sent

Willis Player off to Tehran to conduct talks. Player reported back that it was true. The Shah was serious. He had money to invest—lots of it—and for reasons not entirely clear to the agencies of either government, he had decided that it was in Iran's—which was to say, *his*—good interest to invest in Pan American World Airways.

For Pan Am, it seemed like a deal made in heaven. For the Shah, it was a deal no one could quite figure out. What did he intend to do with Pan Am?

The only answer seemed to be that the Shah was an aviation-minded monarch who had conjured an image of Iran as a major player in world air commerce. He had a vision of his country, until recently a land of goatherds and carpet weavers, taking a role of leadership in the technology of the space age. He was already investing heavily in Iran Air's modern fleet of jetliners. He wanted access to Pan American's global network, and he needed Pan Am's sophisticated training and technological facilities for his mostly recently ordered aircraft.

All of which caused an instant furor in Washington. The Ford administration and the CAB reacted in the most predictable way: *Hey, hold on a minute. Don't you realize that Iran is a foreign power, and that Pan American is vested with our national interest?*

And *that* brought a hoot from every office and conference room in the Pan Am system.

Pan American, of course, *was* the United States' largest international carrier. Pan Am's armada of 747s was the largest contingent of jets in CRAF—the Air Force's Civil Reserve Air Fleet—and was instantly available for military transport use. In every conflict since World War II, Pan Am had provided airplanes, crews, facilities.

Pan Am vested with our national interest? No kidding? What do you think we were trying to tell you for the past year?

And then even the bureaucrats heard their own words and recognized the contradiction. A few weeks ago they were denying Pan Am any relief because the airline was a private—not a government—enterprise. But now they had just declared that Pan Am was, in fact, vital to the government's interest.

So while Seawell and the airline's creditors met with the Iranians, a Pan Am lobbying team descended on Washington to promote the deal. The Shah had made it clear he would not proceed until given a green light from the White House.

The Ford administration took a straw poll of its agencies and found itself favorably disposed. Treasury Secretary William Simon went so far as to tell Congress that he was "very positive on encouraging all the investment by Iran in Pan Am within the constraints of national security."

National security—that was the only hitch. What about the CRAF commitment? What about ownership of the airline in time of conflict? Foreign ownership meant, to an extent, foreign control.

In this instance, the objections had little substance. After all, this was *Iran* they were talking about. Who could get worked up about Iran? Hell, Iran was our *friend,* wasn't it? Iran was so closely allied to the United States it was practically a subsidiary. Iranians *loved* America.

The only real opposition to a Pan Am–Iran deal came from behind the scenes, ostensibly from members of Congress, but in fact from their political fund contributors in the domestic airlines. The strong domestic carriers had been eyeing the decline of Pan Am, hoping to step in and pick up the lucrative overseas routes. Now, with a big infusion of money from the Shah, that happy likelihood was slipping away.

The administration bestowed its blessing, and with that signal from the President, the CAB was sure to follow suit. The board had only to go through its usual bureaucratic deliberations before issuing its ritual approval.

On the surface it looked like a gesture of support for Pan Am. What it *really* amounted to was a collective sigh of relief. What no one was willing to say, at least out loud, was that they were damn glad that someone—they weren't fussy *who*—was getting the Pan Am problem off their backs. The CAB and the White House and the Department of Transportation had been unwilling to *save* Pan Am, but they didn't want to be tagged with the blame when it went under. They didn't really care what happened to Pan Am, as long as it didn't happen on their watch. Now the Shah, bless him, was letting them off the hook.

When the particulars of the deal were made public, an airline financial executive told the press, "This has got to be the most dazzling piece of financial wizardry ever used to rescue a sick company."

Indeed, it *was* dazzling. Probably the most dazzling aspect was the willingness of Pan Am's creditors to write off millions of dollars in loans in order to salvage part of their investment. Iran would foot a $245 million loan that would be used to buy back Pan Am's outstanding notes—at fifty-one cents on the dollar. The airline's long-term creditors, mostly insurance companies, were grudgingly going along with the deal, knowing that the alternative could well be zero cents on the dollar.

Another aspect of the deal was that Iran would buy for $55 million a majority ownership of another lucrative Pan American property, the Intercontinental Hotel chain.

For all this, Iran would receive warrants to buy up to six million shares of Pan Am stock at about $2.50 a share, which gave the Shah what amounted to a call on 13 percent of Pan Am stock. A representative of the Shah would take a seat on the Pan Am board of directors.

For the pilots of Pan Am, especially the old new hires who remembered the promises of the 1960s, the deal had another tantalizing aspect.

The Shah was buying SSTs.

It was disclosed that Iran had ordered a fleet of Concordes. As part of the package, Pan American would provide the operational expertise to fly them.

SSTs? Would they be *Pan Am* SSTs? Would they be flown by Pan Am pilots? That was still too far away. But suddenly the future was wide open again. To the Pan Am pilots it was a fairy tale in which they had gone to sleep as urchins and waked up as the children of a rich king. It was magic. It seemed too good to be true.

And it was.

"We're about a week away from signing the deal," a Pan Am spokesman told the business press in May 1975.

A couple of weeks later, they were still a week away.

And so it went through the summer of 1975. A week away.

The deal was still on, everyone said, but no one could say when. The Shah would make the final decision. By autumn, high-level Iranians were ducking questions about the deal. They would say only that it was "still being considered, but there is definitely less enthusiasm than there was six months ago."

One of the reasons for the waning enthusiasm was that Iran's oil revenue was down 15 percent, forcing Iran to curtail some of its investments. But the Iranians had also taken a closer look at the problems facing Pan Am. "Fuel cost increases have made the airline business a very tricky one," said a representative of the Shah, "and we are wondering where Pan Am will be five years from now."

The fact that the fuel cost increases were wholly the doing of Iran and its OPEC colleagues was an irony he chose not to mention.

By the end of the summer it was obvious that the deal was not happening. What had gone wrong? Why had the Shah changed his mind? No one knew for sure. The palace of the Shah was a place of puzzles.

The dream deal, had it come true, would have metamorphosed into a nightmare. Less than four years later, the Shah was overthrown. America's bedrock ally in the Middle East became, overnight, a mortal enemy. Policymakers speculated grimly about a Pan American World Airways whose principal owner was the Ayatollah Khomeini.

CHAPTER EIGHTEEN

THE CHILDREN'S CRUSADE

Pan Am does a lot more than compete with other airlines. We compete with whole countries, sometimes even our own.

—*NEW YORK TIMES advertisement, September 23, 1974,*
placed by Pan Am employees

The Pan Am mystique was slipping away. And *damn,* it was painful, like a smoldering ember in the gut, to see the domestic airlines—the bus drivers—swarming over what had been Pan Am country.

Pan Am pilots would hear from their former military buddies at American and United and Delta:

"Oh, yeah, we're gonna start nonstop service next month to Tokyo and . . ."

". . . adding Frankfurt and Paris to our new European route system . . ."

"I'm flying the new DC-10s we just bought . . ."

Meanwhile at Pan Am, the news was all bad. The business press had a standard way of writing about Pan Am:

"A spokesman for the *financially troubled Pan American* said today . . ."

"In an effort to secure new credit terms for *financially troubled Pan Am,* the airline's lenders . . ."

"The increase in fuel prices is expected to have a particularly severe impact on *financially troubled Pan American,* whose fortunes . . ."

They never referred to *Pan American* anymore. It was always *the financially troubled Pan American.*

It became a joke in the cockpits: By the end of the century, after all the weaklings in the business had succumbed to bankruptcy or hostile takeover, there would be only three airlines left in the United States: American, United, and the Financially Troubled Pan American.

One day in the spring of 1974, an item appeared on the pilots' bulletin board.

> Pan American director General Charles A. Lindbergh, 72, passed away at his home on Maui yesterday after a brief illness. General Lindbergh's association with Pan American dated back to 1929, when he and Juan Trippe . . .

Lindbergh. The Icon. He had seemed indestructible—exempted somehow from the calamities that visited everyday mortals.

Now the world really *was* different. For the legion of Pan Am airmen, it was like losing their patron saint.

In his later years as a director, he became a roving troubleshooter for Pan Am and spent hundreds of hours in the cabins of Pan Am clippers. He usually rode in coach class, traveling under an alias. His only baggage was the same old brown carry-on he kept for thirty years.

As an anonymous passenger he observed the service, sampled the food, watched passenger reactions. He took copious handwritten notes and made reports back to headquarters. The only thing he couldn't make a judgment about was the wine and liquor quality. Lindbergh didn't drink. "You'll have to ask someone else about that."

It was typical of Lindbergh that no one outside his close circle even knew he was ill. Lindbergh was a man who never asked for sympathy. Nor did he want the maudlin attention of the public.

He still came to meetings of the Pan American board of directors. He looked tired. The ice-blue eyes gazed at his fellow directors wearily, as though he were anxious to get the business over with so he could go home.

In the spring of 1974, at the mandatory retirement age of seventy-two, Lindbergh *did* go home. For most of the board members, it was the last time they would see him.

His malaise was diagnosed as cancer of the lymphatic system. It was terminal, he was told. He said he wanted to die in the house he and Anne had built on Maui, overlooking the sea. In a United Airlines 747, on a specially rigged stretcher in the closed-off first-class compartment, Lindbergh made his last flight. He died on August 26, 1974. He was buried in a plain wood coffin.

The death of Lindbergh seemed to match the rest of the news that year about Pan Am. To the Pan Am pilots it was like a portent of doom. Pan Am was losing *everything* from the old glory days. Even its greatest hero.

One day a column on the op-ed page of the *International Herald Tribune* began with "Who the hell needs Pan Am?"

Captain Terry Beasley handed the newspaper to Jim Hotchkiss, his first officer. They were at ten thousand feet, inbound to Berlin in the southern air corridor.

It was 1974. A month before, on August 15, the CAB had recommended that Pan Am's and TWA's international routes be realigned and that four more airlines be added to the list of competitors. A debate was under way in Congress and in the media about the efficacy of government intervention in corporate debacles like those of Lockheed and Penn Central—and perhaps Pan Am. It was rumored in the business press that Pan Am was near bankruptcy. Should Pan Am be saved? Senator Proxmire of Wisconsin, chief slayer of the SST, thought not. "Let the invisible hand of free enterprise do its work," Proxmire declared. Which was to say, to hell with Pan Am.

"We're going to get screwed again," Beasley said.

"Yup," said Hotchkiss. He was a new hire, 1964 vintage. His bright hopes for Pan Am, like those of his classmates, were going down the drain. "What are we going to do about it?"

They flew to Berlin, and then back to West Germany, and then back to Berlin. And the whole time they talked. The problem seemed to be the public perception that Pan Am's problems were all its own doing.

Okay, decided Beasley and Hotchkiss, a good place to start would be with that particular item of misinformation. They would take Pan Am's case to the public.

They stuck a request on the bulletin board for donations to buy an ad in a major newspaper. Every pilot who passed through the crew room contributed. Within twenty-four hours they had $10,000.

On September 23, 1974, a full-page advertisement in the *New York Times* began with the headline:

AN OPEN LETTER TO THE AMERICAN PEOPLE
FROM THE EMPLOYEES OF THE WORLD'S
MOST EXPERIENCED AIRLINE

The ad took aim at the U.S. government, raising some old questions:

Ask our own government why the Postal Department pays the foreign airlines as much as five times what it pays Pan Am for hauling the same U.S. mail. Not receiving the same pay for the same work costs Pan Am forty million dollars a year.

Ask our own government why the U.S. Export-Import Bank loans money to "underdeveloped" countries like France, Japan, and Saudi Arabia, at six percent interest while Pan Am pays twelve percent.

Ask our own government why it is opposed to letting Pan Am fly passengers within our country . . . it just doesn't make sense. The domestic airlines now have rights to the international routes that we pioneered, and the foreign airlines now serve more cities in the United States than we do.

The ad concluded with a bold-printed summation:

IF PAN AM WERE ALLOWED DOMESTIC ROUTES WITHIN THE UNITED STATES . . . OR TO BORROW FROM THE EXPORT-IMPORT BANK . . . OR TO PAY REASONABLE LANDING FEES OVERSEAS . . . OR TO RECEIVE EQUAL POSTAL RATES FROM

OUR OWN GOVERNMENT, WE WOULDN'T NEED ANY SUBSIDY
AT ALL!

*In fact we wouldn't need to have taken up a collection to run
this ad.*

The Employees of Pan Am

Beasley and Hotchkiss dreamed up the acronym AWARE. It meant Airmen Worried About Remaining Employed. But the scope of their project quickly swelled beyond the pilot roster. As soon as the *New York Times* advertisement came out, the rest of the Pan Am employee group wanted to come on board.

They all felt the same way. They all might be irate with General Seawell. He had slashed the employee force from 42,000 to 27,000. They might be incensed at each other—machinists mad at passenger service agents, flight attendants peeved at pilots—but this was something they could agree on. This was family business.

Thus began the Children's Crusade. An organization of employees—AWARE—sprang up, with Jim Hotchkiss taking the lead. It dispatched teams to Washington, where every congressman and senator received an arm-twisting visit from Pan Am pilots. Thousands of letters flowed into congressional mailboxes. Giant rallies were held on the steps of the Capitol. T-shirts, bumper stickers, more newspaper ads were created.

One morning just after dawn, Senator William Proxmire went pounding down a damp and deserted K Street on his daily jog. In addition to being America's champion of free enterprise, Proxmire was a fitness freak. He jogged nearly every morning at this time. He found it was the only time he could be truly alone.

But alone he was not. The senator became aware of a pounding of feet coming up behind him. Over his shoulder he could see this tall guy with woolly red hair, grinning like a baboon, taking long strides and quickly closing the distance.

"Good morning, senator," said Rich Selph, jogger and Pan American first officer. "I'd like to talk to you about Pan Am."

"Shit," said the senator. "I'm running. I don't want to talk."

"There are some things I'd like you to know about Pan American."

"Call my office."

"I did call," said Selph. "I couldn't get an appointment."

Proxmire picked up the pace. *Damn.* The runner was staying right with him. Proxmire could see by the kid's face he wasn't going to fall behind. He was some kind of freaking zealot.

"Then call again," said Proxmire.

"Will I be able to get in to see you? Just for a few minutes?"

"Maybe. Just let me run in peace."

"It's really quite important, senator."

"All right, all right. You can say your piece. In the office, not out here."

"Thank you, senator. I'll do that. Have a good run."

Washington didn't know what to make of these people.

Historically, when a private industry wanted something from government, it deployed brigades of pinstriped lawyers and professional lobbyists. They rented palatial suites and hosted lavish receptions. Their standard tool of persuasion was almost always *money*, dispensed in the form of campaign contributions and favors and pledges for future support.

In the old days, the Skygodly Imperial Airline days, that had been Pan Am's style. Now Pan Am the corporation stayed conspicuously out of sight. Chairman Seawell conveyed his support to the AWARE workers, then tactfully remained in his headquarters. AWARE, everyone realized, could only be effective as a grass-roots movement.

Never before had the capital seen *employees* of a corporation take up their company's cause like this. Sure, Washington was used to unions lobbying for their pet bills and trade associations applying political pressure. But when had it seen the wage earners of a single business—one not very large airline—get so worked up over the treatment of their employer? There was something quaintly *American* about it—the workers of a venerable old company going to Washington to demand nothing more than a fair shot. It had a down-home, apple-pie appeal. Just take off the manacles, they were saying. That's all. Give Pan Am the same fair shot you give its competitors.

It was hard not to agree. Newspaper editors took up the cause, quoting from the AWARE ad. Congress mumbled collectively about doing something to straighten out the problem. The Ford administration tut-tutted about the need to keep our flag carriers, meaning Pan Am and TWA, alive and healthy.

Even the senator of free enterprise, while not announcing his conversion to the Save Pan Am faith, had enough sense to shut up.

The autumn of 1974 passed, and Congress recessed and then assembled again in 1975. When it opened its doors, the AWARE crowd was still there. They were like tenacious bill collectors. You couldn't get rid of them.

And in the meantime, something amazing was going on: *Pan Am was surviving.*

Actually, very little had changed. Congress passed a bill called the International Air Transportation Fair Competitive Practices Act, which helped Pan Am obtain needed loans. But Pan Am still didn't have domestic routes. There were exactly the same number of U.S. domestic airlines assigned to Pan Am overseas routes. Foreign countries were still extorting outrageous landing and handling fees. Pan Am was paying $4,200 to land a 747 in Sydney versus Qantas's fee of $178 to land in Los Angeles. The only real gesture from the administration was in the form of a directive that government officials travel overseas on United States flag carriers, whenever available. And some adjustments were made in postal rates for airmail.

But Pan Am's fortunes began to improve anyway. It was as if by national consensus the country had decided that Pan Am *would* endure, at least for the moment. Business was picking up—at least in part because the country was pulling out of the recession of the early seventies. The Arab oil embargo and resultant fuel price shock of 1973 had been absorbed.

One of the effects of the AWARE effort was not yet visible. Already germinating in Washington's bureaucratic effluvium was an item of legislation that would transform the landscape of the airline business. It would be called the Airline Deregulation Act, and it would end the life of the inefficient Civil Aeronautics Board. For all practical purposes, deregulation meant that any airline could have domestic route authority. Even Pan Am.

For the new hires now entering their second decade with Pan Am, the AWARE crusade was a surprising revelation. When the dust settled and they looked around, they saw that *they were alone.*

Someone from the press in Washington had hung a label on the AWARE phenomenon—the Children's Crusade—and it stuck. The name was appropriate, because when Pan Am had needed saving, it was the junior pilots who had stepped forward. It was their voices that had been heard in Congress, their rhetoric that had carried the day. Nowhere in sight had been their older, senior, more comfortable colleagues.

The Skygods had stayed home.

For the new hires, it was a coming of age. No more were they willing to politely yessir the Skygods, patiently waiting, waiting for the long apprenticeship to end. The future, for better or worse, belonged to them.

In October 1975, Chairman Seawell convened a secret meeting of Pan Am executives to draw up a contingency plan for taking the corporation into bankruptcy. The plan, as it turned out, did not have to be implemented. Seawell was able to persuade Pan Am's creditors to extend enough credit, taking more 747s as collateral, to see the company through the coming winter slack season.

Pan Am's principal American competitor, TWA, was suffering its own sizable losses on its overseas routes—and for the same reasons as Pan Am. Both airlines had taken delivery of a fleet of jumbo jets at the beginning of the decade, just as international traffic spiked downward. Both were reeling from the effects of the recession on business travel.

Having been rebuffed two years earlier in their merger request, the two airlines appealed once again—this time to the CAB. Instead of a Pan Am–TWA merger, the two carriers wanted approval of a drastic route-swapping arrangement by which they could eliminate much of the costly competition between them.

Since the Richard Nixon and Najeeb Halaby era, times had changed, at least a little. In Washington the AWARE movement had raised bureaucratic consciousness about the unfair treatment of Pan Am. Neither the Ford administration nor the CAB wanted to be tagged with the blame for Pan Am's demise. After its usual deliberations, the CAB announced its approval of the route swaps.

Pan Am agreed to relinquish its United States–Paris service, leaving that to TWA, while TWA would give up its Frankfurt operation in favor of Pan Am. Pan Am would drop flights to Madrid, Barcelona, Nice, Casablanca, and Vienna and give up its routes to London via Los Angeles, Chicago, and Philadelphia. At the same time, TWA would drop most of its Pacific operation, including Guam, Hong Kong, Bangkok, and Honolulu.

Did all this mean that the CAB had developed a more kindly attitude toward Pan Am? Were times changing? Hardly. One historic barrier remained firmly in place: no domestic routes. Pan Am still could not fly in its own country.

The trimming of the airline, it was declared to the press, would mean a saving of something between $17 million and $24 million the first year. It also meant a downsizing of the airline. That meant fewer flights and a reduced number of crews.

For the pilots, it was the F word again.

It was just like the two previous times in the past six years. At bases all around the system they stood there in front of the bulletin boards, their jaw muscles working and their eyes skimming the numbered lists. They looked for their names on the furlough list. A whole new wave of them, several hundred more airmen, were about to join their fellow pilots already out there on the street.

For those not being furloughed, the shrinking of the airline meant moving from their current cockpit seat to another, or from a senior, desirable base, like San Francisco, to the junior, least popular base, which was New York. Newly promoted captains would be demoted back to their old first officer's seat, and new first officers moved back to their familiar old sideways-facing flight engineer's station.

Coping with a furlough was harder than it used to be. The new hires weren't so new anymore. They were ten years into their airline careers. Most were pushing forty. Some were already beyond, and their prospects for another airline job—a *real* airline job—were about nil. The solid airlines, American, United, Delta, were hiring *kids*— hotshot young jocks fresh out of the military—such as they had been a decade ago.

Most had families now, kids in school, mortgaged homes. What were they going to do? Their ancient degrees in engineering or forestry or music didn't translate into any kind of marketable skill. All they knew how to do was fly airplanes.

Predictably, there was anger. "I helped save this goddam airline," said a seething pilot in Berlin who had been a founder of the AWARE movement, "and this is how the bastards treat us."

"That's it," said a pilot, glowering at the bulletin board. He had been furloughed in 1970, and had been recalled, and now was being furloughed again. "To hell with Pan Am. I'm going back in the Navy, and this time I'm going to stay."

"It's Seawell," declared a furloughee-to-be in San Francisco. "That's how he treated pilots in the goddam Air Force. Now he's doing the same thing to us."

Said one discouraged flight engineer in New York: "My mother told me to be a dentist. I should have listened."

Others just shrugged and walked away. They had given up ranting about events they could never control. What was the use? They had grown accustomed to bad news.

Mercifully, 1975 ended. And then in 1976 a most peculiar thing happened: *Pan American made money.*

To everyone's astonishment, the airline was suddenly making *a lot* of money. By the end of the year, Pan American World Airways had racked up a net profit of nearly $100 million.

The financial community was flabbergasted. How had such an incredible thing happened?

The route swaps had helped. Instead of both Pan Am and TWA flying half-empty 747s across the ocean, each airline was now carrying nearly full loads on their noncompeting routes.

But even more significant, people were traveling again. After a long period of stagnation, the overseas travel market was again on the upswing. And the horrific fuel price escalations of the early seventies had stabilized—for the time being—and were now factored into the cost of doing business.

Chairman Seawell was being touted as the airline wizard of the decade. In less than a year he had taken Pan Am on a journey from the abyss of bankruptcy to its all-time peak of profitability.

No one suspected that the journey might be a round trip.

CHAPTER NINETEEN

DEEP POCKETS

QUESTION: How does an international airline acquire domestic
  routes?
ANSWER NUMBER ONE: In the newly deregulated market, it
  purchases new equipment and builds its own route system.
ANSWER NUMBER TWO: It buys a domestic airline.

The phenomenon continued. In 1977, Pan Am earned $45 million.
Even more phenomenally, it kept on making money. In the first nine
months of 1978, the company reported a $123 million profit.

"Seawell is doing a helluva job," declared an airline industry executive to the *Wall Street Journal.*

In his paneled office on the forty-sixth floor, General Seawell could
afford to tilt back and treat himself to some back-patting. He was
aware of the horde of people out there, employees former and current,
who hated his guts. He knew that his enemies would like nothing so
much as to see him blow it.

Well, he had shown them. The past two annual reports vindicated
his drastic head-chopping and route-paring. When he had taken over,
the company had been teetering on the brink of doom. Between 1969
and 1976, Pan Am had lost $364 million, enough to spur dark rumors
that Seawell would be the guy who took Pan Am into extinction.

Seawell knew he could take credit for much of Pan Am's recovery.
But there was also overwhelming evidence that luck had played a role.
After the setbacks of the early seventies—the price hikes of the oil

cartel and the numbing recession—business was resurging. Travelers were taking to the skies in record numbers.

The truth was, it would have been difficult for an airline *not* to make money in 1978.

The other carriers were doing even better. Since the Johnson and Nixon administrations the foreign route award process had become thoroughly politicized. With its handouts, the Carter White House was reaching new heights of munificence: Delta from Atlanta to London; National from Miami to Paris, Amsterdam, and Frankfurt; Braniff from Dallas to London; Northwest from a number of U.S. cities to Copenhagen and Stockholm.

Even the foreign airlines were recipients of the Carter generosity. The administration was making deals with foreign governments, using Pan Am routes as bargaining chips. British Airways received new routes to San Francisco; KLM to Los Angeles; Laker Airways to New York and Los Angeles; Lufthansa to several new U.S. destinations, including Miami and Atlanta; British Caledonia to Houston.

United Airlines was pressuring for a new air agreement with Japan, exchanging rights for Japan Air Lines to land in more American ports of call so that United could compete directly with Pan Am on the Tokyo route.

So even though Pan Am was making money—at the moment—its future was filled with peril. Pan Am's piece of the overseas market had dwindled from 20 percent in the 1950s to only 7.5 percent in 1978. Pan Am wasn't even the front-runner across the Atlantic anymore after Seawell's cutbacks. TWA now claimed that distinction.

All this, of course, was well known both in and out of Washington. During the 1940s and 1950s, Trippe had lobbied hard in Washington to preserve Pan Am's "protected" status. Pan Am's routes to Europe and Asia were still artificially profitable because of mail subsidy. Whenever the specter of competition on its routes came up, Pan Am historically pulled all the stops on its lobbying machine.

It was Pan Am's legacy of arrogance, and despite the brief respite brought about by the AWARE campaign, it still lingered in Washington, like a bad hangover. "They were autocratic twenty-five years ago," observed the *Wall Street Journal*, "and they're still autocratic today."

One businessman, persuaded by a Pan Am director to visit congressmen on the airline's behalf, got a violent reaction. "They threw me out of their office," he reported.

Pan Am's most entrenched opponent in Washington was, arguably, the five-member Civil Aeronautics Board, created during the Roosevelt administration. The CAB's purpose was to regulate air commerce—set fares, approve routes, and control competition, all, supposedly, in the public interest. Over the years the CAB consistently thwarted Juan Trippe's efforts to make Pan American the "Chosen Instrument." Always citing the need to stimulate "competition" and "free enterprise," the CAB diluted Pan Am's market share by parceling out routes to Pan Am's competitors. The CAB board members, being political appointees, reflected the economic philosophy of the current administration.

President Jimmy Carter's choice to head the Civil Aeronautics Board was a bespectacled, feisty, sixty-year-old economics professor from Cornell named Alfred E. Kahn. Kahn was familiar with Pan Am's history, and he didn't like the Trippe legacy any better than his predecessors had. "Pan Am can go to hell," he snapped to the press one day after he'd heard enough about Pan Am's problems.

Later, when he'd had time to cool down, Kahn thought about what he'd said. Actually, he told a reporter, for Pan Am "that *would* be an interesting new route."

In the fall of 1978, the rules changed. A long-simmering item of legislation called the Airline Deregulation Act was finally signed into law. What it meant, in effect, was that anyone could fly anywhere, at least within the United States. Deregulation was a trendy idea whose time had come during the inflation-ravaged 1970s. The traveling public— and its elected congressmen—were fed up with runaway airline fares and the inability of the bureaucratic CAB to regulate anything. Laissez-faire economics was being touted as the cure-all for the country's ills. According to the laissez-faire crowd, the airlines would have a wide-open marketplace, which would promote new airlines, cut fares, reduce inflation, and serve the public splendidly.

Alfred Kahn, CAB chairman and free market disciple, was the spiritual leader of the deregulation movement, and it would be his responsibility to make it happen. In the process he was also putting himself and his fellow board members out of a job, since one key aspect of the act, in addition to removing regulation, was to remove the regulator. The new law mandated a dissolution of the plodding, inefficient Civil Aeronautics Board.

And *that,* at least to Pan American World Airways, was the best news of all.

After half a century of trying, Pan Am could finally have domestic routes. But how? Where to begin?

Chairman Seawell had a purse full of money, thanks to Pan Am's recent profitability. Already Pan Am had placed orders for new airplanes, but *not* more of the gargantuan 747s to haul amphitheaters full of passengers from continent to continent. Pan Am was buying the smaller, three-engine, long-range Lockheed 1011, with an eye on the lesser-traveled routes, destinations like Madrid and Nice and Hamburg that didn't produce enough passengers to fill up a 747 but would provide a profitable load on the Lockheed.

Now Seawell faced a critical decision. Should he invest Pan Am's hard-earned capital in the wild free-for-all that was developing in the deregulated domestic market? It would take millions, possibly a billion, to put such a domestic airline system in place. And years.

Pan Am didn't have years. Nor did it have a billion dollars. Time was running out both for Pan Am and for Bill Seawell. Seawell was sixty years old. He wasn't at the end of his run, but the finish line was in sight. If Pan Am was going to return to its old prominence in air commerce, if Pan Am was ever again to reward its shareholders with dividends, if Pan Am was to recapture its technological leadership in aviation, then Seawell wanted history to record the fact that those glorious events happened under his generalship.

There was no time to waste building a domestic fleet, buying short-haul airplanes and building facilities, hiring qualified managers and training crews, before Pan Am could start flying across the hinterlands.

Instead, Pan Am would *buy* an airline.

What Seawell wanted was an acquisition, one in which Pan Am totally absorbed a lesser entity, not a merger in which Pan Am shared or surrendered its autonomy. That ruled out a deal with Eastern. And a TWA deal had already been explored more than once and dropped.

Forget Braniff, which was expanding like an omnivorous animal, driven more by appetite than good sense. Forget the mainline domestics—American, United, Delta—which were getting what they wanted in the international market anyway, thanks to Carter and company.

And that was when Seawell's attention fixed on National.

National Airlines? Pan Am's analysts took a look. They could see that National was a Miami-based airline, meaning that it was brash, a little on the folksy, Florida cracker side, strong traffic growth, erratically managed, overextended, restive unions, a mixed fleet of airplanes . . .

It was what Seawell wanted. By now the general and his paint-peeling tantrums were well known on the forty-sixth floor. From his staff the chairman heard nothing but voices of agreement.

Yes, sir, general. Why not?

The question was making the rounds of the crew lounges, the cockpits, the layover hotels: *Why National?*

Why buy any airline, for that matter? If Pan Am had so much money it could buy out someone else's mess—employees, airplanes, and trash cans—why didn't it just build on what it already had?

Crewing new airplanes was not the problem. Pan Am already had a legion of pilots out there on the street, some of them furloughed since back in 1969. Training them in newly acquired equipment would cost something, but it was an expense that would have to be borne anyway, sooner or later.

There were two views about what was good for Pan Am: a *them* and an *us.* A merger might be the best thing—for *them,* meaning Pan Am, the corporation and its stockholders. But what was good for the *them* wasn't always good for the *us,* meaning the pilots—the aging, disillusioned, bleary-eyed, time-zone-crossing, so-called new hires about to enter their seventeenth year of apprenticeship. And not by any extrapolation of merger rationale could it be considered a good deal for the legion of furloughed airmen out there on the sidewalk, noses pressed against the window, waiting to be let back in. They would see their cockpit seats filled with fresh-faced new National pilots.

A box of pins showed up one day in the pilot lounges. On the pins was the message WE HAVE THE URGE TO MERGE.

"We do?" a pilot asked, picking up one the pins.

The pins were distributed by the AWARE group, the grass-roots movement originally started back in Berlin by pilots who wanted to do something about saving Pan Am. But that was six years ago, and the crisis had passed. Gradually AWARE had metamorphosed into a pro-management bunch who went around parroting the company line. Most of the pilots now regarded AWARE with suspicion.

Now here was the box full of pins. AWARE was promoting the company's—and Chairman Seawell's—bid to buy National Airlines.

"Why do we have the urge to merge?" a pilot asked the AWARE representative, a flight attendant in her thirties.

"Because the company will grow," she said. "It's good for Pan Am."

"But if we add all the National employees to our list, how will that be good for *us?*"

"We'll be a bigger airline," she said.

"But we'll have a bigger seniority list," he said. "I don't see how that will help *us.*"

"Oh, but it will," she said. "You just don't understand."

And she was right. He didn't understand. Nor did anyone else.

CHAPTER TWENTY

THE NATIONAL CAPER

If an airline's business persona truly bore the spirit of its founder, then National Airlines was a corporate incarnation of George Ted Baker.

Baker was a tough guy from Chicago who smoked cigars. "If you steal a chicken," Baker liked to say, "don't pluck it on the way home." This precept he learned as a teenager when he, in fact, purloined a chicken and rowed it home across a lake. The owner caught up with him by the trail of plucked feathers across the lake.

What Baker learned from the experience wasn't that it was wrong to steal chickens. It was wrong to leave a trail.

Baker was type-cast for the thirties. It was generally believed— and he would not deny it—that he had been a rumrunner during Prohibition. Short, stocky, tough-talking, cigar jutting from his teeth, Baker was a ringer for Edward G. Robinson. But it was no act. Baker was a *real* tough guy. He loved nothing so much as a good fight.

George Baker acquired National Air Taxi back in 1934. National's archrival then was—and continued to be for the next third of a century—Eastern Airlines. Baker elbowed his way into Eastern's territory, bidding on its mail routes, undercutting its fares, stealing its customers.

Eddie Rickenbacker, who headed Eastern, hated George Baker's guts. National's fly-to-Florida advertising theme, the "Route of the Buccaneers," had to be changed when Rickenbacker started denouncing Baker as "an old pirate."

Rickenbacker was not alone. Most of Baker's employees hated his guts too. Baker was a bully who constantly changed his company officers' titles and salaries, hiring and firing them at whim. At lunchtime he conducted what they called "noon bloodlettings," at which he verbally pistol-whipped every errant executive who had screwed up in the past twenty-four hours.

And he was cheap. Instead of buying shades, Baker covered the windows of his headquarters with wrapping paper and masking tape. He went over the records of all the company's long-distance calls. He was in a constant range war with his employees, who formed themselves into seven separate snarling unions to do combat with Baker. Labor war was a way of life at National, and that was okay with Baker, who would just as soon fight as do anything else.

In 1946, National expanded its route system into Cuba. It was a big moneymaker for National until 1959, when Castro overthrew the government. During its last month of flying to Havana, National flew empty airplanes in, then departed full of anti-Castro Cubans. Cuban officials confiscated five thousand cigars from National airplanes.

One day when he saw photos of Castro smoking cigars, Baker came unhinged. "Those are my goddam cigars!" he roared.

No one could have been more unlike George Baker than Bud Maytag, who took over National in 1962. Maytag had grown up as a rich kid, grandson of the Maytag washing machine company founder. He was a pilot, a *real* pilot who liked aerobatic airplanes and who personally test-flew National's new jetliners. He was tall and thin, given to understatement in speech and style. When he was young, he wanted to be a concert pianist.

Maytag didn't like cigars, and he didn't like to fight. So when Bud Maytag took over National Airlines in 1962, there was every reason to believe that things would change at National.

But they didn't, really. National would never change. It was in the company's blood, stamped on its stationery, embedded in the skin of the airplanes. National was imprinted with the Edward G. Robinson tough-guy, cigar-chomping, ass-kicking personality of George T. Baker.

Bud Maytag, though, turned out to be a competent businessman. Under his management, National made money and grew. In 1964 it became the first all-jet airline. In 1970 it became the third U.S. trans-atlantic carrier, flying nonstop between Miami and London. And then came service to Frankfurt, Paris, and Amsterdam, and nonstop flights to Europe from Tampa and New Orleans. In 1974, Maytag began construction of a dazzling new hangar-and-office complex at Miami Airport. The building won the "Grand Conceptor" award of the American Consulting Engineers Council.

But the fighting went on. It was just something they did at National. The airline's seven unions had not forgotten what they had learned from George T. Baker. Almost every contract dispute culminated in a strike. During the seventies, National suffered through successive strikes by the mechanics, ground agents, and flight attendants. In 1978 a long strike by the flight attendants wound up in federal court.

That was it for Bud Maytag, who had never loved fighting. He started looking for a way out. "Running an airline is no fun anymore," he said.

Out in Houston, Texas, in the manicured suburb of River Oaks, it was another clammy, heat-shimmering, asphalt-melting July midafternoon. For the slender, dark-haired young man pounding down the sidewalk, the searing heat was no problem. He was a marathoner, comfortable with adversity. On this torpid afternoon, Frank Lorenzo's thoughts were half a continent away. He was thinking about National Airlines.

Francisco A. Lorenzo was an unlikely player in such a high-stakes game. He was the son of Spanish immigrants who ran a beauty parlor in New York. He worked his way through Columbia driving a Coca-Cola truck. After graduating from Harvard Business School in 1963, he went to work for TWA, and then for Eastern, as a financial analyst. In the late sixties he and his Harvard classmate Robert Carney put together $2,000 to form an airline financial advisory firm, which evolved into a company called Jet Capital Corporation. With a public stock offering they were able to raise $1.5 million, a grubstake with which they bought a little, almost-defunct company called Trans Texas Airlines—known by locals as Tree Top Airlines.

Lorenzo changed Trans Texas to the grander-sounding Texas International. This company became his test bed for his first experiments with no-frills, fly-on-the-cheap, serve-'em-peanuts airline operations.

He loved it. He restructured TI's debt, slashed fares, and managed to resuscitate the company. "The airline was on its deathbed," said Bob Garrett, Lorenzo's financial adviser. "Yet Frank managed to pull all the various sides together. He kept working and working after everyone else had stopped."

This was all before deregulation. Then came 1978, the year of the Airline Deregulation Act. It was a unique moment in airline history— a time just made for someone like Frank Lorenzo.

Who the hell is Frank Lorenzo?

That was what they wanted know at National's Miami headquarters on July 9, 1978, the day Frank Lorenzo informed the CAB that he had bought 9 percent of National Airlines' stock. He had also informed the board that, by the way, he intended to buy up to 15 percent, or as much as it took to have controlling interest. In the process, Lorenzo had not bothered to consult National's chairman, Bud Maytag.

Maytag received the news with dismay. It was no secret that he was fed up with running an airline, but he wasn't so fed up that he was ready to turn over seventeen years of unstinting work to this guy with a Latin name from somewhere out in Texas. He wanted National Airlines, if it couldn't continue under its own banner, to be amalgamated with a strong player like Pan American.

And in New York, in his command post on the forty-sixth floor, General Bill Seawell wondered alike: *Frank Lorenzo?* And more to the point, *Texas International?* It seemed like a classic minnow-swallows-the-whale caper. But it was just the kind of challenge to get the old Cold War gladiator's combative juices running. General William Seawell, by God, had set out to capture National Airlines, and he was not going to be outflanked by some cracker-assed outfit from Texas.

The general plunged into the fray. In short order, Pan Am owned 20 percent of National's stock, exceeding Lorenzo's share.

And so Lorenzo bought more.

Seawell countered. Pan Am bought more National stock.

So Lorenzo bought more.

And so on. By the end of July, Pan Am and Texas International each owned about 24 percent of National Airlines. The stock market reacted to the frenzy quite predictably. National Airlines stock, which had been trading below $20, took off like a Texas jackrabbit. By July 24, the price of National stock had doubled, and it was trading in blocks as large as half a million shares.

Finally it came down to a vote by the National stockholders. Pan Am or Texas International? The biggest offer on the table was from Pan Am—$41 a share—and that seemed to be the upper limit to the madness.

And then, three hours before the proxy material was supposed to go out to the stockholders, another player jumped into the game: Astronaut Frank Borman, down from outer space and now the chairman of Eastern, was offering $50 a share.

The game was on again.

Regardless of who made the most outrageous offer for National Airlines, any such merger still required the approval of aviation's most plodding, bureaucratic agency. Even though the Airline Deregulation Act of 1978 imposed a death sentence on the Civil Aeronautics Board, the CAB was still around in the summer of 1979. The five-member board would have to study the matter and make its recommendation. The President, Jimmy Carter, would render a final decision.

While the CAB deliberated—the CAB *always* deliberated—the fight for National became a prime morsel for the business press. Everyone, it seemed, in and out of the industry, felt obliged to express an opinion.

Alfred Kahn no longer headed the CAB—he was now President Carter's anti-inflation czar. That didn't keep him from expressing his feelings about Pan Am. It would be better for everyone, Kahn told the press, "if Texas International won control of National."

Whereupon General Seawell's temper reached the flash point. To the *Wall Street Journal* he suggested, not too delicately, that the President tell his former CAB chairman to "keep his views to himself."

The case dragged on for a year. Never had little palmetto-hopping National Airlines been the object of such courtship.

It was hard to take one of the bidders, Eastern Airlines, seriously.

Eastern owned no more than a token hundred shares of National and hadn't joined in the rush to buy more. Eastern had no real chance of taking over National, because neither the CAB nor the Justice Department would approve a merger giving a single airline a virtual monopoly on the East Coast.

Why, then, was Eastern pursuing National?

Eastern and Pan Am were major airlines, nearly equal in size. Even though Eastern almost surely wouldn't be allowed to have National Airlines because of the antitrust implications, it certainly didn't want a competitor the size of Pan American moving into its neighborhood. Of the other two candidates, the less threatening to Eastern was tiny Texas International.

Seawell, stating the obvious, told *Forbes,* "Borman is acting as a spoiler because of his fear of competition."

To which Eastern's vice-chairman, Charles Simon, said of Seawell and company, "I don't think they know their butts from a hole in the wall."

The repartee was getting nasty.

Through it all, Frank Borman kept right on smiling his disingenuous astronaut smile. Eastern's intentions were honorable, he insisted. Spoiler? Certainly not. The airline only wanted to solidify its "historical presence in the eastern seaboard market." "We're going to make it happen," he told the *Wall Street Journal.*

Not if General William T. Seawell had anything to do with it.

At first, Seawell told the press that Pan Am wouldn't match Eastern's ridiculous $50 offer. "We don't have to," he said. "An Eastern-National merger would be a textbook case of antitrust." And that was a matter for the Justice Department.

But there was this guy out in Texas, Lorenzo, still sitting on a load of National stock—*and* voting shares. He could vote for or against Pan Am's proposed takeover.

So Seawell did something he hated to do: He made a deal with Frank Lorenzo. If Pan Am would raise the ante to $50 a share, matching Eastern's offer and, most important, raising the value of Lorenzo's investment, Lorenzo would not vote against Pan Am at the shareholder meeting scheduled for May 16.

Fifty dollars a share. It was outrageous. Even Borman knew it was outrageous. He had no intention of paying that much.

So Seawell raised the ante, and the National shareholders, especially Frank Lorenzo, loved it.

Pan Am could have National Airlines—if the CAB approved.

The CAB kept on deliberating. The Justice Department kept on ruminating. Lobbyists from all three sides kept tugging at the sleeves of anyone in Washington who might influence the outcome of the National case.

Seawell wanted the employees of both airlines to get on the bandwagon. At Pan Am he already had the AWARE people out there with their URGE TO MERGE buttons. Now he needed to convince the National employees that merging with Pan Am was *their* best deal.

Down in Miami, they didn't think so. The National pilots were not keen about a merger with Pan Am. They were worried about how they would be swallowed in Pan Am's gray-headed pilot roster. "Have you seen those guys? They're *old!* Most of 'em were hired back when Christ was a copilot. Their junior pilot was hired in *1968!*"

Which was true. Pan Am, by age and longevity, was a much more senior airline than National. The National pilots had much to lose in such a merger. Most thought it would be better to be bought up by some benevolent entrepreneur like this guy Lorenzo, whoever he was.

Seawell went to Washington to spearhead the lobbying campaign. He appeared before the CAB. He had briefing papers printed explaining to newsmen why the National acquisition ought to be approved. He flew to Miami and spoke to the Chamber of Commerce.

He appealed to National's unions. "Not a single employee would lose his job as a result of the merger," Seawell promised them.

And *that* was some promise. National had 8,350 employees, many of whom were doing jobs already being done by Pan Am people. The two employee groups overlapped in administrative, maintenance, and operations functions. Seawell was making an expensive promise.

Back in the Imperial Headquarters a question hung in air, like the first hint of an incoming artillery shell. The question was: *General, is buying National Airlines really a good idea?*

But no one was brave enough to give voice to the question. No one within earshot of the chairman was clearing his throat and saying,

"General, excuse me, but I think we're going to lose our hat and ass if we go ahead with this."

Seawell's mind was made up. A fire was burning in the eyes of the Cold War gladiator, and anyone on the forty-sixth floor who had the slightest instinct for self-preservation was keeping his mouth shut.

So that's what they did, all the general's lieutenants. They kept their mouths shut and wore their WE HAVE THE URGE TO MERGE pins.

And so it came to pass. On January 7, 1980, National Airlines was merged with Pan American World Airways. It cost Pan Am $374 million. All 8,350 National employees came to Pan Am, less one. Part of the merger deal was that Bud Maytag would be a vice-chairman of the merged airline at an annual salary of $375,000. But now that the deal was done, Maytag said to hell with it. He had seen enough of Pan Am's Cold War gladiator to know he couldn't work with him. Anyway, he was by now thoroughly fed up with the airline business. He took his $54 million and went home.

Francisco A. Lorenzo also went home. He felt obliged, at least publicly, to complain about how things had turned out. "Pan Am," he told the press, "has bought politicians and lobbyists from coast to coast, from Maine to Florida."

Privately, Frank Lorenzo could gloat. He was taking home $40 million. It was the easiest money he ever made.

CHAPTER TWENTY-ONE

ORANGE PUKES AND BLUE PUKES

If nobody is happy, then it's an equitable merger.
— *Maxim of airline seniority list arbitration*

Make National disappear.

That was the idea. General Seawell's obsession to buy National Airlines was now supplanted by a burning desire to erase it from the planet. He needed to do this because that flaming orange sun—National's logo—over Pan Am's new equipment was a constant reminder that he had committed an egregious blunder.

Only a few weeks after the merger the press was saying things like "Pan Am Overpays for National" and "Is National More Than Pan Am Can Swallow?"

What *really* ignited the general's afterburner was the name they'd taken to calling his purchase: Seawell's Folly. "It made him furious," said a former vice president. "That's why he was in such a hurry to integrate National."

There was only one thing to do: get rid of those lurid orange National Airlines sun balls. Paint the whole damned mess Pan Am *blue!*

At the same time there were suggestions, some from his critics in the press, that it might be smart for Pan American to *ease* into the integration of the two airlines. Go slowly. Let National continue to be National for a while. Operate it as a subsidiary of the Imperial Airline. Let the employees and the public get used to the idea. It would save money and heartburn.

Seawell wasn't having any of that. *Get rid of that goddam flaming orange logo.* Without delay, all National's airplanes were stripped and repainted in proper Pan Am livery. All uniformed ex-National employees—pilots, flight attendants, gate agents—were told to trash their old outfits and suit up in Pan Am costume. All ex-National flights were renumbered and fed into the Pan Am schedule.

But what about the pay scales? It was pointed out that the ex-National employees, who were historically spring-loaded to strike over *any* inequity, would probably slip right back into their George T. Baker pugilistic mode. National's pay scales had always been lower than Pan Am's. Now here they were, wearing the same uniforms and doing the same jobs on the same airplanes—for considerably less money than their Pan Am colleagues.

The general had a fix for that, too. He would make them forget all that crap. He would *pay* them to forget it.

And so all in one swoop, without incremental raises or timed increases, the ex-National employees' paychecks were upped and their benefits packages expanded to match those of the Pan Am workers, most of whom themselves had just gotten a generous pay hike.

The cost of the National acquisition was already immense, nearly $400 million. Now it was soaring beyond half a billion dollars.

The other migraine headache that attended the merger was the airplanes. The National fleet bore almost no resemblance to the Pan Am armada, had almost no compatibility. National had 727s, which was okay, because Pan Am did, too, but it also had *sixteen* trimotor McDonnell Douglas DC-10s. Only four months before the National buyout, Pan Am had bought its own fleet of trimotor jets—Lockheed L-1011 Tri-Stars.

It was a maintenance and supply nightmare. Previously, all of Pan Am's airplanes were Boeing-built, and all its engines were by Pratt & Whitney. Pan Am's new Lockheeds, which went into service in May 1980, had Rolls-Royce engines, a puzzling new British-built power plant Pan Am mechanics had never seen. The DC-10s had yet another engine, built by General Electric, also an item new to Pan American. Both the trimotor jetliner models—Lockheed and McDonnell Douglas—were high-tech, state-of-the-art vehicles, but they were vastly different from each other in design concept.

The cost of the acquisition went up some more.

Salaries. Maintenance facilities. Spares. Offices and stations Pan Am didn't need. The National price tag was inflating like a hydrogen balloon. Not only was Pan Am's treasury dwindling at warp speed, the United States was being visited by yet another recession in 1980 and a concomitant fall-off in foreign travel.

It happened so quickly. On January 7, an instant before Chairman Seawell put his pen to the National contract, Pan Am had been an airline with deep pockets and few bills. Its success was a testament to the stewardship of William Seawell. Eight years before, when Seawell took over the chairmanship, Pan Am had been going broke. He had nursed it to record profitability. *Seawell is doing a helluva job,* reported the business press in 1978.

Now it was broke again.

General Seawell had accomplished his goal. He indeed had made National Airlines disappear. With it, he had also made nearly a billion of Pan Am's dollars disappear.

What didn't disappear was the low rumble out there, gradually swelling in volume. It was coming from the press, from the stockholders, from the directors. *What the hell was happening to Pan Am?*

And what also wasn't going away was the catch-all explanation for Pan Am's troubles: *Seawell's Folly.*

It stuck. The general could curse and kick and glower with his Cold War gladiator's eyes, but it wouldn't go away.

The pilots—Pan Am and ex-National—eyed each other warily across the crew rooms. They were all wearing the same uniforms now, but that was their only common bond. They were like new stepchildren being forced to hug each other. They hated it.

Because National's logo had been a flaming orange sun emblem and Pan Am's logo was a blue globe-shaped ball, the two groups sorted themselves into dissimilar factions—the Blue and the Orange. The colors clashed.

On one side you had the smaller and more tightly knit group, called the Orange Pukes, who referred to the Pan Am pilots as the "blue bloods." The implication was that the old, snooty Pan Am bunch were so inbred, with no new blood, that they had gotten a little queer in the head.

On the other side there were the Blue Pukes, who liked to call the National pilots the "pig farmers," an inaccurate reference to their fondness for pickup trucks and chewing tobacco and their supposed good-ol'-boy ways.

Both appellations were insulting, of course, and deliberately so. The Pan Am bunch, when they were in their most blue-blooded mode—which was whenever two or more gathered at a layover bar —would fret endlessly about the sacred turf of the Skygods becoming soiled with pig effluvium.

To be sure, the National pilots weren't all crackers. In fact, only a few were, but they, more than the others, reflected the airline's distinctive persona. Unlike the Pan Am group, a minority of National's captains had been military pilots. Most had learned flying as civilians, instructing and charter flying and crop dusting and banner towing. A significant number, all hired in a cluster, were former Miami cops.

For half a century, Pan Am had flown the flag from Capetown to Moscow to Buenos Aires to Oslo. Now, suddenly, airplanes with the Pan Am blue ball were palmetto-hopping from Tampa to Pensacola to Tallahassee and across the hinterlands.

It was an audible culture shift. The dialect was changing from a Skygodly, Eastern, sometimes European, patrician inflection . . . to a crackerized twang.

Within days of the merger announcement in January 1980, the two pilot groups began their own negotiations. Each side, Blue and Orange, had granite-hard notions about the *new* seniority list. The Blue side insisted that the new seniority numbers correspond with length of time with the airline. Nothing else would do. First hired, first on the list. That was the only fair way. They even made up bumper stickers that appeared on cars, baggage, and lockers all over Pan Am property: SENIORITY BY DATE OF HIRE.

In the airline piloting profession, seniority was everything. Promotions, new assignments, vacations, monthly schedules—*everything* was dispensed according to the numbers. The pilot one number ahead of you on the seniority list would always receive his preference before you. And it would never change. There was no passing, at least not while you both worked for the same airline.

To the Orange pilot group, seniority by date of hire wasn't fair at all. Pan Am was a much older airline than National in terms of age versus position. While Pan Am had not hired a new pilot since 1968 and had furloughed many since then, National was still hiring in 1978, even while the merger was beginning to take shape. National had *captains* who had been hired *after* the most junior pilot at Pan Am.

A youngish National captain summed it up: "It wasn't our fault," he said, "if someone was dumb enough back in the sixties to go to work for a shrinking company like Pan Am. Now it's fourteen years later and they want *our* jobs."

What the Orange pilots wanted was to be dovetailed into the Pan Am list. It meant seniority by ratio. You fit into the new, integrated seniority list at the same *relative* position you held on your previous list. Captains would remain captains. Copilots would remain copilots. Engineers stayed engineers. Everyone would have a new seniority number corresponding to the seat he occupied.

In such a negotiation, there was little room for compromise. Each of the negotiators knew what would follow if he went back to his own pilot group and reported that "in all fairness to the other side, I decided to give them your seniority numbers."

He would be disemboweled and fed to fire ants.

Predictably, the negotiations stalled. The next step was mediation, which meant an outside labor mediator, chosen from a list from the Air Line Pilots Association, would try bring the two sides to agreement. Just as predictably, mediation failed.

The final phase was arbitration. This meant that a mutually agreed upon neutral would listen to the case of each side. The neutral would decide for them how the seniority lists would be integrated. The two parties agreed that the arbitrator's decision would be binding.

A neutral was chosen the way sandlot baseball teams choose up sides. They started with a list of candidates, and then the two sides, alternately, eliminated names until one was left—the neutral.

For the Pan Am–National merger arbitration, a list of half a dozen professional labor arbitrators was drawn up. When they had eliminated all but one name, they came up with Lewis B. Gill.

Gill was an experienced labor mediator who had previously arbitrated the integration of the old Mohawk and Allegheny seniority lists. His purpose in a seniority list integration, as he saw it, was to protect the *prospects* of each group of pilots. Those prospects depended, in his view, on whether the airline was contracting or growing, and on whether pilots could have expected advancement or regression.

That particular argument, of course, was bad for the Pan Am bunch. Pan Am's fleet had not grown at all since the early seventies, because of the massive seating capacity of the 747s, each of which replaced several smaller 707s. As a result, Pan Am's pilot roster had contracted, and with it the promotion prospects of the junior airmen.

That was then, argued the Blue negotiators. This is now. We're talking *domestic expansion.* In the newly deregulated market, Pan Am would acquire a fleet of smaller jets. Pan Am would need more pilots, and that would mean advancement.

Wait a minute, chimed in the National negotiators. We *are* the domestic expansion. This is what we're here for. And our prospects for promotion have *always* been better than the old Pan Am guys'.

The arguments went on. Sessions were held in New York, Philadelphia, and Phoenix, and again in Philadelphia. Gill listened, and he asked for briefs on the anticipated fleet sizes of each airline had they not merged. Each side argued that its fleet size was growing, thus providing the prospect of advancement for pilots.

It was becoming quickly evident that the Pan Am pilots' problem would be to convince Mr. Gill that Pan Am was, in fact, a going concern, that Pan Am's pilots, prior to the merger, had prospects of steady advancement. Their expectations ought to be preserved in the new list.

Shrinking or expanding? The argument went on for the rest of 1980 and into 1981. Finally, in March 1981, Lewis Gill announced that he had made his decisions about integration. He handed to the negotiators copies of his new Pan Am seniority list.

It rippled through the system like a seismic upheaval. The first roughprinted versions of the Gill Award were posted on the bulletin boards.

The junior Pan Am pilots—first officers and engineers—couldn't find their names on the list. They weren't where they should have been.

They looked further down the list.

And then further.

When they found their names, with several hundred National pilots' names ahead of theirs, the crew rooms reverberated with a single outpouring of opinion about the Gill Award: *I don't fucking believe it.*

It had to be a joke. How could years and years of accumulated seniority instantly evaporate? Pilots hired in 1967 were suddenly junior to pilots hired in 1977.

Gill had devised a complicated ratio method. He decided to preserve the captaincies—and relative seniority—of the National 727 captains, most of whom were younger than and junior in longevity to their Pan Am counterparts. His reasoning was that the junior Pan Am pilots would, in any case, have *expected* to remain copilots for a very long time, but they would graduate to a bigger airplane, the 747. And so, under his terms, they still would. But they would be copilots.

There was more. None of National's flight engineers were pilots. The career starting point for a young National pilot was in the right seat—the first officer's station—of a 727. And according to the Gill dictum of *expectations,* that's where they would rightly remain. The older and grayer Pan Am flight engineers—who *were* also pilots—would stay right where they had begun more than a decade earlier, in the sideward-facing flight engineer's seat.

And so at each of the crew bases—San Francisco, New York, Miami, Berlin—pilots stared at bulletin boards, jaw muscles working, fists clenching and unclenching. Their disbelieving brains processed the unbelievable numbers.

Some, like Hans Bernick, who had been thirty-five when he was hired and who was still a junior first officer, quickly calculated that he would probably retire at age sixty. *Still a goddam copilot.*

Rob Martinside, who was a more senior first officer, realized that he would not be graduating to the left seat of a 727 as he had expected. Those jobs were now *reserved* for more junior Orange captains. He would continue to be a copilot.

For engineers like Roger Bledsoe, who had been about to progress from the engineer's seat to the first officer's station, it meant he would be flying and yessirring and raising the landing gear for ex-National captains ten or more years his junior.

For First Officer Cliff Parker, the new list contained special irony. He had been a National pilot at the beginning of his career. He'd resigned when Pan Am drafted him in 1966. Then it had seemed his great fortune to be plucked from puddle-jumping National Airlines to join mighty Pan American. Now his old National classmates—all captains by now—preceded him on the seniority list by nearly a thousand numbers.

Seawell's Folly. The full meaning of the general's purchase began to settle on the pilots. Everyone had agreed that Pan Am had to have a domestic route system. That was good for all parties—the company as well as the pilots. But it was becoming clear that Pan Am did not have to acquire an entire airline—planes, pilots, and pot scrubbers— to do it. Even if that *was* good for the company, which was already looking doubtful, it was a disaster for the pilots.

As always, it came down to *Them* and *Us*.

A few days after the Gill Award was out, some fool showed up in the crew room at Kennedy wearing a WE HAVE THE URGE TO MERGE pin. It was supposed to be a joke. One of the pilots standing there at the bulletin board, reading the list and working his jaw muscles and clenching his fists, took one look at the URGE TO MERGE pin and went crazy.

Before they could pull him off, the crazed pilot had done some surface damage to the pin-wearer's sport coat as well as his lower lip. But under the circumstances, no one felt like making an issue of it. It was just a bad day for jokes.

CHAPTER TWENTY-TWO

THE CROWN JEWELS

If the old Imperial Skygod felt any resentment or rancor about the way *his* airline was being managed, he kept it to himself. Juan Trippe left the board of directors in 1975, and in his waning years he did what no one had thought possible: he stayed out of Pan American's affairs.

What did Trippe think of General Seawell's slashing and swapping of Pan Am's routes? How did he react to the overtures of the Shah of Iran? Was he pleased about Seawell's capture of National Airlines and its domestic routes, a prize that had eluded Trippe for his entire career?

The old man wasn't saying. He appeared at functions like the Wings Club banquets and Business Council meetings, where he accepted awards for his lifetime of accomplishment.

At those events it was difficult to visualize, watching him, that this stooped, pear-shaped figure had once been a giant. It was hard to remember that in his day Juan Trippe commanded the attention of kings, presidents, prime ministers. You could forget that Trippe, with his astonishing clarity of vision, had peered into the future of aviation—and then made it happen.

The famous vitality was gone now. In his late years he could hardly remember *anybody's* name, not without his wife, Betty, there at his side to cue him. In conversation he rambled and digressed as he always had, but more so. His thoughts seemed to dwell in another time.

He kept his silence during the last years he sat on Pan Am's board, when his hand-picked lieutenant, Jeeb Halaby, was faltering. And he likewise remained silent while Bill Seawell grappled with the problems of Pan Am's immense debt and an indifferent government.

He listened stoically to the insinuations that it was he who had sown the seeds of Pan Am's ruin by burdening the airline with a half billion dollars' worth of 747s. He wouldn't reply to such talk. It wasn't Juan Trippe's style to answer the Primitives.

In September 1980, three months after his eighty-first birthday, Trippe suffered a massive cerebral hemorrhage. For another seven months the old Skygod clung to life.

It was a funeral to which they all came, those who had loved or despised or been compelled to reckon with Juan Terry Trippe. The service was held, of course, in New York, in St. James Episcopal Church. They sang the Mariner's Hymn and listened to a reading from Ecclesiastes. Beneath a splendid April sun, his seven grandsons bore Juan Trippe's coffin, draped in the American flag.

It was a fitting farewell to the Imperial Skygod. Just as fitting was the rechristening a few weeks later of a Pan American 747: *Clipper Juan T. Trippe.*

The Primitives still had to look at Juan Trippe's monument. Each morning of every day of the year, it had stood there astraddle Park Avenue, smacking Trippe's enemies in the eye. The building was the monument to his triumph over the Primitives.

Back in 1963, when he first stuck the Pan Am logo up there over the Manhattan skyline, Trippe had also laid the groundwork for Pan Am to eventually take over the whole package. And so in 1969 and again in 1978—following profitable years—the airline exercised its options to increase its ownership. Pan Am bought out the original British investors for $15 million, and then the estate of the developer, Erwin Wolfson, for $8.6 million. Pan Am wrapped up the whole package by buying the land under the building from the Penn Central Corporation for $25 million.

That was 1978, when the airline was making money. This was now, 1980.

Pan Am was in serious trouble. The banks had lost patience with Pan American and, particularly, with General Seawell. The year 1980 was shaping up as the grimmest in company history. The general had spent $374 million for National, and then continued to run the tab to nearly a billion dollars, wiping out all Pan Am's reserves and taking the company into the financial gutter.

Now Pan Am was losing over a million dollars a day. Something had to go. General Seawell would have to sell the monument.

It didn't take long to find a buyer for the Pan Am Building. The Metropolitan Life Insurance Company stepped forward, agreeing to pay $400 million. Even in the inflationary early 1980s, that was an outrageous sum—the highest price ever paid for an office building in Manhattan. It amounted to a $294 million profit on Pan Am's investment.

With the stroke of a pen the deal was done. Juan Trippe's monument became the property of an insurance company.

Outwardly, nothing much changed. Part of the deal was that the airline could lease its several floors of executive office space until the end of the century. More important, the building would still bear the company logo. Manhattan would still be smacked in the eye every morning with the fifteen-foot-high salute to Trippe's Primitives: PAN AM.

But inwardly, *everything* had changed. To the executives and staffers who still rode the elevators to their respective floors in the airline headquarters, it wasn't . . . *their* building anymore. "We're only tenants now," said a staffer. "Just like the shopkeepers on the mezzanine." The change in status spoke volumes to them about where the company was headed. The Imperial Airline had surrendered its crown jewel.

The worst part was, the monumental sum Pan Am had received for the building—$400 million—still wasn't enough. The airline was losing money faster than even the sale of the world's most expensive office building could cover.

After the ghastly losses of 1980—$248 million for the year—the sale of the Pan Am Building was mourned but accepted. At least the worst of the National Airlines assimilation was behind Pan Am. Now, it was hoped, the hemorrhage would stop and Pan Am could get back to the business of making money.

But the hemorrhage *didn't* stop. The recession that began in the late seventies was paralyzing the airline industry. In the first quarter of 1981, the airline lost a record $115 million. Pan American World

Airways, which had earned record profits of $118.8 million in 1978 and $76.1 million in 1979, had blown its cash reserves. Even the proceeds of the Pan Am Building sale evaporated like a vanished contrail. Pan Am's debt and lease obligations swelled to more than $1.3 billion.

Seawell was in a corner. Feeling the hot breath of the bankers as well as his own board of directors, he frantically cast about for something else to sell.

It was then that the pilots—the Blue Pukes—came up with a good idea. They sent the suggestion to the chairman: *Did Pan American want to sell something? How about National Airlines, General? Maybe you can sell it to Frank Lorenzo.*

Chairman Seawell, even if he got the joke, didn't respond. It was too late, in any case. National Airlines didn't exist anymore. The general had spent a billion dollars making it disappear.

That summer Pan Am's executives, led by Seawell, met with the airline's lenders. The Pan Am officers delivered a briefing wherein they predicted the company's losses for 1981. They would exceed $300 million, the greatest deficit ever sustained by an airline.

The bankers were stunned. They had had no idea it was that bad. "Do you *really* plan to lose that much?" asked one horrified financier.

Glum headshakes. "Yes, that's the way it looks."

The banker was speechless. He rose and stalked out of the meeting.

The bankers turned the screws on Pan Am. Led by Citibank, the lenders proceeded to slash Pan Am's revolving credit in half. They demanded a first mortgage on all outstanding shares of one of Pan Am's profitable subsidiaries, the Intercontinental Hotel chain, as well as a mortgage on nine of the Douglas DC-10s acquired from National.

But the losses continued. Pan Am's cash crunch was getting worse, not better. It was hardball time. Something—or someone—had to go.

By now, even Pan Am's lethargic board of directors, most of whom had been selected by William Seawell, had had enough of the general. And it wasn't due just to the enormous losses and the National Airlines mess.

Nobody could get along with Seawell anymore. Reports were coming to the board about the tantrums and shouting matches on the forty-sixth floor. In November even easygoing Dan Colussy, whom Seawell had appointed president, stormed out after a series of fights with the chairman. Since the door slammed behind Colussy, the office of president had been empty. No one wanted it. Chairman Seawell was running the whole show, and not doing very well at it.

The August 8, 1981, *Wall Street Journal* reported the inevitable: SEAWELL TO RETIRE EARLY. . . .

The new president and interim chief executive officer was Bill Waltrip, a bright and bland forty-three-year-old executive vice president. Waltrip had taken the job with one crucial stipulation: He would not be accountable to Chairman Seawell. He would report directly to the board of directors. Though Seawell would continue to hold the title of chairman until his replacement was found, the job, for the time being, was mostly ceremonial.

"For Mr. Seawell, it would mean retirement a year before he reaches sixty-five, the normal retirement age at the airline," said the press notice.

The official line was that the chairman was *retiring early*. The public relations department took pains to point out that General Seawell, after all, had been around for over eight years, longer than any other chairman except Trippe.

As part of the same shake-up, the board of directors announced that the corporation was being restructured to consist of three subsidiaries: the airline itself, Pan American World Airways, which would be headed by Waltrip; Pan Am World Services, Inc., an aviation services contractor, under Tom Flanagan; and the Intercontinental Hotel chain, managed by Paul Sheeline.

What the announcement didn't say was that one of the three subsidiaries was already gone.

Eleven days after the announcement of Seawell's retirement, the August 19 *Wall Street Journal* reported a move that had been in the works for the past month:

PAN AM TO SELL ITS HOTEL UNIT; CANCELS PLANES

Pan American World Airways announced a series of drastic financial steps in an apparent attempt to avoid insolvency.

The airline said it will sell its hotel subsidiary, Intercontinental Hotels Corp., its only major money maker. . . .

Though the announcement didn't name a buyer, the deal had already been cut. The new owner of the Intercontinental chain would be the omnivorous British conglomerate Grand Metropolitan. Its products included Alpo dog food and Watney's beer. It would ante up $500 million for the luxury hotels.

The announcement went on to report that Pan Am was canceling its order for eight Boeing 727 jets costing $200 million. "While the order had been a firm one, Pan Am told Boeing it didn't have the money to buy the planes. . . ."

Besides canceling the 727s, Pan Am announced that it would also postpone delivery of two new Lockheed L-1011s with which it intended to service European destinations. Already the airline had sold eight 747s to a leasing company, then rented them back.

After this drastic surgery, Pan American would live on, at least for another season. But for how much longer? How long could its real estate business support its airline business?

"We're selling the last of the family jewels," said a Pan Am executive.

The sale of the hotel chain was the final act of the Seawell era.

Around the system, pilots stood in front of the bulletin boards and read the company wire reporting the dramatic changes in the corporation. There was little celebration. There was no mourning whatsoever. Mostly they stood there, working their jaw muscles, thinking.

It had been a hell of a ride. During the reign of Chairman Seawell their careers had undergone profound change. For many, their dreams—their sweetest and most hopeful aspirations—had turned to dust.

Gone was the SST.

Gone was all the prideful ballyhoo about flying to the moon.

Gone—at least for the thousand or so who'd been clotheslined by the Gill Award—was their chance to command a Pan Am jet.

Gone, literally, were the several hundred furloughed pilots whose jobs had vanished in the Seawell cutbacks.

Now Seawell was gone. And for most of the pilots reading the bulletin board, that was okay with them.

A special committee of the board was appointed to select Seawell's successor.

During the summer of 1981 the committee members combed the industry. They were looking for candidates from outside the company. They wanted a man who had both financial and airline experience, dual criteria that narrowed the list considerably. Most of the candidates who possessed those qualifications responded with words to the effect that they had no interest in taking over the *Titanic*.

The search went on. What Pan Am needed, everyone agreed, was someone *dynamic*. Someone who would take *command*. Someone who would seize the faltering company by the scruff of the neck, give it a good shaking, and restore Pan American to its old imperial glory.

In short, they were looking for a Skygod.

Down South, at a little airline called Air Florida, they found someone who seemed to fit the description.

PART III

IMPACT

CHAPTER TWENTY-THREE

THE TEXAS HUCKSTER

Never trust a man who uses an initial for his first name.
—CAPTAIN JIM WOOD

He thrust out his big hand and said, "Hi. I'm Ed Acker."

The voice was forceful. Through the framed spectacles the eyes drilled into you like lasers. C. Edward Acker was a big man, well over six feet, and you could tell that he had once been an athlete. The jawline had gone a little soft, but the handshake was hard as granite. He was hoisting the liter-sized steins of Pilsner as if they were thimbles.

He had come to Berlin—as he came to all the other pilot bases—to introduce himself. So the pilots hoisted beers with the new CEO and looked him over. And, generally, they liked what they saw. The guy was clearly *in charge*.

But what he was telling them wasn't exactly what they wanted to hear. Here he was, new in the job, and he was talking *pay cuts*. It was hardly the way to endear yourself to the Pan Am workaday grunts. But he was also talking *growth*. He intended to return Pan Am to profitability, Acker said, by increasing the volume of operations. "We're going to *fly* our way to profitability," he told the troops.

And to that they raised their beer steins and cheered. Finally some-

one up there was making sense. This guy Acker was light-years removed from the aloof and lordly Pan Am executives they'd known in
the past, who used to talk down to them in their clipped old-school
accents. Never before had they seen a chairman of the board like this
one, hoisting beers and going on in his Texas twang about how Pan
Am was going to rise up and kick ass again.

They were ready to believe it. *Count us in, Ed!*

The tall Texan, C. Edward Acker, entered office boldly. For a while a
kind of euphoria pervaded Pan American. General Seawell was gone,
and that in itself was a reason for feeling good. The general, after all,
had been the architect of the National debacle, which had done for
the pilots' careers what tornadoes did for Kansas.

Now they had this fellow Acker, who seemed to be a real leader.
He was encouraging them to believe that maybe . . . just maybe . . .
they were still riding a winner. Pan American might just *still* be aimed
at the stars.

The AWARE crowd, aware of which way the wind was blowing,
got rid of all their old WE HAVE THE URGE TO MERGE pins. They
stamped out several thousand new pins that declared I'M AN ACKER
BACKER. All over the airline, on uniforms and coveralls and blouses,
the new pins appeared. Suddenly the place was full of Acker Backers.

Ed Acker was fifty-two years old. A native of Dallas, he was the
first CEO in Pan Am history without an East Coast pedigree. Acker
had never set foot within the ivied halls of Yale or Harvard. He had
stayed close to home, graduating from Southern Methodist University,
where he studied psychology and economics.

Acker had made his reputation in the airline business as president
of Braniff International. That was back when Braniff was flying high.
He left in 1975, with Braniff still declaring big profits, and for a year
he worked as president of Transway International, a New York–based
freight forwarding company. For another year he headed Gulf United
Corporation, a financial holding company.

And then he went to a little regional airline called Air Florida. In
1977, the year Acker assumed the top post, the airline had an annual
revenue of $7.8 million. In 1980, during its last year under Acker's
directorship, Air Florida took in $161.2 million.

Air Florida was one of the deregulated era's big success stories, and Ed Acker was getting all the credit.

From the beginning it was clear that Ed Acker's management style was unique. "You never knew what the guy was going to do," said a soon-departed executive. "He was a vest-pocket CEO. He carried stuff around in his pockets—airplane deals, new routes, asset sales—that *nobody* else knew about. Then he'd spring them on you."

Acker was as different from Seawell as a salesman was from a soldier. Acker dismantled the general's bureaucratic management structure and instituted, instead, "round table" management, in which problems were aired in open sessions of department chiefs. Seawell appointees quickly began to vanish from the meetings. Acker brought in new managers from his old airline, Braniff, which in 1981 was teetering on bankruptcy. Bill Waltrip, who had become the airline president just before Seawell's departure, sniffed the air and concluded that Acker intended to be not only the chief executive officer but the chief *operating* officer as well. Waltrip took his leave.

As the CEO of Air Florida, Acker had tinkered constantly with the little airline's southeastern routes, adding and removing destinations at his whim. Now Ed Acker had a *global* route system to tinker with. According to an industry article, "his favorite reading is the OAG (Overseas Airline Guide), which he thumbs through in search of new cities to connect." The trade journal *Aviation Economist* predicted that "for an airline the size of Pan Am to be scheduled by a peripatetic one-man research department could lead to nothing but trouble."

During the summer of 1982, Acker added dozens of new international destinations. By the end of autumn, he was closing most of them. He severed Pan American's historic round-the-world route by eliminating the India–Bangkok–Hong Kong segments. Pan Am's Caribbean destinations, which had been dropped because of their low profit yield, he cranked up again.

In the last year of the Seawell regime, a new marketing strategy had been announced: Pan Am would shift from its strong domestic presence, for which it had paid a total of nearly a billion dollars (Seawell's Folly!), to concentrating on its profitable international routes.

In the new strategy, the only real purpose of the domestic system was to feed the international routes.

Forget all that, said Ed Acker, the new CEO. Back to a domestic strategy. Pan Am's domestic revenues, which accounted for 30 percent of Pan Am's activity, would have to be increased to 40 percent.

Within six months, Acker had changed his mind. Domestic expansion was forgotten about, for the time, and Pan Am was back to the old hub system—connecting its now-anemic domestic network to the international route system.

Meanwhile, Pan Am was losing money by the bargeload, and Ed Acker knew of one sure place to get some of it back.

Ten percent.

The chairman was laying it on the line. Up front, he wanted a 10 percent giveback in salaries from all the airline's employees. Such a concession would improve the balance sheet in the amount of some $160 million. Acker and his entourage made the rounds of the airline. He pumped hands and gave Texas-style pep talks, and soon he had the Acker Backers cheering and reaching for their wallets. *Ten percent? Outa my paycheck? Well, hell, Ed, if that what it takes . . .*

The heads of the five labor unions at Pan Am were not so quick to become Acker Backers. The unions represented 24,000 of the airline's 33,000 employees. Acker was asking not only pay concessions but contractual rule changes that would increase the average productivity of the Pan Am worker. In the case of the pilots, this meant items like extended monthly flight time maximums, reduced vacation time, and longer daily flight time limits.

Throughout the autumn of 1981, negotiations went on between the unions and the company. Marty Shugrue, onetime new-hire flight engineer and furloughee, had by now risen to the job of vice president for personnel. With each union Shugrue carved out a new working agreement that would net a 10 percent reduction in labor costs.

In October an accord was reached. Four of the five unions—the Independent Union of Flight Attendants had cut a separate deal—agreed to the 10 percent cut and a wage freeze through the end of 1982. But in exchange, they demanded—and received—an employee stock ownership plan that would amount to $35 million of Pan Am shares. To represent their block of stock, the unions were granted a seat on Pan American's board of directors.

It was a unique arrangement. Pan American became the first of the thirteen major American carriers to seat a representative from its labor force on the board. After a noisy caucus, the union contingent chose the chairman of the Pan Am pilot's union, a forty-three-year-old first officer named Bob Gould, to represent them on the board of directors.

The unions were becoming nervous. They had deep suspicion about the move, taken under Seawell's chairmanship, to turn Pan Am into a holding company, of which the airline was one subsidiary, and the other was Pan Am World Services, a small but profitable maintenance and technical services supplier. Now the unions feared that Acker might spin Pan Am's airline operation off to a *new* subsidiary —a low-cost, nonunion airline.

The Acker honeymoon was brief—less than a year. A few weeks after the ink had dried on the pay-cut agreement and the contract freeze was in place, details about Chairman Acker's own contract appeared on a back page of the *Wall Street Journal*. For his first four months as chairman, C. Edward Acker was paid $416,667, which included a $250,000 lump for giving up his benefits as Air Florida CEO. His regular annual salary would be $350,000, with bonuses ranging from a minimum of $100,000 to a maximum of $750,000. In addition, he had received options on *one million* Pan Am shares, with his price locked at $2.77 a share.

An even more disquieting statistic concerned Acker's predecessor, the Cold War gladiator. General Seawell, it was reported, had received $516,881 for his services in 1981, the year in which he was sacked as CEO. And for the next two years he would continue to be compensated $100,000 per year as a consultant.

Consultant? That one got a laugh all around the airline. Consultant for what? For how to convert a billion dollars to vapor?

There were more tidbits that stuck in the craws of the Pan Amers. In February, a few months after Acker joined Pan Am, it was quietly announced that Pan American was paying Air Florida the sum of $6.6 million for an option to lease six 737s at a "predetermined" rental for at least three years.

Workaday grunts' eyebrows rose all the way to their hairlines. *Hey, wait a minute. Wasn't Air Florida Mr. Acker's previous airline? And now he's handing them six and a half million. . . .*

Then another thought: *737s?* Pan Am didn't even operate 737s. Why was it spending a ton of money to lease an odd breed of airplane for its already mismatched fleet?

Because the chairman said so, of course. Acker had taken a look at the Berlin operation, with its fleet of fuel-inefficient trimotor 727s, and made a decision. *We need smaller airplanes with two engines and two pilots. Just like we had at Air Florida.*

And that was that. A $6.5 million deal was made.

Was Chairman Acker getting a cut? Undoubtedly not, but the troops seized on the story. The rumor of skimming would be just part of the growing myth of plunder that everyone figured *had* to be going on at Pan Am.

The 737 affair was, in fact, an example of Acker at work. That was Ed Acker's strong suit—deal-making. He loved it, and over the years he had become very good at it. In the grim years ahead, it would be Acker's deal-making, not his managerial ability, that would keep Pan Am alive.

But in 1981 the workaday grunts didn't see that. Even if they had, they wouldn't have thought any more highly of him. Ed Acker was opening a gulf between himself and his employees as wide as Texas.

A peculiar thing was happening. The pay cuts and the contract freeze were in place. The chairman did manage to trim a big piece off the airline's overhead, just as he had promised—in the form of the employees' wages. But by some astonishing inversion of economic law, the airline was losing *more money than ever before.* In 1982, Ed Acker's first full year as chairman, Pan Am racked up a loss that amounted to $485.3 million.

To the workers who had just given up a tenth of their paychecks, it was a joke, almost. Rounded off, the 1982 loss came to half a billion dollars. How could any company lose that kind of money and remain in business?

Huge losses had become so commonplace that most Pan Am employees no longer believed them. They *knew* it had to be some kind of bookkeeping sleight of hand. The losses were just on paper. The airline was *supposed* to lose money, right? It had to hide it from the creditors and the IRS.

Some believed the company was being looted. There was no way the airline could *lose* that much money. Somebody had to be *stealing* it. Regional managing directors, vice presidents, even their CEO, whom they were now calling "Fast Eddie," were probably dipping into the till.

There were the "eyewitness" accounts: *I heard firsthand from a passenger service agent who knows this purser who actually saw Acker and his wife with this suitcase full of, hell, a million, maybe two million in cash. They were sneaking it out on a flight to . . .*

Such tales were outright lies, of course, and most employees, in their less hysterical moments, knew it. But the stories fed their discontent. The tales became part of the mythology of a deeply troubled corporation.

What the embittered workaday grunts didn't know was that Ed Acker wasn't getting rich from Pan Am. Acker was *already* rich. He had made a tidy fortune from his previous ventures, including the profitable years at Braniff and Air Florida, and as president of Gulf United Corporation.

It hadn't taken long for them to stop loving C. Edward Acker. It didn't take much longer before they were hating him. The employees came to hate Ed Acker for the same reasons the soldiers of a retreating army hated their commanding general: They hated losing. *Why doesn't he do something? Why are we losing this goddam battle?*

It was Acker's own style that soured his relations with the troops. Ed Acker liked the good life, and he was never careful to hide the fact. He particularly liked the perquisites the Imperial Airline had always showered on the chief executive—the limos and red carpets and receptions in his honor. That was the way it had been since the boat days, when the original Imperial Skygod, old Trippe, journeyed around the empire in a manner befitting a celestial deity.

The problem was, the Imperial Airline wasn't quite so imperial anymore, being a billion or so dollars in the red. And the troops out there on the line no longer thought it appropriate that the boss, who was demanding big sacrifices from *them,* comport himself like the Aga Khan.

To go with the success of his middle years, Ed Acker had taken a new, youngish wife. Sandy Acker was blond and pretty and vivacious. Unlike the meddlesome Mrs. Seawell, Mrs. Acker smiled and left business to her husband.

When the Ackers traveled, which was frequently, they liked to be deposited right at the front doorstep of the Clipper Club, at the Kennedy Worldport. They would emerge, King Edward and his queen, from their tinted-glass limousine onto the plush carpet. Uniformed attendants scurried to fetch bags and open doors. Like visiting monarchs they would be escorted to their waiting jumbo jet.

Sandy Acker liked champagne. She especially liked to drink the stuff while she and her husband rode on Pan Am airplanes. On one such occasion, the Ackers were flying aboard a Pan Am 747 to Moscow. By the time the Clipper rolled up to the terminal, Mrs. Acker was ready for more champagne. So she asked for a bottle to take along, carrying it under her arm while she trooped down the deplaning ladder.

And that was a mistake, at least for labor relations. The flight attendants stood there, mouth agape and eyes wide, watching the chairman's wife committing an act for which *they* would lose their jobs. Taking *anything*—booze, food, cutlery—off a Pan Am airplane would get them instantly fired.

That such an act might offend, of course, never occurred to the chairman's wife. For her part, she *was* gracious and friendly to the cabin crews on Pan Am airplanes. She just liked champagne.

But the story got around, adding weight to the legend. The truth no longer mattered, because by now the troops were willing to believe *anything* about the Ackers—that they were looting the treasury . . . building their Bermuda house with marble purloined from Pan Am stations . . . living the good life—*too damn good*—at Pan Am's expense while the airline was doing a death dance.

The tall Texan had ridden into town in a swirling cloud of hope and optimism. The troops had wanted to believe. They wanted to embrace him like a savior. *Right on, Ed! You lead, and we'll follow.*

They expected too much. Ed Acker wasn't a Skygod who would lead them to new victories. Nor was he a visionary—a reincarnated Juan Trippe—who would again aim Pan Am at the stars.

Something else dawned that they had overlooked: *Acker wasn't a pilot.* And that was something different. There had never before in Pan Am's history been a CEO who wasn't a pilot.

As vain as pilots tended to be, most understood that being an aviator maybe wasn't a qualification for running an airline. It was probably a handicap, considering what they'd been through with pilots like Bill Seawell and Jeeb Halaby. Managing a corporation and flying an airplane were different job descriptions.

But Acker was letting it be known in a variety of ways that he wasn't fond of pilots. He thought they were being paid far too much for performing far too little service. He was tapping into a theme that had become popular with the CEOs of ailing airlines:

Pilots only work seventy-five hours a month and they make a hundred and umpty thousand a year. . . .

Pilots make more money than the vice presidents of our company. . . .

Pilots are overcompensated and underworked. . . .

And, of course, *pilots are prima donnas. . . .*

The pilot group always had trouble refuting such accusations. There was just enough truth to them to open a breach between the pilots and the other employees. Pilots *were* the highest-paid of the unionized employee groups. And it was true that their actual flight time per month totaled only about seventy-five hours. It was difficult for pilots to convince the ground employees that in terms of time spent on duty and service performed, they *did* work every bit as much as mechanics or gate agents or vice presidents.

Okay, maybe they weren't underworked. But were pilots really prima donnas?

Indisputably. It went with the job.

CHAPTER TWENTY-FOUR

HOW SWEET IT IS

The toughest thing about being a new captain is to keep from
grinning all the time.
> —CAPTAIN DON ARNESON, *circa 1981*

Prima donnas or not, the pilots didn't think the job was what it used
to be. They could still remember the glory days.

Martinside recalled what Vern Kennedy, one of his instructors,
had told his new-hire class in San Francisco:

"We have a deal with the baggage handlers all around the world,"
Kennedy said. "They don't fly airplanes, and we don't carry bags."

It was true. When you checked in for your trip at the crew complex, there were baggage carts marked with the numbers of the departing flights. You tossed your bag onto the right cart, and, magically,
the bag was there waiting for you on the customs belt at your destination. From there it was transported by loaders, van drivers, bellboys,
until you found it deposited in your hotel room.

In those days Martinside hauled an international-size, aluminum-
shelled Halliburton. It contained a week's clothes, reading material,
snorkel gear, tennis racket, a mini-bar, jogging shoes, and other oddments. In the big Halliburton you could carry almost an entire ward-
robe. You never knew what might be needed.

Over the years, things changed. The contract with the world's baggage handlers—*They don't fly airplanes, we don't carry bags*—was

rescinded. For their part, the baggage handlers were keeping the bargain—they still didn't fly airplanes—but the pilots were carrying a hell of a lot of bags. It was just another part of the changing times— the budget-slashing, frill-cutting, giveback era. The world's most glamorous airline was getting less glamorous.

Some blamed it all on the arrival of the 747. "It ruined our airline," complained Jack Gaugler, a captain who, perversely, loved flying the jumbo. The *airplane* was wonderful, at least from a stick-and-throttle viewpoint. The trouble was that there were too damn many *people* in the act—not just the horde of passengers, but as many as twenty-some crew members on each flight. Gone were the small-crew amenities like having your own crew limousine, and bellboys running to fetch your bag. Now the entire crew of two dozen—pilots and flight attendants—waited at the airport curb for their crew bus, tired and scratchy, looking and feeling like migrant farm workers.

And they hauled their own bags.

It was in the late seventies that someone showed up with the first "wheelies," collapsible carts on which you could stow your bags with bungees. At first only the flight attendants rolled their baggage around on the contraptions. Pilots sneered at such things, continuing to lug their massive Halliburtons like *real* men, which is to say Skygods. "Wimp wagons," they called the baggage carts. But then realism and a few hernias began to change their attitudes. Before long it became a common sight—uniformed Skygods strolling down airport corridors, towing their wimp wagons behind them like U-Hauls.

One lost luxury from the old days was the hotels. Back in the glory days, Pan Am owned the Intercontinental Hotel chain, and that was where Pan Am crews stayed. The elegant Intercontinentals with their somber clerks and haughty doormen provided an appropriately grand accommodation for the Skygods.

But those days were gone. Now crews spent their layovers in Holiday Inns, and Ramadas and Best Westerns, where blocks of rooms at discounted rates were reserved for the airline crews.

If you were a pilot, that's where you lived much of your life. You stood there on countless mornings, waiting at check-in desks, eyes red-rimmed from crossing five, six, maybe ten time zones, unshaven, needing a bath and a beer and, most of all, sleep. You waited while a prim clerk told you you'd have to wait for a while longer because the rooms weren't ready, and by the way, would you mind standing over there, a bit out of the way, so the *other* hotel guests, the ones paying full rate, could do their business? And after you fought back the compulsion to seize the little peckerhead by his neatly knotted cravat and yank him over the counter, you tiredly got out of the way and waited some more.

The hotel drill never changed. You schlepped your baggage wheelie onto the same whirring elevators, trooped down the same endless hallways, fought the same spring-loaded doors while you maneuvered your baggage into the room.

If it was one of the lesser destinations—Lisbon, Nice, Budapest—the room tended to be spacious. Big beds, furniture, steeping baths, room to spread out. In the major capitals—London, Paris, Rome—you had a broom closet. When you opened the blinds to check the view, you saw the brick wall of the building next door. There was room to undress if you stood in the corner. There was the same little fold-out rack for your suitcase, with no place to fold it out. There were the same unstealable hangers in the closet that forced you to hang your clothes with the hangers still attached.

The first thing most pilots did was turn on the television. It didn't matter what was on. The noise and flickering image filled the little cell and made you feel not quite so alone and fatigued. There was usually a mini-bar, and if you were in that beyond-tired, too-fatigued-to-sleep mode after an all-nighter across the ocean, you might have a beer. You drank this while you sat in a hot bath. And then you slept.

But not for long.

Ratatatatatat! Whang! Whang! Ratatatatat!

It sounded like the hammers of hell.

The daytime world of London and Paris and Rome didn't care a fig that you'd been up all night. Nor did the hotel. Crews stayed in the *cheap* section—the airline rooms—and that was where the renovations were going on. Every Pan Am layover hotel in the Western world had renovations in progress, and they were timed to commence *precisely* when you put your head down on your pillow.

There was the standard call to the front desk and the usual argument with the manager about the noise, and, maybe, you could get another room if you wanted to get dressed again and move all the stuff you'd unpacked.

To hell with that. You stuffed plugs in your ears and put a pillow over your head and went to sleep, more or less.

There was no satisfactory way to deal with the time zone problem. Some pilots tried to stay on home time, sleeping in Tokyo when it was bedtime in Connecticut, eating when it was dinnertime back home. But that meant doing everything contrary to the local clock. Where did you find dinner at six in the morning? And who could face the dreariness of being up all night in a sleeping city, locked in a room watching *Bonanza* reruns in Japanese?

So you dragged your carcass out of bed after three hours of dozing through the jackhammers and went to dinner with your crew. And then you went to bed again. You were so tired you ought to be co-matose for eight or more hours, making up the sleep deficit.

Wrong. The body clock wasn't buying it. At three in the morning you were awake, bone-tired, restless, impatient. Six hours before pickup. So you read and watched the television reruns and thought about nothing in particular. Thirty minutes before your wake-up call, you fell asleep.

Jim Wood used to do this. He stumbled around, packing his stuff and getting himself dressed. He stared at himself in the mirror, not liking what he saw, and he thought: *I hate this goddam job.*

And then one day everything changed. He didn't hate the job anymore.

Sixteen years. *Sixteen egg-sucking, yessirring, three-striping, pride-swallowing years.* That was how long it took Jim Wood to progress to the left seat of a Pan American jet. He was the first of his class of new hires to do so.

It happened all of a sudden. Pan Am's pilot seniority list, measured by the age of the pilots, looked like a large rat passing through a snake. The list was constricted by an entire generation of pilots, all nearly the same age, hired during and just after World War II. They were the second wave of the Skygods, direct descendants of the Masters of

Ocean Flying Boats. When their group reached the captain's seat, beginning in the early sixties, the top of the seniority list remained
plugged for the next decade and a half.

Now, all in a collective gaggle, they were reaching the pumpkin
hour of their careers. As each hoary Skygod hit the mandatory retirement age of sixty, the occasion triggered a new captain's vacancy.

Sixteen years was an unnaturally long apprenticeship. Too long
for some, because after that many years of responding to commands,
of *thinking* like an apprentice even when you already had more time
in your seat than the captain had in his, it was simply too overwhelming to assume responsibility for the whole show.

Most, like Rob Martinside and Jim Wood and Pat Dryer, laughed
about it. *The loneliness of command.* It was a joke. They made mock-
serious statements like "Ah, what a relief to have that burden off my
shoulders" when they took off their four-striped coats. "The toughest
thing about being a new captain," observed Don Arneson, "is to keep
from grinning all the time."

But for a few of the longtime new hires, it *was* very damn lonely.
The mere thought of being in the left seat *alone*, totally responsible
for the fate of a two-hundred-ton aluminum dreadnought and its load
of human flesh, was more than they could handle. The first officer's
seat had gotten to be a comfortable niche. None of the final, truly
difficult decisions was theirs. In the right seat all they were expected
to do was *fly*, which was something they could do pretty well after
this many years. All the deciding, the head-scratching, the worrying
was accomplished by the guy in the left seat. And that was just fine
with them. Now here they were, forty-some years old, having expected
to be a copilot all their lives, and they were suddenly supposed to be
a *commander*. It was like suddenly appointing the helmsman of a ship
the captain. Steering was one thing; deciding the *course* of the ship
was quite another.

Pat Dryer had no such problem. In the early days of his copilothood,
Dryer had been a respectful and polite young crew member. By the
seventeenth year of his servitude in the right seat, he was insufferable.
He would walk into the operations office, peruse the flight schedule,
and inquire, "What asshole am I flying with today?" He had taken to

flatly ignoring captain's orders that he regarded as inane. If a captain so much as *suggested* a modification of his flying technique, Dryer would slide his seat back, fold his arms over his chest, and say something like "Okay, it's your airplane. You fly." He was often written up for his attitude. He would be chewed out by the chief pilot, then go back to his ways. Even the good guys, the easygoing captains, had come to dread flying with Dryer.

And then came the day when Dryer graduated to the left seat. It was a different Dryer. He appeared in the operations office, resplendent in his new regalia. No one had seen him smile for years. Now he was beaming like a Cheshire cat.

"What asshole are you flying with today, Pat?" asked the operations agent.

Dryer grinned and pointed to his chest. "This one."

The advancement of new captains continued. The old constriction in the seniority list—the fat rat stuck in the snake—had finally worked its way to the exit point. There were almost too many parties for the pilots to attend. Every week contained an agenda of retirement bashes for old captains and wetting-down parties for new ones. Every day someone showed up in a crew room looking like Lord Nelson in his glittering new captain's outfit. Shiny stripes glinted like veins of gold.

An old airline ritual was revived—cutting off the necktie of a newly promoted captain. In Skygod culture, it amounted to symbolic circumcision. Now freshly severed necktie remnants were littering the crew-room floor.

One effect of the new promotions was that the generation gap in the cockpit all but disappeared. No longer were captains white-haired sages who, when so inclined, shared their wisdom with worshipful junior pilots. Now captains and copilots were nearly the same age. Almost all of them—captains, first officers, flight engineers—had been hired between 1965 and 1968. All three airmen in the cockpit had similar histories, which made them peers in experience if not in rank.

Given this new equality in the cockpit, it was natural to believe that the day of the Skygodly Master of Ocean Flying Boats was over. After all, the new captains were enlightened, weren't they? *They* would never insult their junior airmen. They would be fair and generous with their crews. They would be admired and respected by their copilots. They would inspire reverence and, most likely, secret yearning in the hearts of the flight attendants.

All this turned out to be dead wrong. One of the anomalies of airline training is that years of schooling and practice go into learning to fly, but virtually no formal training is given in the nuances of command. Many pilots just happen to be natural leaders. For them the command of an airliner comes easily. A small number happen to be naturally quarrelsome or uncommunicative. For them the management of a cockpit crew is an exercise made in hell.

It was a maxim in airline flying that the most insecure captains were also the most monumental pains in the ass. Those who doubted their own skills were quick to believe that their crew members were trying to kill them. They sat there in lonely trepidation, worrying that disaster was about to strike, snapping at the copilot and imagining that the crew were conspiring against them.

Such a captain was John Demura. Demura's name always popped up in after-hours debriefings in the layover bars and lounges. As a captain of the new vintage, Demura was already getting himself compared to Attila the Hun and Ivan the Terrible.

As a new hire, Demura had slipped through the normal airline screening process—the interviews and background checks and probationary period. For sixteen years he sat there stewing in the right seat, waiting to explode like a land mine.

"Get the London weather," he would order the copilot right after takeoff in New York.

"But we've got six and a half hours to go, John."

"I *know* how many hours we have to go. I want the weather *now*."

Demura didn't trust the weather any more than he trusted copilots. Everything, even the elements, was conspiring against him. He checked the weather at least once every hour all the way across the ocean.

Captain Demura made frequent trips to the chief pilot's office to report the shocking inadequacies of his crews. He told the chief that most of them were grossly incompetent. Some of them were so bad they ought to be fired.

"Funny," said the chief. "A lot of them have been coming up here and saying the same thing about you." He counseled Captain Demura to go out and have a beer with his crew. "Take a stewardess along. You might even learn something," he said.

Demura didn't, of course. He continued to enrage planeloads of people. Other captains tried talking to him, mainly because they were anxious for the new breed—*their* generation—to be known as kinder and saner captains than the leather-nosed Skygods that had preceded them. It didn't work.

Eventually a significant number of copilots refused to fly with Demura. Flight attendants walked en masse off his airplane. Engineers debated whether to poison him. "I think he's nuts," declared a first officer after getting off a trip with Demura.

The chief pilot became concerned. He removed Demura from flight status and had him examined by the company flight surgeon. The flight surgeon referred him to a psychiatrist. The psychiatrist spent time with him and then delivered his judgment: Captain Demura was sane. A little neurotic, perhaps, but undeniably sane.

So he returned to flying duty. The story got around, of course, about Demura's troubles and his stamp of approval from the shrink. Captain Demura had earned a unique distinction: He was the only pilot in all of Pan American who was certified sane.

Most of the problem captains smoothed out. They got over their insecurity in the new job and relaxed. Of the corps of new captains, only a tiny minority never changed their act. These Jim Wood attributed to the Jerk Factor.

"Every profession—doctors, lawyers, cowboys—has its quota of jerks," Wood explained one night at the Hundekehle. "Even the profession of flying. And that's not all bad. Think about it," he said, wiping the ribbon of foam from his upper lip. "Remember Art Gilson? If we didn't have a few jerks among us, who would we pick on?"

One day in 1982, it was Rob Martinside's turn. He showed up an hour early. He felt conspicuous in the new uniform. The four gold stripes glowed like neon bars. The braid on the visor of his new hat weighed, it seemed, about forty pounds. He felt like a player in a costume drama.

He could feel people looking at him. Did they know he was wearing this regalia for the very first time? How could they tell that until today he had never actually *been* an airline captain?

The hardest part was the crew room. The crew room was a place where you could get eviscerated for any gesture that might be interpreted as taking yourself seriously. Wearing something like a new captain's outfit into the crew room in Berlin was a sure sign that you were taking yourself seriously.

So Martinside slunk in the door, doing his best to be invisible. No one looked up. The inhabitants were reading newspapers, perusing bulletin boards, slouching in the beat-up leather chairs.

Martinside had already stashed the gold-bedecked hat. Uniform hats, in any case, were seldom worn in the Berlin base. The only pilots who wore their hats were new captains and check captains and a few suck-ups who aspired to be check captains. It was a joke that copilots never wore hats *except* when they ceased to be copilots and were suddenly issued their splendid new gold-encrusted captain's hats. Then they wore their hats everywhere—in the crew room, in the bedroom, in the toilet.

In the cockpit, Martinside noticed something strange: People kept asking him questions. *Him.* "How much stored fuel do you want, captain?" "Okay to load the restricted articles in the aft cargo, skipper?" "What airport do you want for a takeoff alternate, captain?" "Captain, what do you want to do about . . ."

Martinside stared at them blankly. *Captain?* They were talking to *him*, for Christ's sake! For seventeen years he had sat there in the right seat, invisible and mute. No one ever asked a first officer's opinion about anything. Now he was supposed to be an oracle. They were deluging him with questions about everything from jet fuel to toilet paper.

His first officer was a short, freckled pilot named Red Parsell. Parsell and Martinside went way back together. Parsell had been hired about six months after Martinside, and trailed him on the seniority list by some five hundred numbers.

Red was acting funny. "What's the matter, Red? You act like your hemorrhoids are kicking up."

"Aw, hell," he said, "I'll get used to it. It's just seems . . . peculiar.

Us junior pukes all alone up here. After all these years. You know, like they let the monkeys run the zoo."

Red was right. It *did* seem peculiar. They had been copilots for so many years they were brainwashed to think it wasn't safe unless they had a real card-carrying Skygod there in the left seat. Well, screw all that ancient thinking, Martinside thought. It was high time the monkeys *did* run the zoo.

After they landed in Hamburg, Martinside said, "Your leg, Red. You fly us back to Berlin."

Parsell stared. "Aren't new captains supposed to fly all the legs until they have a hundred hours in command?"

"So we'll record it that way in the logbook. The captain flew all the legs. Do you want to fly or don't you?"

Red Parsell smiled for the first time that day. "Well, hell. Sure I want to fly."

And so he did. He flew every other leg, and by the end of their six-leg day, when they touched down back at Tegel Flughafen in Berlin, seventeen years of brainwashing had been laid to rest. They told jokes. They kidded each other. They made bets on who could make the slickest landings.

The monkeys *were* running the zoo. They were loving every minute of it.

Martinside was in no hurry to leave the cockpit. He sat there for several extra minutes, savoring the moment. He looked at the instrument panel. He gazed out at the new view from the left cockpit window.

Seventeen years. Here he was. It was worth it.

He pulled out his ballpoint. For the first time he placed his signature in the aircraft logbook. He signed his name directly over the printed words *Aircraft Commander*.

By the time he had stuffed his manuals and headset and flashlight back into his briefcase, Red was packed and gone. So were the passengers.

Martinside walked out through the jetway. That was where they got him.

He barely saw it coming—an apparition lunging at him from the shadows, large, mustachioed, wielding a—*what the hell?* It looked like a huge shears.

It *was* a huge shears. Martinside thought he was about to die a grisly death. The apparition seized him by his black uniform tie, snatching him nearly off his feet. Martinside saw the shears coming for his throat.

Rrripp! Martinside's tie was slashed away just below the knot.

The apparition was Larry Phillips, a first officer of immense size, black-mustached and evil-looking. "Gotcha, captain," said Phillips.

The rest of the ritual followed. This happened at the crew watering hole, the Hundekehle. It was Martinside's responsibility to provide an uninterrupted flow of Pilsner Urquel for the rest of the night.

CHAPTER TWENTY-FIVE

STRIKE

We're mad as hell, and we're not going to take it anymore.
                    —*From the film* Network, *reiterated by Pan Am employees,*
                    February 28, 1985

It should have been a normal day in Berlin. You could feel the wet winter fog gathering out there on the runways of Tegel Airport. You knew that at sunrise, when the temperature and the dew point came together on the thermometer, it would be another gray-murk, phlegm-thick German morning.

At five-thirty the crews began checking in for the first wave of departures to their destinations throughout West Germany. A half hour later, while they were sitting in the cockpits, going through pre-flight checklists, swilling their first coffee, a runner from the pilots' union office made the rounds of the cockpits. The word had come from New York: *The strike is on.*

Strike? It was the news they dreaded—and expected—on this be-fogged morning. *Well, damn . . . I guess so. . . .* Charts and manuals and flashlights back into the flight kits . . . slide the seats back . . . hats and coats back on . . . leave the cockpit . . . looking and feeling sheepish . . . avoiding the perplexed stares of the boarding passengers. . . .

It was the most unnatural act of their airline careers. They hated it. They thought of themselves as professionals. You didn't walk off your airplane and leave your passengers in the lurch.

But that's what they were doing, all over the Pan Am system, climbing down the boarding ladders, bags in hand, leaving pilotless airplanes behind them like ghost ships in the darkness.

And each in his private thoughts wondered: *Why the hell are we doing this?*

A strike at Pan Am was as rare as a visitation by aliens. The former National employees had seen a lot of it during their years at the George T. Baker airline, where labor brawling was a way of life. But at blue-blooded Pan American, the Imperial Airline, a strike was viewed with the same distaste as getting sucked into a bar fight. It besmirched the airline's image. There was something about it that just wasn't . . . *imperial.*

But that was before Ed Acker. Times were changing.

"We don't expect profitability until the third quarter of this year," Ed Acker had told his employees. That was in 1983, following his first full year as Pan Am CEO. The 1982 loss of nearly half a billion dollars put Pan Am in history books—it was an airline industry record.

The third quarter of 1983 came and went. Another loss.

The third quarter of 1984. A loss of over $200 million.

You could hear a loud metallic sound reverberating across Pan American property. It was the sound of ACKER BACKER pins hitting the trash bins. The mood was turning ugly.

Pan Am's United States–based employees were represented by five separate labor unions: the Air Line Pilots Association; the Flight Engineers International Association; the Independent Union of Flight Attendants; the Transport Workers Union, representing the airline's 5,700 mechanics; and the Teamsters, whose membership included clerks, ticket agents, and reservations personnel.

Traditionally, labor disputes at Pan Am had been settled in a Runyonesque atmosphere. Union spokesmen sat down with the company negotiators. Everyone talked tough for a while, made preposterous demands, and hinted at shutdowns and lockouts. Then they would get around to arguing about the real issues—pay scales, work rules, contract renewal.

Such a negotiator was Jim MacQuarrie, the pilots' union chairman. MacQuarrie was a gruff, cigarette-smoking former fighter pilot with the face of an ex-pugilist. His negotiating style was to lock gazes with the guy across the table and tell him, just for openers, that he was going to break his balls. That got the talks started on the right note.

Eventually the negotiations would come to a sticking point. The negotiators would hunch over their legal pads, scribbling meaningless notes. Nobody would have anything to say. MacQuarrie would glower at his counterparts across the table, and then, when he'd had enough, he'd bang his fist down. "You guys are stalling. Get off your asses and negotiate, or we're gonna slam the door so hard it'll be heard in Juan Trippe's tomb."

That usually broke the deadlock. They would resume negotiating. Afterward MacQuarrie and his union people and Marty Shugrue and his company people would go down the street to the Cattleman to knock back a few scotches and talk airplanes. It was great fun, like a private club. For years that was how labor problems were negotiated at Pan Am.

And then appeared C. Raymond Grebey.

Ed Acker hired Ray Grebey in 1984 to be Pan Am's vice president for industrial relations, making him the airline's chief negotiator with the unions. Grebey was fiftyish, with a ruddy complexion and the arrogant strut of a banty rooster. He brought with him a reputation for bare-knuckle, spit-in-your-eye brawling with unions. Grebey had spent twenty years in labor and personnel jobs at General Electric, where labor relations were consistently fractious. From 1978 to 1983 he represented the owners of major league baseball teams in their disputes with the players. It was principally Grebey who precipitated the bitter players' strike of 1981.

In Pan Am's private little labor negotiating club, the arrival of Ray Grebey was like throwing a pit bull into an alligator pen. Grebey instantly insulted the labor representatives. "You guys," he told the union officials on a first meeting, "have had it too good for too long. Now it's giveback time."

Union leaders hated him. "That little sonofabitch," said a pilots' union negotiator. "Grebey can piss off more people than Idi Amin and the IRS together."

Grebey didn't care what they said. He figured that went with the job. He explained to a newspaper reporter, "There's a bad guy at every airline trying to wring wage concessions from labor." Grebey was the bad guy at Pan Am.

In August of 1984, the unions were informed that Pan Am had stopped its contributions to the employees' pension funds. And then on January 1, 1985, Pan Am announced that it was unilaterally extending the pay freezes the unions had accepted back in the short-lived Acker Backer euphoria. The freeze was supposed to be temporary, with a "snapback" provision—an automatic reinstatement of the previous, higher wage scales. Now it was time for the snapback, and Acker was reneging on the deal—withholding scheduled pay increases of 26 percent for the pilots, 14 percent for the mechanics, 12 percent for the flight attendants, and 2 percent for the clerical employees.

Labor relations at Pan Am plunged to an all-time low.

While the unions took the company to court over the pay freeze extension, they gained access to an evaluation of Pan Am's management done for the board of directors by the consulting firm Lazard Frères. The report indicated Pan Am had damaged its credibility by saying that concessions from labor could solve the airline's financial problems. Most stinging, though, was the consulting firm's conclusion that "by far the most significant failure has been Pan Am's inability or unwillingness to confront its own problems."

To the embittered work force, this translated to Pan Am's willingness to blame labor for its own failings. The Lazard Frères report noted that Pan Am workers were being paid significantly less than their counterparts at other major domestic airlines and "the quality of labor relations had deteriorated into anger and accusation."

Anger and accusation—that was an understatement for the rage the employees were feeling. By court order, Pan Am was forced to abide by the snapback agreement. In the meantime, all the union contracts were up for renewal. Ray Grebey kept up the pressure on the unions for *new* wage freezes as well as a host of new "productivity" improvements. "Productivity" was a popular labor relations term that had an ancient meaning: more work for the same pay. Pan Am also wanted to institute a trendy new two-tiered airline wage scale—A and B scales—under which newly hired employees, the B-scalers, would be paid as much as 50 percent less than current workers.

Negotiations dragged on through the early winter of 1985. Even the union leaders, at least in private, understood that Pan Am could not afford the snapback pay increases and a restoration of the pension contributions. The snapback alone would cost $170 million per year. Pan Am's unfunded pension liabilities came to a staggering $650 million.

In February the pilots were the first union to give the company generous concessions in productivity and health care. It was necessary, Jim MacQuarrie told the *Wall Street Journal,* "to ensure the future health and profitability of the company." The company's hope was that with the pilots leading the way, the other unions would follow.

They didn't. The Transport Workers Union, representing the 5,700 mechanics, was led by a feisty Irishman named John Kerrigan, who was finding it especially difficult to bargain with a man like Ray Grebey. Throughout February the two sides haggled. The deadline for the contract was fixed at 12:01 A.M., February 28, 1985.

Midnight came, and there was still no contract. Grebey told the mechanics they could take it or leave it.

The mechanics left it. The other four unions, equally fed up with Ray Grebey and Ed Acker and Pan Am management in general, walked with them. The strike was on.

Later, if you asked employees why they had gone on strike, most could not put a specific reason to it. That was because the Great Strike of 1985 had less to do with wages and pensions and productivity than it did with . . . *dignity.* It was bad enough, they thought, that the old airline of the Skygods should be so hideously mismanaged that it couldn't afford to pay its workers a decent salary. But *this*—to be insulted by hired guns like C. Raymond Grebey—just wasn't . . . *dignified.*

Not all the pilots were on strike. "Management" airmen—those assigned as check pilots and instructors, and administrative airmen who had jobs as chief pilots and operations managers—had been alerted to fly that morning. They were supposed to maintain a skeleton flight schedule.

The management pilots found themselves in a no-man's-land. They were regarded by Pan Am management to be exempted from union obligations. They were expected to carry the company flag. But on the other side was ALPA—the pilots' union—which didn't see it that way.

"Pilots are pilots," said a union official in a letter to the management pilots. "When we go on strike, we *all* go. No exceptions."

But there they were, the exceptions.

"There go the fucking scabs," yelled a man wearing a sign that declared he was a striking employee. He stood with a group of strikers on a picket line outside the Pan Am check-in counters.

Martinside had been recently assigned as a check pilot. It was supposed to be something of a distinction, being selected as a check pilot. No one had told him that the job would place him at ground zero in a labor war. Now he wondered how he could have been so naive. He hadn't foreseen the vehemence with which the group—the striking pilots—would turn on him.

Martinside had no particular feelings about the strike one way or another. He knew there were no gut-burning, Bastille-storming, banner-waving issues at stake. The pilots were on strike because they were union members and that's what the union had declared. The check pilots were flying because they worked for management and that's what management had declared. Both sides were doing their jobs in the collective bargaining process.

But it was more complicated than that.

A note appeared in Rob Martinside's mailbox: *I presume that by now you have seen the light and resigned your check pilot position. If not, consider our friendship ended.* It was signed by an old friend from his new-hire class.

Another old friend called up to say he thought Martinside was a gutless traitor. A man on the picket line spat at him as he walked past.

The strike was getting expensive. Losing old friends was a price he had not expected to pay.

Jim Wood wasn't bothered by such things. He told Martinside to grow up. "Friends?" said Wood. "Quit kidding yourself. What makes you think people who spit at you are *friends?* Friendship doesn't have anything to do with strikes."

The war went on for nearly a week. Nothing in the pilots' airline experience had ever aroused so much passion. Paranoia was running wild on both sides. The striking pilots gathered every night at the Tempelhof Officers' Club to pump up morale and exchange their deepest fears.

"They're bringing in scab pilots to take our jobs."

"Pan Am is going out of business and reorganizing—*without us*."

"If we go back to work, we go on the bottom of seniority list."

"We've all been fired."

And *that* one was true, at least on paper. Every pilot who didn't show up for his scheduled trip received a notice of termination. Most said they thought it was very funny and they intended to keep it as a remembrance. But deep down, they were scared. This goddam strike . . . it wasn't funny at all.

One of the odd things about the strike was that both sides claimed to be trying to *save* Pan Am. Which raised a question—who was Pan Am? The employees? Management? The guy who signed the paychecks? The grunts who had given most of their adult lives to the company? Who were they saving it for?

A few asked an awkward question: How are we *saving* Pan Am by shutting it down?

Support for the strike, at least by the unions that had walked out in sympathy with the TWU, quickly waned. Slowly, picket signs came down and people took up their jobs. Back in New York, Jim Mac-Quarrie signed an agreement with management to put the pilots back to work. The others, the flight attendants, the clerks, the flight engineers, followed suit. The TWU held out longer, then reached its own compromise with management.

When it was over, both sides were claiming victory. The employees felt that they had fired a torpedo directly into Ed Acker's throne room.

The company did some chest-thumping of its own. Pan Am's management had made its point, at considerable expense, that it would not be held hostage to demands from its unions. The Imperial Airline would do business exactly as it saw fit. Even if it went broke in the process.

Who won? It was hard to find a winner. The Financially Troubled Pan American looked as if it had been gut-shot at a time when it was already limping.

That, perhaps, was why they had gone on strike.

The pilots' strike-ending agreement with the company included a "no hostages" clause, which meant that everyone—strikers and scabs—was supposed to forgiven. No reprisals. Bygones were supposed to be bygones. At least, that's what the agreement said.

But it would never be the same. The pilots had lost something intangible. The carcasses of old friendships lay like corpses on a battlefield. No longer were they, the Skygods and Skygods-to-be, a cohesive team fighting the bureaucracy, the competition, the rest of the world. They had been reduced to fighting with each other.

CHAPTER TWENTY-SIX

PACIFIC

This is one hell of a good deal for United Airlines.
—RICHARD FERRIS, *chairman, United Airlines*

We're cutting off our right arm.
—A PAN AM PILOTS' UNION
REPRESENTATIVE

It was a classic Ed Acker hip shot. He had carried the secret with him, telling no one, for three months. And then one day over lunch at the Sky Club in the Pan Am Building, he spilled it to Marty Shugrue.

"I've sold the Pacific," Acker said.

Shugrue slowly lowered his fork. Outside he could see the long rays of the April sun flooding Manhattan. It was 1985, and spring had mercifully come. The airline was still reeling from the strike in March. Shugrue stared at the chairman. Surely he had misunderstood. *Sell the Pacific?* What did that mean? How can you sell a goddam ocean?

It was true. Acker explained how he had made a deal with United Airlines to sell Pan Am's Pacific Division. The Pacific happened to be one of Pan Am's rare moneymakers. It also happened to be the fastest-growing market in the world. It was a route system that had been virtually invented by Pan American.

243

And Acker was selling it. He was lopping off an entire ocean of airline routes and destinations, all pioneered by Pan American going back to the *China Clipper* days.

He had done it in typical Acker vest-pocket fashion. No one else had known, just he and Richard Ferris, chairman of United Airlines. Part of the deal, Acker revealed, had even been done on a golf course.

Why did United want Pan Am's Pacific routes? By the 1980s, United had managed to extend its reach into the Pacific, dominating the mainland-to-Hawaii market and obtaining rights to Tokyo and Hong Kong. And United already had a powerful domestic system poised to feed a new Pacific route expansion. But two Far East destinations were not enough to make an impact. United needed an extensive Pacific route system to make it work. To build up such a system through the burdensome application process, adding one route, one destination, at time, would take decades.

The quick solution was to buy Pan Am's routes. Since 1982, Ferris had been probing. When he first suggested a Pacific deal, Acker was still new in his own job as chairman of Pan Am. Anyway, Pan Am wasn't hurting *that* bad, since the airline was still living off the proceeds of the sale of the Pan Am Building and the Intercontinental Hotel chain. Pan Am didn't *have* to sell. Acker said no.

Ferris kept trying. Again in 1983 he approached Acker on the subject. The answer was still no.

By 1985, Pan Am's situation had changed. Ed Acker was wrestling with demons that exceeded even his Texas-sized imagination. Pan Am wasn't just losing money. It was going through cash faster than a Middle East emirate. While the Atlantic and Pacific divisions were showing small profits and the South American operation was just breaking even, the domestic routes were racking up a projected 1985 loss of $250 million. Since the beginning of the eighties, Pan Am had transformed *one and a half billion dollars,* including all the proceeds from the assets sales, into a fine invisible vapor.

Richard Ferris, aware of all this, telephoned Acker in early February 1985. Would he *now* like to talk about a possible sale of Pan Am's Pacific routes?

Acker was in a corner. His growing conflict with Pan Am's unions, if it came to a strike, would cause another disastrous loss for the year. It was apparent that Pan Am would be soon be forced, no matter what, to make another asset sale. The airline's only marketable assets left were its routes.

Ed Acker thought it over. He called Ferris back in late February.

In absolute secrecy the two executives haggled through the winter of 1985, and into the spring. The Great Strike came and went. While the strikers stood on the picket lines raging about Ed Acker, they didn't know about the three-quarter-billion-dollar secret Acker was carrying around with him, like a derringer in his boot.

The Texas deal-maker was doing what he did best, and this was the biggest deal of his life. At three o'clock on a Monday morning, April 22, after a weekend of haggling, they came to terms. The announcement knocked the wind out of the airline business.

Pan Am Agrees to Sell United Its Pacific Unit

Price of $750 Million Includes 18 Planes, Routes to Asia and Australia from U.S.

The business press made more of the gargantuan sum paid by United than of the shrinkage in size—about 21 percent—it represented for Pan Am. The *Wall Street Journal* obtained a secret thirty-six-page analysis of the transaction prepared by the aviation consulting firm of Simat, Helliesen & Eichner. It focused on the fact that the average purchase price of airline acquisitions over the years amounted to 9.5 times one year's earnings. In the case of the Pan Am–United sale, United was paying *twenty-two* times the annual earnings of the division. At that rate it would take United over twenty years to recover its investment.

Ferris shrugged it off. "Our studies indicate the return on invested capital will be very good. Our feed of domestic traffic to the West Coast can do marvelous things to the load factor." Load factor meant the percentage of seats filled in the airplanes. Because of United's extensive domestic system, it could feed more passengers to its Pacific flights than Pan Am had ever dreamed of.

The deal scared the hell out of the other airlines. United was already the biggest carrier in the country. "This deal will only make the nine-hundred-pound gorilla a twelve-hundred-pound gorilla," warned

C. E. Meyer, president of TWA. Northwest Airlines, which had recently overtaken Pan Am as the biggest Pacific carrier, declared that it would oppose the sale on antitrust grounds.

Part of Acker's rationale for selling the Pacific routes was that Pan Am would have had to invest one billion dollars in new equipment just for the Pacific in order to remain competitive. Pan Am didn't have a billion dollars.

Wait a minute, critics of the deal began saying in the business press. A billion dollars? Hadn't Acker, just the year before, in 1984, placed an order with Airbus Industries, the European aircraft consortium, for sixteen A-320 short-haul jets and twelve A-310 twin-engine wide-bodies, which were transatlantic jetliners? The deal had a purchase price of $1.1 billion. Wasn't that approximately the amount Acker was saying it would cost to reequip the airline's Pacific operation? In other words, the profit-making and expanding Pacific market was being sacrificed for the already-saturated and questionably profitable Atlantic.

Well, as a matter of fact, yes. But as Acker's people explained, there really wasn't any choice.

"We can't afford to be a two-ocean airline any longer," said a vice president close to the deal. "Something had to go. Ed decided it was the Pacific."

Meanwhile Acker was telling his board of directors what a good deal it was for Pan Am. Pan Am would not only reap a huge cash infusion, he told them, it would save itself the huge investment it would have to make to upgrade the airplanes that served the Pacific. Pan Am had a fleet of dogs. Now it was selling them to United.

"We're not overjoyed about the airplanes United is getting," Ferris admitted. United was taking eighteen airplanes off Pan Am's hands, including the 747 SPs. The "SP" meant "special performance." They were shortened models of the 747 that, because of their reduced weight, had lower fuel consumption and thus longer range. Because of the shorter fuselages, they also had fewer seats, only 233, compared to the nearly-400-seat versions of the normal 747. Now the SPs were anachronisms from the seventies. Boeing was delivering full-size 747s with new, more powerful engines that had the same range as the undersized SPs. They also had upper decks that allowed a total load of as many as 500 passengers.

A Pan Am executive said, "To equal the seats in one of those new planes, you have to fly two SPs in formation."

United was also taking the fleet of six Lockheed Tri-Stars, which Pan Am had been trying for several years to unload. Though pilots loved the technically advanced Lockheed, the trimotor jet with its clunky Rolls-Royce engines had an uncompetitive cost per seat-mile. One other unwanted airplane, a single model of the trimotor DC-10, was also included in United's package.

Not everyone was ecstatic about the deal. Pan Am's labor unions, still battle-weary from the Great Strike, were dubious about *anything* served up to them by Ed Acker. "It's cutting off our right arm," said a pilots' union official. "What's next?"

The board of directors, as well as Acker's own executives, already knew how strapped the airline was for cash. *Something* had to be liquidated, and the Pacific was the only route system that had a ready buyer. The Atlantic could not be sold, because that was the bulk of the Pan Am system and was the principal reason for the domestic feeder network. Pan Am had never gotten around to constructing a similar domestic feeder system for its Pacific destinations.

When the board of directors voted on the sale, pilot Bob Gould, representing the labor coalition, voted no. It was the only dissenting vote.

Even Marty Shugrue, who was initially horrified by the deal, shrugged and conceded that, okay, maybe the sale *was* the only way to survive. But after that, what? If the proceeds were used to fund more losses—business as usual—then all they had done was convert more assets to vapor. It would be only a matter of time before they were selling something else.

"We have to expand," Shugrue told anyone who would listen. "New *domestic* routes, new equipment."

And that, paradoxically, had always been Pan Am's burning ambition—before deregulation and before the National acquisition. Somewhere during the Seawell-Acker assets sell-off, the domestic priority had been dumped. Now they had to undo the errors following the National acquisition and try to rebuild what they had dismantled.

Was Ed Acker listening? With Acker, it was hard to tell.

* * *

One aspect of Acker's deal would be looked back upon with appreciation. Besides bargaining for the sale of assets, Acker negotiated the transfer of *people*. As part of the package, United Airlines would hire 2,700 Pan Am employees, including 1,000 non-U.S. workers, about 100 managers, 1,200 flight attendants, and *410 pilots*.

Had Acker been looking out for the interests of Pan Am people when he shook Ferris's hand? So it seemed. In this instance, it was a fortuitous arrangement for both sides. United *needed* the Pan Am people, because it was in one hell of a hurry. By acquiring the Pacific routes, it had just plunged itself into competition with powerful Northwest Airlines as well as the strong foreign carriers, Japan Air Lines, Cathay Pacific, Singapore Airlines, and a host of newcomers. There was no time to learn the new territory, train crews, hire station personnel, establish offices. United needed a quick-start, turnkey operation.

The Pan Am personnel were already there. All they had to do was change uniforms.

Whatever the reason—altruism or hard-nosed business reality—it was a principle that Pan Am employees would later wish had been painted on the airplanes and engraved in the aluminum: *Employees go with the assets.*

In future transactions, it would not be so.

So 410 airmen would transfer to United. But *which* 410? Like everything in the airline business, it went by seniority.

For those eligible to transfer—the most senior captains, first officers, and flight engineers who were already qualified in the 747s and L-1011s—it was a time for soul-searching. And reality-checking. Stay with Pan Am, or emigrate to the domestic, bus-driving turf of United Airlines?

Captain Rich Selph was one of those who agonized over the decision. Go or stay? Few pilots were more dipped in Pan Am blue than Rich Selph. He had been one of the early AWARE pushers. He had made the pilgrimage to Washington. It was Selph who had hounded the senator of free enterprise, Proxmire, on his dawn jogs. Now Selph was a fast-rising young management pilot who had just been offered a chief pilot's desk.

Like many pilots, Selph was an analytical person. He believed numbers. One night until past midnight he sat in his kitchen filling a steno pad with his calculations. He kept coming up with the same answer.

Maybe Pan Am would hang in there. He hoped so. Did he think it would? Not really. There was no question that *United* would be around until long after he had retired. And despite all the romantic reasons for sticking with Financially Troubled Pan Am, Rich Selph had some overriding considerations. Four of them. They were all approaching college age.

Decision made. He *had* to go.

So it was with most of the eligible pilots. They had been through a decade of uncertainty with Pan Am. United was a sure thing. United was offering them the rarest of all commodities in aviation—a second chance.

Not all were so analytical. There was Harry Shepard, for example. A 747 pilot, Shepard went through the interview and took United's prehiring physical. He even attended United's indoctrination class. While he was there he took a look around. He didn't like the dark hats, or the tacky bus-driver uniforms. He didn't like the silly sixth-grade-level pilot's manuals they issued him, and he sure as hell didn't like the officious, patronizing bureaucracy of the huge airline. *Take a number and have a seat over there. We'll call you when . . .*

For Shepard, that did it. "Never mind," he told the officious clerk. "Here, you can have your manuals back."

"I beg your pardon . . ."

"I won't be needing them. I changed my mind."

Shepard trudged across the parking lot. He got in his car and drove back to the Financially Troubled Pan American. He felt like a convict who had just declined a pardon. *That was really dumb*, he told himself. *Why did you do that? I don't know. Because it felt good, I guess. . . .*

Les McDivitt, a 747 captain, summed it up for the stay-behinds: "I started out in this business wearing a white hat. I'll finish up wearing a white hat."

It was like breaking up a family. Twenty and more years they had been together at the Imperial Airline. They were new hires together, navigators, engineers, copilots, captains, Skygods-in-training.

No one was very happy about it. There were the inevitable jokes. The transfer was raising the average IQ of both airlines. Someone likened the exodus to a boat lift of refugees. They were applying for asylum at United.

Nobody wanted a farewell ceremony. It just looked too foreboding when guys like Rich Selph and most of the senior check pilots were jumping ship en masse. The departing pilots quietly came by to collect their final paychecks. They shook a few hands and mumbled stuff about good luck and keep your nose up and stay in touch and all that. And they were gone.

The Financially Troubled Pan Am set about reinventing itself. One happy manifestation of the United boat lift was that most of the transferees—the boat people—left from *the top of the seniority list*. That meant everyone left behind took a giant leap upward in seniority. Pan Am suddenly needed new pilots in every category. Longtime first officers were suddenly catapulted into the left seat. Flight engineers began their long-awaited training to be *real* pilots. It was an orgy of training and promotion unlike anything the company had ever seen.

And that wasn't enough. Pan Am needed *more* pilots. Recall notices went out to furloughed pilots. Soon, every furloughed Pan Am airman had been summoned back to the Imperial Airline.

Amazingly, even that wasn't enough. So rapid was Pan Am's reinvention of itself, so great was the need to fill cockpit seats, that the most stunning announcement the pilots had heard in twenty years came forth: Pan American would be hiring new pilots.

Hiring? The long drought was over. It meant the new hires weren't new hires anymore. Now they would have some real new hires to kick around.

CHAPTER TWENTY-SEVEN

WHITE KNIGHTS AND THE MAXIMUM SKYGOD

It beats working for a living.

That was what you heard when you ran into the recalled furlough-ees after their ten-year-plus exile. They showed up in the crew lounges, the hotels, the crew hangouts. They were wandering back to Pan Am like bedouins from the desert.

And everyone asked them the same question: "Why did you come back to Pan Am?"

It beats working for a living. It was part joke, part truth. For some, being furloughed had been a trauma like a hit-and-run. They had been rudely hurled out of the warmth of their airline job and onto the mean streets. And they weren't prepared. Until the day of the F word, they had lived their entire adult lives beneath an institutional umbrella—home, college, the military, then the airlines. Not one minute of their lives had been spent languishing in unemployment lines or perusing classified job ads.

Flying jobs out there were scarce. Another airline job—a *real* job with a company like American or Delta or United—had been out of the question. For one thing, the other airlines didn't want *old* guys, pilots like them who were pushing forty or more, and in any case they didn't want pilots furloughed from another company, because they figured you would jump ship and go back when your old airline recalled its furloughed pilots. It was a Catch-22. You couldn't *get* a job because you'd already *had* a job.

Bernie Giere was furloughed in 1976. With a young family at home, he hoped to find a job near where he lived, on Long Island. Weeks went by. Nothing turned up. There were no flying jobs, no slots available in the Air National Guard, not even *ground* jobs with an aviation company. Bill collectors were closing in. His savings were gone. So Giere took a job in which he had previous experience. It was the same thing he'd done during his summers between college semesters. He went to work for a construction company laying an extension of the Long Island Expressway. It was entry-level work, meaning he had to crawl down into the bottoms of the excavations where they were pumping out mud and silt before sinking the supports and pouring concrete for the expressway.

It wasn't fun. It was dirty, sometimes dangerous work. But it was a job, and it beat the hell out of *not* working.

The hardest part for Giere was when he was down there slinging mud and wrestling machinery—and he would hear a jet pass over. Through the mouth of the excavation he would glimpse a silhouette, flashing past like a subliminal image. For a minute Giere would gaze around him. He'd look at his mud-caked boots, at the wet cement and the jackhammers. He felt like a prisoner on a chain gang.

This went on for almost a year, the mud and the glimpses of airplanes. One day he got a call from the Air National Guard unit based at Suffolk County, on Long Island. "Bernie, we've got an open slot out here flying F-4s. You're next on the list. Do you want it?"

The F-4 Phantom was the fighter he had flown on active duty with Air Force. You didn't make a lot of money flying in the Guard, scarcely more than construction work. But it was *flying*.

Giere thought it over—for less than a microsecond. He had seen enough subliminal images from the excavations. He threw his mud-caked boots away.

Some of the furloughees found jobs with the nonscheds—fly-by-night charter operators with cast-off Boeing 707s and Douglas DC-8s—hauling freight and cattle and produce up from Latin America and out to the Middle East. The pay was lousy. The airplanes had peeling paint and anemic engines.

But the furloughees grabbed up the nonsched jobs, when they

could get them. It was flying. And it kept some of the bills paid until
. . . *the recall.*

Someday there *had* to be a recall. The first Pan Am furloughees
had hit the street in 1969. Another gaggle, several hundred strong,
joined them in 1976.

Five years went by. For some, ten. It couldn't go on forever, they
told themselves. Someday Pan Am would *have* to require more pilots.
In 1979 came deregulation. The furloughees checked their mail for the
recall notice. *Now* Pan Am, after all these years, would be expanding
in the deregulated domestic market. Pan Am would *have* to recall the
new pilots it would need.

Then came the nastiest shock the furloughees had received since
their first furlough notices. Pan Am was buying *National Airlines.* It
was freaking unbelievable! And with the purchase, *Pan Am was taking
aboard all the National pilots.* Pan Am didn't need the furloughees.

So the furlough went on, like an endless drought. Five more years.
Six. Seven. Not until 1986 did Pan Am start calling back the pilots it
had furloughed more than a decade before.

They were changed. Gone was the fighter pilot swagger, the clear-
eyed optimism of the new-hire days—"Sure, in no time we'll be flying
747s and new Lockheeds and SSTs and . . ."

Now they were glad to be on the payroll. Never mind all the
flimflammery about supersonic flight and new airplanes and how
quickly they would be captains. It was enough just being in the cockpit, sitting sideways in the flight engineer's seat of a beat-up 727.

They wore reading glasses and combed their graying hair in peculiar ways to cover the bald spots. They all had stories. Some had
established successful new careers. They were coming back to Pan Am
because during all those years they thought they were *missing* something. Flying was something they loved.

Some came back because things hadn't gone so well for them out
there. They had tried selling insurance and used cars. Some had built
houses. A few, like Bernie Giere, had done construction work. Flying
for Pan Am, even on the bottom of the seniority list, was still a hell
of a good job. *It beats working for a living. . . .*

Some didn't come back. Denny Smith had always been interested
in politics. While he was furloughed he ran for office in his home state
of Oregon. When he received his recall notice from Pan Am, he re-

spectfully declined. Congressman Smith already had a full-time job serving his district in the U.S. House of Representatives.

Dave North didn't come back. North was a Naval Academy graduate with a master's degree and four hundred carrier landings. When Pan Am furloughed him, he didn't find a flying job, but he found a job *writing* about flying. He went to work as a correspondent for the McGraw-Hill publication *Aviation Week*. Within a few years he had progressed upward through the editorial hierarchy, serving as an editor, then a bureau chief, then managing editor of the magazine. And that was where he intended to stay.

Marty Shugrue didn't come back either, at least as a pilot. Shugrue had never actually left Pan Am. He had spent his furlough years in Pan Am management, ascending the corporate ladder—all the way to the top rung. Shugrue was now Pan Am's vice-chairman and chief operating officer.

Many, like Kurt Axelsson, returned because they wanted to see what they had been missing. Axelsson came from a family of New Jersey fishermen. When he was furloughed he went back to Cape May, where he had grown up. He and his wife and his kids established a restaurant, working twelve-hour days, seven days a week, for ten years. Now their restaurant, the Blue Claw, made more money in a summer month than he could earn in a year flying for an airline. Now Kurt Axelsson was tired of the hard grind. It was time to do something that was fun.

Marc Born ran a successful executive jet charter business. When he was recalled by Pan Am, he "retired" from his business. "I was fed up with having a phone stuck in my ear eight hours a day," he said. "Flying is more civilized."

Several pilots, like Gus Littlefield and Mike Pipkin, went back to school and earned law degrees. But that wasn't wholly satisfying either. "I'm glad I did it," said an attorney-pilot. "I'm more glad I'm done with it. What the world needs is good pilots, not more lawyers."

Everyone was back who wanted to be back. Pan Am even had new hires—*real* new hires—bright-faced young men and something *very* different—*women*—in the cockpit.

But nobody was kidding himself. Things were not as they used to be at the old Imperial Airline. Not only was the Pacific gone, so was all the high-flying talk about SSTs and the moon. Pan Am was in a survival mode. There were even hushed whispers about . . . *Tango Uniform.*

You heard it a lot around the crew rooms these days. It was an old military euphemism, exported to the airlines. Tango Uniform was radio-phonetic pronunciation for the letters TU. It stood for *tits up.* In normal usage it meant flat-on-your-back dead. Defunct. Moribund. Inert. Inoperative. When your radio quit, or your engine stopped, or your lights went out, they were Tango Uniform.

Airlines could go Tango Uniform. Like Braniff. Like Air Florida. Now they were talking about . . . of all things . . . Pan Am! The old Imperial Airline . . . Tango Uniform.

In the wake of the great fratricidal strike and the loss of the Pacific, the specter of Tango Uniform preyed on the thoughts of the pilots. It made them want a less warlike way of conducting employee-management business.

Jim MacQuarrie, the bellicose chairman of the pilots' union, was replaced. Into his job came a union leader of a different stripe. Errol Johnstad was articulate, in his early forties, and possessed of an appetite for politics. Johnstad's real skill was to stand in front of gatherings, as he had during the strike, and whip them into a bug-eyed, foot-stomping frenzy.

Most pilots who held union jobs saw the work as a sort of civic duty, like serving on the town council. It gave them the feeling, however fleeting, that they had some control of their destinies. It was a tiny measure of real Skygodly power.

And so it was with Johnstad, only more so. Beneath the smiling, conciliatory exterior, Johnstad was hungry for power. *Real* power. Running the union was okay, but that was small potatoes in his greater vision. From the union chairmanship at Pan Am, Johnstad saw himself ascending to the presidency of the national ALPA organization. Or, better yet, to an office in airline upper management. Even better, a vice presidency at Pan Am. Or even better. Johnstad aspired to be nothing less than a Maximum Skygod.

He was a farm kid from Wisconsin who had earned scores of merit badges, become an Eagle Scout, been class president, done his hometown proud by graduating from the university, then gone on to win

his Air Force wings. He had even become a pilot for Pan American
World Airways. Errol was the kind of kid that the folks back home
liked to have give talks at Kiwanis Club lunches.

But being a Maximum Skygod, for Johnstad, involved more than
honors and offices. Johnstad had a list that he liked to show his colleagues of feats that he intended to accomplish in his lifetime. Most
of the feats were macho undertakings. For reasons not even he understood, Johnstad was driven to hang his carcass far out over the
edge of the Great Abyss. To satisfy that compulsion, he took up sky
diving. And he took a course in sports car racing. And he pursued
sport aerobatics. And then he became obsessed with air racing. He
went so far as to buy a Formula I race plane and in 1986 entered the
national air races at Reno. To everyone's astonishment except his own,
he won.

Errol Johnstad wasn't at all like his predecessor, Jim MacQuarrie,
whose inclination was to punch the other guy's lights out. Johnstad
was more cerebral. As union chairman he did things like retain a psychology clinic to aid stress-impaired pilots. He introduced computers
to the union office. He dragged his pilots into the information age by
hooking them up to an electronic bulletin board.

And he preached to his flock.

"*We* are Pan Am," he told the flock. "And we must save our-
selves." By *we* he meant the pilots, and by extrapolation, all the employees. By Johnstad's definition, the *employees* were the substance of
Pan American World Airways, not the stockholders, not the board of
directors, and certainly not the tall Texan, Ed Acker, for whom Pan
Am was a third and probably not last airline.

We are Pan Am. It was a novel idea. It struck a chord in the
disgruntled grunts at Pan Am. Who in the company had more to gain
or lose than they did? Who else but them, the employees, had their
careers, their futures, their dreams invested in the airline?

And so with Johnstad and the pilots' union leading, the employees
took on the task of saving themselves. Their avowed mission was to
find a "white knight," a person or entity that would take over Pan
Am. As an enticement for the investor, Johnstad let it be known that
the pilots were willing to consider substantial pay concessions to make

Pan Am an attractive property. To that end the coalition of Pan Am unions—the Joint Labor Council—retained as its advisers the investment firm of Drexel Burnham Lambert, Inc., and the law firm of Skadden, Arps, Slate, Meagher & Flom, specialists in corporate mergers.

Throughout 1987 the search went on for a white knight. The first serious candidate *was* a knight, a real one named Sir James Goldsmith, who seemed interested enough to sit down with the Pan Am unions and talk business. In the proposed deal, Sir James would invest at least $100 million in Pan Am. For their part, the unions would agree to pay concessions of about $180 million, for which they were to receive an increased equity in the airline.

The Goldsmith deal made a brief splash in the business news, running up the price of Pan Am stock nearly 40 cents and making it the sixth most active issue in trading that day.

Nothing more happened. Goldsmith lost interest. Quietly, the white knight sheathed his umbrella and went home.

The next knight rode into town in October 1987. He was the Los Angeles high roller Kirk Kerkorian, who owned, among other properties, MGM Grand. Since August, when he had been recruited by the unions' adviser firm, Drexel Burnham, Kerkorian had a contract with Pan Am for an exclusive right to review the airline's books. What he had seen interested him enough that he was now willing to make an offer. He wanted to spin off the airline unit from the parent Pan Am Corporation and take over total management of the airline. The only other properties of consequence still living with its parent, Pan Am Corporation, were the Northeast Shuttle, which Acker started in late 1986; Pan Am Express, the little Northeast commuter acquired in 1987; and the aviation services subsidiary, Pan Am World Services.

As with the Goldsmith deal, the unions would agree to large wage concessions in exchange for Kerkorian's investment. The amount of Kerkorian's investment depended on the size of the concessions.

There was a kicker to the deal, a condition attached to the labor concessions: *Acker had to go.* The Kerkorian group would bring in its own team to take over management of the airline.

Whether or not this prospect influenced Acker's thinking was not revealed in the announcement of November 13, 1987, in the *Wall Street Journal*. Pan Am had to turn the deal down, Acker said, because "the proposal is too highly conditional in many important respects. . . ."

What Acker meant was, Kerkorian was trying to buy controlling interest in the airline with contingency financing that might or might not materialize. Kirk Kerkorian's offer was mostly smoke and mirrors.

Another white knight had come and gone. But before the Kerkorian troupe had left the city limits, yet another knight appeared, this one in the unlikely form of Towers Financial Corporation Towers was a New York debt-collection agency. No one was taking it seriously. It paraded a list of "consultants" that included Edward Nixon, a geologist and brother of the deposed President; the former and also deposed Attorney General John Mitchell; and former Federal Reserve chairman Paul Volcker, who vehemently denied any connection with Towers, as did the firm of Paine Webber, which disputed the report that it was representing Towers in a Pan Am acquisition.

The Towers team, on close inspection, appeared neither white nor even knightly.

And then came a new player in the game: Jay A. Pritzsker, who controlled Braniff Inc., a resurrected shell of the once-mighty airline that had gone Tango Uniform in 1982. Pritzsker had become convinced that the Financially Troubled Pan Am would dovetail nicely with the similarly troubled Braniff, which he was managing under Chapter Eleven of the bankruptcy code.

Unlike the Towers group, which was still trying to put together an investment package, Pritzsker clearly had the backing. The union coalition was taking him seriously, though what Pritzsker wanted from it was steep—$200 million worth of pay concessions annually over three years, for which he would give them a 20 percent equity in the merged company.

All this took place in the autumn of 1987, the season of the white knights. And out in the high desert of Reno, Nevada, it was again the season for the national air races.

Captain Errol Johnstad, Maximum Skygod-in-Waiting, had sometimes wondered how he would handle himself and his race plane if the engine actually *quit*. But it was one of those calamities you didn't let yourself think about, not too much. In air racing it was better not to dwell on calamity. You just did what you had to do when the time came. Anyway, engine failures in real life happened so rarely they were hardly worth considering. So Johnstad put the possibility out of his mind. There were other things to consider.

As he settled himself into the sleek-winged little race plane, Johnstad's pulse rate accelerated another twenty beats. He could see the wind sock snapping and the sagebrush bending in the twenty-five-knot gusting winds. It was still morning, but heat waves shimmered from the concrete. Johnstad knew it was going to be hellishly rough out there when he went skimming along the floor of the desert at two hundred miles an hour.

This was supposed to be a practice session, to get a feel for the course. He would just fly a few laps around the circuit to learn the location of the turn pylons and to acclimate to the spine-jolting turbulence that was gathering over the high desert.

He took off, and . . . *holy shit* . . . sure enough, no question about it, it was *rough* out there. The little race plane slammed through the bumpy air like a dune buggy on a washboard. It was all Johnstad could do to keep his eyes focused on the rapidly passing terrain outside. Inside, the instrument panel jiggled so hard the gauges were blurred.

He flew one lap, hugging the ground and fighting the bumps. Then another. And another. On the fourth lap the event so rare in real life that Johnstad had deliberately banished its very likelihood from his conscious thoughts . . . happened.

The howling 0-200 Continental engine delivered one great retching, gasping, gulping noise.

And then nothing. Utter dreadful silence.

The adrenaline level in Johnstad's body shot through the saturation point. He yanked on the stick, hauling the race plane's nose up . . . up . . . all the way up to the vertical . . . soaring way up above the airport and the high desert . . . losing airspeed rapidly . . .

The idea—it was only an infinitesimal microbe of an idea in Johnstad's adrenaline-charged brain—was to slow the airplane so that the propeller would stop rotating in the windstream, which would give the airplane a longer gliding range. It wasn't a great idea, all things considered, but it happened to be the *only* idea Johnstad could come up with.

The propeller did stop. And immediately thereafter the airplane ran out of airspeed. It fell off on a wing and commenced *a spin* back toward the earth.

After a turn-and-a-half spin, Johnstad regained control. Now the airplane was gliding normally. All he had to do was land.

But where was the damn airport? It was directly beneath him, but the effects of a hard vertical climb, an inadvertent spin, and several gallons of adrenaline had skewed Johnstad's internal gyros. His once-formidable brain had shrunk to the size of a pea.

There was the runway. But, Christ, he was going *away* from it!

A hard turn back. He was on a sort of base leg now. He could still make the runway. But the wind, gusting more violently than ever, was blowing him away.

Turn tighter. Johnstad's energies fixated on the slab of concrete that was trying to slip away from him.

Turn tighter still. He yanked back more on the stick. The powerless airplane responded. It shuddered once, then snapped wing downward into another spin.

Johnstad saw the sagebrush and gullies whirling toward him, filling up his windscreen. The little racer hit the floor of the high desert with the force of a freight train.

They stood around the chapel at Kennedy a few days later, pilots, union types, company executives, eulogizing the late Errol Johnstad. It was an overflow crowd. Vice-Chairman Marty Shugrue added his own eulogy. He praised Johnstad, calling him "a formidable adversary," meaning that the union leader had caused him fits at the bargaining table. But that, of course, was what union leaders were supposed to do.

Now that Johnstad was departed, and having managed it in a flamboyant, show-stopping manner, it seemed that perhaps he *had* been larger than life. It was, everyone had to admit, a hell of a finale. As exits go, it was almost . . . *Skygodly.*

CHAPTER TWENTY-EIGHT

MISTER NICE GUY

There's no way Acker and Shugrue can work together after this. One will have to go.

—A PAN AMERICAN WORLD AIRWAYS DIRECTOR,
December 7, 1987

Never had such a thing happened. Never in the long and glorious history of Pan American World Airways had there been a *fistfight* in the boardroom. It was unthinkable, a brawl in the imperial court of Juan Trippe and the blue-blooded Skygods.

But that's what it was coming to.

The chairman of the board was on his feet. He was red-in-the-face, spittle-dripping, lip-curling *furious*. C. Edward Acker was so enraged his finger trembled when he aimed it at the vice-chairman. "Shugrue is trying to sabotage the Braniff deal!"

Which was a true statement. And Marty Shugrue was just as nostril-flaring, pop-eyed furious as the chairman. He had placed himself in vehement opposition to a sellout to Jay Pritzker, and over that issue the two top executives of the Financially Troubled Pan American were about to punch out each other's lights.

Astonished, the directors watched the two glowering executives. Someone had the sense to step between them. Another director moved that the meeting adjourn until things cooled down.

Acker thought he nearly had a deal with Pritzker and the Braniff crowd. In his view, Braniff represented the best and last hope for Pan Am to salvage something from its current nosedive. Jay Pritzker wanted to spin the airline off from the Pan Am Corporation, leaving the parent company—and Acker—with the Pan Am Shuttle and Pan Am Express. The key to the deal, however, was pay concessions from the airline's labor coalition amounting to $200 million. This meant that the employees, by giving up part of their wages, would be partly subsidizing the buyout of the airline for the new owner. In exchange, Pritzker was giving the unions assurances of no layoffs and representation on the Braniff board.

Pay concessions. For months Acker himself had been sparring with the unions over that very issue. Pan Am needed payroll givebacks.

The key to getting the concessions was, as usual, the pilots. The pilots were the most conspicuous and the most highly paid group in the labor coalition. Acker knew he had not one hope in hell of extracting concessions from the unions unless the pilots ponied up their share first. The airline was nearing the point where they had to have it. No alternative. None except Tango Uniform.

It began the week before, when Shugrue put his job on the line. You didn't just throw a stink bomb into your boss's office and then expect to get patted on the back for your diligence.

After the dust had settled, some heads would roll. Shugrue figured that one of them would very likely be his. But, dammit, he knew the Pritzker deal *had* to be stopped. He couldn't stand on the sidelines and watch the airline get spun off to the oblivion of Braniff Fly-on-the-Cheap Airlines.

But there was another reason, even stronger and more abstract, that was compelling him to place his carcass on the line. Shugrue had been with Pan Am for nearly twenty years, longer than any other senior executive and certainly longer than C. Edward Acker, who was an itinerant airline manager. Pan Am was Shugrue's life. He had begun his career as a new-hire pilot—a Skygod-in-training—and then through the furlough and chaos of the seventies had clawed his way to the second-highest job in the Imperial Airline.

There was something faintly . . . *sinister-looking* about Marty Shugrue, with his slicked-back hair and riveting eyes and demonic expression. It gave you the feeling that you should be glad he wasn't mad at you.

"I fix things," Shugrue liked to say. "That's what I'm good at—fixing things." That's how Shugrue had ascended the pyramidal management structure at Pan Am, bottom to top. He was a guy who could fix things. Shugrue could conjure solutions to problems no one else had the guts to tackle. When the boss had a problem that needed fixing, he learned that he could give it to Marty Shugrue.

Shugrue's skill at fixing things had gotten him all the way to the summit. Officially, he was Pan Am's chief operating officer. *Maximum Skygod.*

Now he was about to step off. He was trying to wreck the chairman's carefully wrought merger plan. Shugrue guessed that his efforts would produce roughly the same effect as ramming a lighted cigar up a bull's rectum.

But he was running out of time. The board was scheduled to meet on Tuesday, when Chairman Acker would present the details of the Pritzker deal. Jay Pritzker himself would be there to explain how the deal would work, that it was contingent on the unions' agreeing to Pritzker's requirement of $200 million in concessions.

Shugrue wanted to put together a cost-savings plan of his own to present to the board. So he dispatched vice presidents Bob Gould and Ray Grebey to negotiate with the pilots' union.

Gould and Grebey were a good-guy-bad-guy team. Gould could talk to the pilots because he *was* a pilot. He, in fact, had been the union chairman only three years before. But Ray Grebey was another matter. Since the 1985 strike, the very mention of C. Raymond Grebey in a union office produced epithets that peeled paint and shattered glass.

All Monday night, Grebey and Gould bargained—good guy, bad guy—with the deadline of Acker's board meeting the next day hanging over their heads. Twenty minutes before the board meeting was to convene, they had an agreement with the pilots. They delivered it to Shugrue.

The meeting convened. The chairman brought up the Pritzker proposal. And then Marty Shugrue cleared his throat and put his bombshell on the table. He told the directors that he had a cost-savings agreement from the pilots that amounted to $55 million. When the other unions came aboard it would net a total savings of $180 million. They didn't need Jay Pritzker and Braniff.

The board members were stunned. All heads turned toward Chairman Acker, to observe his reaction.

It was just as Shugrue expected—the same effect as a lighted cigar up a bull's rectum. . . .

The forty-sixth floor divided itself into Acker backers and Shugrue backers. The fighting went public, with the press reporting the comments of both sides.

"Here's Acker trying to put together a *must* deal with Braniff, and some goddam staffers come in at the last minute with a pilots' agreement that aims to sabotage the Braniff deal," an Acker backer told the *Wall Street Journal*.

Of course, replied the Shugrue camp. "Slicing up Pan Am's operations doesn't make any sense. The Braniff deal is lousy."

On the surface, the infighting appeared to revolve around the value of the concessions offered by the pilots. Acker insisted that the cost saving didn't add up to $55 million, that it was more like $42 million. Shugrue said it did, and offered an outside accounting firm's audit to prove it.

But the *real* dispute, as everyone knew, was more a gut issue. Ed Acker wanted to merge with Braniff. Marty Shugrue wanted to keep Pan Am independent. It was an issue of life or death of the Imperial Airline. In such a dispute, there could be no middle ground.

The board of directors observed the feud with growing horror. It was like watching their own generals slug it out while the enemy was torching the camp. "This just can't go on," an executive told the press.

And so it didn't. In the first week of the new year, 1988, Pan Am's labor coalition announced that the unions were ready to concede $180 million in givebacks—but for a price: new management. They wanted Ed Acker's head.

By now the board was of a similar mind. Not only were the directors appalled at the schism in the executive ranks, they had grown steadily dissatisfied with the tall Texan's management of the airline. In particular they had become critical of Acker's 1986 creation of the Northeast Shuttle, the Pan Am commuter operation based in the old marine terminal at La Guardia Airport. The shuttle operated like a separate airline, competing with the Eastern Shuttle hauling commuters between Boston, New York, and Washington. Acker had spent $150 million of the proceeds from the Pacific sale on the shuttle, and though the operation was breaking even, it didn't feed passengers to Pan Am's overseas routes. The $150 million, the board believed, should have gone into a *real* domestic system—a route network connecting America's heartland to Pan Am's international hubs.

That week the word leaked out to the street: *Pan Am was looking for a new chairman.*

Ed Acker, the Texas deal-maker, was on his way out.

And not just Acker. It was a package deal. The chief operating officer went with the chairman. Marty Shugrue's career at the Imperial Airline was over too.

The *Titanic* was again looking for a captain. The search was led by the same trio of powerful directors who, seven years earlier, had engineered the replacement of General Seawell: Jack Parker, former vice-chairman of GE; Donald Kendall, former chairman of PepsiCo; and William Coleman, a former Transportation Department secretary.

To replace Shugrue as chief operating officer, heading the airline's day-to-day operations, the board settled on Hans Mirka, fifty-one, a fast-rising star in the business who had come to Pan Am four years before from American Airlines and who was currently a senior vice president of field sales and services.

Finding a new CEO—the next in the lineage of Imperial Sky-gods—was not so easy. The leading candidate for a while was the ex-chief of Piedmont Airlines, William R. Howard. But Howard was bound to a contract with the pilots of United Airlines, whom he was representing in their bid to take over United. There was brief talk of drafting Paul Sheeline, a longtime director who had formerly headed the Intercontinental Hotel subsidiary. Neither Howard nor Sheeline was inclined to accept.

After the internecine warring of the Acker years, what the Imperial Airline needed, everyone agreed, was someone with the persuasive clout to bring them all—unions, managers, executives—together. Someone dynamic enough to rebuild what had been lost. Someone with the same vision and guts Juan Trippe had possessed when he *built* the airline.

In short, Pan American needed a *Skygod*.

On January 20, 1988, the board announced that it had found its man. And when it revealed his name, a single collective question reverberated around the offices and crew rooms and work shops of Pan American.

Who?

"He's a nice guy."

That's what you heard when people talked about Tom Plaskett. *A nice guy.*

How strange it sounded, referring as they were to the chairman of the board of Pan American. *Pan Am!* Over the decades, Pan Am's CEOs had been called many things, but never *nice guy*.

In the past, throughout Pan Am's years of decline, it had been easy, fashionable even, for the pilots to hate the chief executive, especially someone like General Bill Seawell. And the Cold War gladiator with the ice-blue eyes had returned their contempt in full measure. Seawell always maintained that level of arrogance that made him so satisfyingly hatable.

And then it became just as easy for them to hate Ed Acker, because the Texas huckster had promised them things, and then instead of delivering, had dismembered their airline. And Ed Acker, in his high-rolling style, was also arrogant.

Ah, the *arrogance!* The *Skygodly loftiness*—the champagne, the tantrums, the much-loved rumors of looting and plunder. Both Seawell and Acker had reigned over the Imperial Airline like potentates of a medium-sized monarchy—and the grunts loved it because they could hate them for it.

Now they had Mister Nice Guy. No icy-blue-eyed tantrums, no hucksterism, no arrogance. Here was a bland-faced little guy who was telling them to their face that things weren't looking so good at Financially Troubled Pan Am, that he was going to do his best, whatever that was, to turn it around. But he wouldn't promise them the moon. The moon days were over.

He was a little guy, diminutive both in stature and in manner. Standing in a room full of six-footers, Tom Plaskett looked like a kewpie doll in a business suit. Roundish of face, bland of expression, he stood there and recited his numbers, dismal as they were, and took hits from the audience, who had just agreed to pay $180 million to get rid of Ed Acker.

"Mr. Plaskett, tell us why you and the other top executives aren't taking pay cuts just as we are."

He didn't even blink. "Because Pan Am needs the best talent it can recruit right now," he said. "We can't recruit good managers unless we offer attractive salaries."

Whaaaat? That answer made no one particularly happy. But how could they argue with it? At least the man wasn't dodging and weaving.

Plaskett brought with him decent, if not impressive, credentials. He had a Harvard M.B.A. and had begun his career as an engineer at GM. He had served a term at American Airlines, where he earned recognition for creating the first frequent-flier program. He played classical piano. He was a self-avowed computer freak who carried a laptop with him wherever he traveled. He disdained strong drink and language. When Tom Plaskett became irate, truly *seething,* he would let fly a salty epithet like "Oh, *poop.*"

With his engineer's roots, Plaskett was known as a detail-oriented manager, methodical perhaps to a fault, disinclined to shoot from the hip. And that, of course, suited the Pan Am staffers just fine, because for the past seven years they had worked for the king of the hip shots, Ed Acker.

Plaskett's sole experience as an airline chief executive was at Continental Airlines. Frank Lorenzo had hired him for the top job, then decided that Plaskett was too plodding, too unflamboyant for his taste, and summarily fired him. But no one was holding that against Plaskett. In the stormy world of deregulation, being fired by Frank Lorenzo was like winning a public service medal.

Chairman Plaskett put together a fresh management team. As the new senior vice president, operations, he named Bob Gould, the pilot who had first represented the labor coalition on the board of directors, and who had been drafted by Marty Shugrue as a vice president for planning.

Gould was a young man in a hurry. Seven years ago he had been a junior Pan Am first officer. Now he was in charge of *all* Pan Am operations—flight ops, maintenance, in-flight service, dispatch—everything that had to do with how Pan Am moved airplanes.

One of Gould's first acts was to shake the whole foundation of the flight operations department. He fired the vice president of flight operations, the airline's chief pilot—an avuncular, highly experienced manager named Jim Duncan. And he replaced him with a bellicose union officer named Dan Affourtit.

The pilots were furious. Duncan fired? Duncan was one of the few managerial pilots the line pilots trusted. Duncan was one of them, everyone said. Duncan would stick up for his troops.

Now he was replaced by a union hack.

Until then the pilots had believed that Bob Gould, one of their own, was endowed with a Skygodlike judgment. No more. Gould's brain had apparently turned to toast.

Gould had a specific purpose in mind. He had witnessed previous "concessionary" contracts. The pilots would agree to change the scheduling and duty limit rules in their contract so that the company would gain a specified dollar savings. It never worked that way. Somehow all the little "productivity" changes were never fully implemented. Too much slipped through the cracks. A $50 million contract concession never yielded half that much.

Which was why Gould hired Dan Affourtit. It amounted to hiring your adversary to tell you what you were doing wrong. As a union representative who had *negotiated* contract givebacks, Affourtit understood the nuances of the new contract better than anyone. Gould gave Affourtit his orders: *Get our money's worth out of this contract.* Squeeze the pilots' agreement like a wet chamois.

Gould figured they had a year. Two at the most. Pan Am had to extract full value from the employee contract concessions quickly, or the game was up. Tango Uniform.

More heads rolled. Most of them were experienced managers who had been around flight operations for years. They were mostly replaced with former union officials.

And that troubled the line pilots, both pro- and anti-union. Despite its financial troubles, Pan Am had earned one of the most enviable operational records in the business. The old appellation "the world's most experienced airline" meant something, because over the years Pan Am's checklists, procedures, manuals, and flight-training curriculum had set the industry standard. And the standard had been maintained by a succession of professional managers like Duncan and his lieutenants.

Now what? There were predictions of disaster. What did these union hacks know about flight operations? To those with clear recollections of the Great Strike, it seemed a variation on an old theme: The monkeys were running the zoo. This time the monkeys were from the union. Striking pilots who had strived to bring the company to its knees during the labor war were now striving to resuscitate it.

It did seem peculiar, but after a while people stopped thinking about it. Pan Am wasn't flying airplanes into the ground. There were no headline-making breaches of safety. Nothing changed.

As the Financially Troubled Pan Am lurched through 1988, good news came in strange forms.

The *Wall Street Journal* confidently reported that the airline would have "a much narrower loss in 1988 than in 1987," which provoked minor celebrations at Pan Am. Hell, what else did they have to celebrate? Sure, they were still losing money by the shipload, but—*hallelujah!*—not as many shiploads as before.

And then Chairman Plaskett told the business press he expected the airline "to have a modest operating profit this year."

Which triggered serious celebration. Profit? Could it be? It was almost more than the dispirited, pay-reduced grunts dared let themselves imagine.

Much of the previous two years' monumental losses had been attributed to terrorism—the negative traffic effects of a TWA hijacking in the Mediterranean, and a terrorist takeover of a Pan Am 747 in Karachi, which was climaxed by a bloody shootout. Overseas passengers stayed away from Pan Am in droves.

Now they were coming back. The threat of terrorism was fading from the public consciousness. The number of summer travelers to

Europe had risen by 30 percent. Pan Am's share of the North Atlantic market was actually growing—from 13.5 percent in 1986 to a current 16.7 percent. The airline was embarked on a refurbishing program for its flagships, the 747s. Plans were announced to hire an additional eleven hundred flight attendants.

Small gains, maybe. But in them were the minuscule seeds of a miracle. It was beginning to look as though the old Imperial Airline was turning itself around. Pan Am just might make it into the next century after all . . . unless, of course, something unforeseen, something unthinkable, happened.

And then four days before Christmas, 1988, something did happen. Something unthinkable.

CHAPTER TWENTY-NINE

A VILLAGE IN SCOTLAND

It was the day the heart of Pan American died.
—A PAN AM PILOT

Some things never changed. Captain Jim MacQuarrie was exasperated. Here they were, ready to push back from the gate at six o'clock in the evening—exactly on time—but *still* they were going to be late. Out there on the blue-lighted taxiways, MacQuarrie could see the airplanes with the anticollision beacons winking, backed up like cattle in a chute. It was a classic Heathrow winter evening. Too many departures in too short a time.

In his mid-fifties now, MacQuarrie was becoming something of a curmudgeon. He liked to bitch about things—the delays and the beat-up airplanes and the mush-witted executives that he thought were running the airline into the toilet. But for MacQuarrie the bitching was mostly a reflexive activity. Hell, it was his *duty* to bitch. *Somebody* had to keep the jerks on the forty-sixth floor honest, and it might as well be him. For nearly a decade MacQuarrie had been a mover in the Air Line Pilots Association. It was MacQuarrie who, as chairman of the union, had led the pilots into the Great Strike of 1985.

All that was behind him now. All except the bitching. He was out of union work, content to enjoy his job as a 747 captain. MacQuarrie was senior enough to fly to the destinations of his choice, which, for him, meant London. He didn't care about Rio or Delhi or Moscow. London was civilized. In London they spoke English, served decent beer, and didn't honk their horns in traffic. He liked that.

And as a senior captain, MacQuarrie could pick his time off. After this trip he would be home in New Hampshire spending the Christmas holidays with his family.

People liked Jim MacQuarrie. Once you knew him, you could see behind the curmudgeonly bitching and tough-guy role-playing. MacQuarrie had a twinkle in his eye.

The truth was, he enjoyed the union-versus-management scrapping. It was good fun. It was a game where you got into the ring with the other guy and you slapped each other around awhile. Then you shook hands and repaired down the street to knock back a few.

And MacQuarrie's bitching also concealed his true feeling about Pan Am. As much as anyone, he *wanted* the old Imperial Airline to make it. He liked to say, not too discreetly, that if the morons in management would just get their shit together, the airline could be great again. Like all the old new hires of the sixties, MacQuarrie remembered the lofty talk . . . *Congratulations, gentlemen, you're going to be SST captains* . . . the rich legacy of the Clippers . . . the reservation list for Pan Am's first commercial moon flights . . .

Well, maybe it hadn't worked out. But there was a new generation. MacQuarrie had a son, Mike, who had been a naval aviator and was now a Pan Am pilot himself—one of the *new* lineage of new hires. Maybe, just perhaps, *he* would be flying an SST.

Clipper Maid of the Seas was working its way in the queue toward runway 27R. When they were third in line for departure, MacQuarrie leaned back and told the flight engineer, Jerry Avritt, he could start the two inboard engines, which had been shut down to conserve fuel.

It had taken nearly half an hour to get there. Finally they were number one. "Clipper one-oh-three, cleared for takeoff on two-seven-right," said the tower controller.

MacQuarrie reached up and snapped on the landing lights, illuminating the concrete a hundred yards ahead. He eased the four throttles forward.

Weighing over 700,000 pounds—nearly her maximum weight—

the great ship lumbered down the darkened runway. Vortices of mist spiraled from her wingtips as *Clipper Maid of the Seas* lifted from the concrete and climbed into the sodden English sky. In less than a minute she was enveloped in the slate-gray murk.

It was the busiest time of a flight, the first half hour. Air traffic control kept them down at six thousand, under the inbound arrivals. After Burnham VOR, they were steered north. "Clipper one-oh-three, fly heading three-five-zero and climb to flight level one-two-zero."

That was better. They were on their way northward, toward Scotland, and climbing. A few minutes later they were cleared all the way up to 31,000.

MacQuarrie handled all these chores just as he had hundreds of times before. The jet leveled at its initial cruising altitude of 31,000 feet. Avritt, the flight engineer, was busy at his panel managing the fuel supply to the four thirsty Pratt & Whitney engines.

They checked in with the air traffic controller in Prestwick. "Good evening, Scottish. Clipper one-oh-three with you. We're level at three-one-zero."

"Good evening, Clipper one-oh-three," responded the controller. "Squawk zero-three-five-seven. Ident, please."

MacQuarrie inserted the transponder code—0357—and pushed the tiny "Ident" button on the control head. This would produce an image on the controller's radar screen identifying the Pan Am flight by its number and confirming its altitude of 31,000 feet.

Six miles below, invisible under the dank layer of cloud, lay Scotland. Through the undercast MacQuarrie could pick out the soft glow of the cities. They shimmered through the cloud like lamps under a blanket.

The clearance was to an airways position called Margo, in Scotland, then oceanward, directly toward fifty-nine degrees north by ten degrees west. They were bucking a headwind, a jet stream of over a hundred knots that howled down out of the Arctic, nearly on their nose.

Despite the torrent of high-altitude wind, the ride was smooth. *Clipper Maid of the Seas* was cruising the night sky as serenely as an ocean liner.

Jim MacQuarrie tilted back in his seat. His feet found their usual perch on the two rests at the bottom of the instrument panel. The busiest part of the flight—the hectic climb-out and postdeparture activity—was behind them. All the pilots had to do now was obtain their oceanic clearance and check it against their printed flight plan. Then they could relax and work on something important. Like dinner.

In the first-class cabin the flight attendants were already into the cocktail service. The first round of appetizers was on the way. That's what MacQuarrie liked about Flight 103. You left London at dinnertime, and it was still early evening when you landed at Kennedy. A very civilized schedule.

"Oceanic clearance, Jim."

"Okay, I'm listening."

On the second VHF radio, Shanwick Control was delivering Clipper 103's oceanic track across the North Atlantic. To preclude a misread clearance, both pilots monitored oceanic clearances.

The time was 7:03 P.M. The pilots were still copying the clearance. The unthinkable happened.

A loud *whump*—from somewhere below and behind the cockpit. A lurch. The sucking, ear-popping *whoosh* of an explosive decompression.

The hull of the pressurized jetliner split like a burst balloon. A maelstrom of fog and cushions and paper and luggage and bodies swept through the fuselage. As the cabin lights extinguished, there was a bewildering roar.

It took less than three seconds. *Clipper Maid of the Seas* was transformed from a colossus of the skies to a plummeting aggregation of scrap metal and human life.

A few lucky ones died in the violence of the airframe disintegration.

Most did not. They spent the last forty-six seconds of their lives trapped in the belly of a raging beast . . . whirling, twisting, plunging in darkness toward the earth . . . their screams lost in the vastness of the night sky.

It was a vision of hell.

Nothing in Bob Gould's years as a Marine Corps officer or as a Pan American pilot had prepared him for this. The stench of kerosene assailed his nostrils. A pall of smoke still rose from the torn hunks of metal that littered the landscape. As Gould slogged through the wet grass, the mud sucked at his shoes like soft cement.

The ghastliness was almost too surreal to register on the senses. Bodies lay in gardens, by the roadside, on rooftops. They hung in trees, their clothing fluttering in the dismal wind. They lay in the fields, half buried in the mud. Some were horribly dismembered. Some appeared to be unmarked, as if in a deep sleep.

In the center of the town was a crater thirty feet across. Gould walked to the edge of the great hole and peered inside. It was still smoldering, filled with fragments of the doomed jetliner. Nearby were three of the engines, planted vertically in the concrete.

The still-smoking crater was on the site of what had once been a house. It was the home of a family named Flannigan. Now the house was gone, and so were the Flannigans, every trace of them. They had been literally vaporized in the thirty-foot bubbling hellhole.

The village of Lockerbie had been visited by horror. One Scottish family rose that morning to find a handsome young man with blond curls lying in their front yard. There was no visible sign of injury, but the body was lifeless.

On the golf course north of town, the greenskeeper discovered corpses scattered fifty to a hundred yards apart on the fairways. They had tumbled from the sky like bales of laundry.

Outside the village, a farmer found his flock of sheep spooked and stampeded into a fenced corner of the field. One of his ewes, he discovered, had been killed by the falling body of a young woman.

Gould looked at a large section of the fuselage that was still intact. It was filled with debris and oddments of passenger's belongings—Christmas gifts, eyeglasses, shaving kits, driver's licenses, shoes, dolls. And corpses. The cabin looked to Gould as though it had been whirled in a devil's caldron.

When the bulletin came in on the night of December 21, 1988, that Pan Am's Flight 103 had inexplicably fallen from the sky, Gould assembled his team of maintenance and operations people and boarded Pan Am Flight 2 for London. From London they took a chartered light airplane to Scotland.

On the way, Gould had time to think. He already knew the names of the crew. There wasn't anyone in Pan American he had known better than Jim MacQuarrie. When Gould was the chairman of the pilot's union, his vice-chairman was MacQuarrie. And when he had vaulted the fence over into management, it was MacQuarrie who had succeeded him in the union job.

Gould and MacQuarrie. Their styles were as different as velvet and sandpaper. Gould, the Yale graduate, liked to keep union affairs on a businesslike, genteel level. MacQuarrie, more the street fighter, was apt to aim for the solar plexus. Together they made a formidable team. Even after they took opposite sides at the negotiating table, they remained fast friends.

It was raining in Lockerbie. The muck and mire of the soggy ground made it difficult to inspect the extensive crash site. There were six separate impact areas, including the one in the center of the village where eleven residents had been killed by the falling mass of metal.

Soldiers and constables and policemen were formed into search teams to comb the hills and forests and fields for articles from the wreck of Flight 103. The total search area amounted to 845 square miles of soggy, wooded, hilly Scottish terrain. In the jet stream at 31,000 feet, fragments from the disintegrated jetliner had scattered like chaff in a hurricane. Debris from the jetliner was turning up as far away as eighty miles from Lockerbie.

In an open meadow, looking like a piece of abstract sculpture, lay the nose section and cockpit of *Clipper Maid of the Mist*. The smoothly contoured bow of the jetliner had been neatly severed from the rest of the fuselage. At a glance it appeared to be an intact airframe component waiting to be joined to the fuselage.

Gould didn't want to see what was inside. He had to, he told himself. It was his job. So he took a deep breath and looked.

The interior was a jumble of debris. The throttles were jammed full forward. Trailing from them, fifty or more feet from the cockpit, were the cables that had once connected the throttles to the mighty Pratt & Whitney engines. Two crew members were inside. Gould could tell by the uniforms and insignia that both were pilots, the first officer and the flight engineer.

They walked on. Bodies lay in clusters across the open meadow. A few had been covered with tarpaulins. Most were not.

As Gould and one of his team, John Pagnotta, were walking along the impact path of the doomed jetliner, tracing the sequence of its collision with the Scottish countryside, Gould spotted what he had been dreading—and expecting—to find.

The body was partially covered by a tarpaulin. Someone had marked it "Captain." Partly visible beneath the tarp was the white uniform shirt with the four-striped insignia.

Gould stood there for a moment gazing down at the shape on the ground. He stooped to pull back the tarpaulin.

Pagnotta caught his arm. "Jesus, Bob, I wouldn't do that."

Gould drew another deep breath. He pulled back the tarp. For a long while he stood there, looking down at the lifeless body of his old friend Jim MacQuarrie.

Late that night, Gould latched the door in his hotel room. Except for a nap on the flight across the Atlantic, he had not slept for over twenty-four hours. He was bone-weary, chilled by the dismal wind, numbed by the daylong exposure to unbelievable horrors. He sat on the bed and stared at his mud-encrusted shoes. The leather soles were already rotting.

It would be the hardest thing he'd done all day. He picked up the telephone and called New Hampshire. Gould delivered the news that Jim MacQuarrie's wife had been waiting for. "I found him," Gould told her. "I found my friend."

How could this happen?

One of the tenets of accident investigation was that you didn't leap to conclusions. You methodically collected all the facts, without bias. Then you studied them. It was a very analytical process.

But the media weren't waiting for analyses. Already the press was offering speculation that *Clipper Maid of the Seas* had experienced an in-flight structural failure. Weren't Pan Am's 747s the oldest in the industry? CNN reported that of the 710 Boeing 747s constructed, *Clipper Maid of the Seas* was number fifteen. Her maintenance records contained a history of cracks, corrosion, one on-board fire, and an incident of smoke in the cabin.

Clipper Maid of the Seas had a phenomenal history: *72,000 service hours.* That placed her in a twilight zone far beyond what anyone knew about airframe flexing limits and metal fatigue. It amounted to fifteen hundred circumnavigations of the planet. Television news programs hosted experts who explained how such an old bird could literally come apart at the seams after so many years of service.

Such speculation was making the Pan Am team furious. For one thing, *Clipper Maid of the Seas* had just been through a hugely expensive six-month-long structural retrofit to qualify it for the CRAF, the Air Force's Civil Reserve Air Fleet. This particular 747, old as she was, possessed the strength of the Brooklyn Bridge. Gould and all his staff knew there was no way this airplane would have experienced a structural failure.

But here it was, smashed over the earth like a dropped watermelon. If not a structural failure, then what?

By the end of the first day, they suspected. By the end of the second day, they knew. The wreckage was yielding tiny, telltale clues. Bud Perry and Walt Winkler, Pan Am's maintenance executive, identified certain fragments of the fuselage that were charred—but not in the manner of an after-impact kerosene fire. They bore the residue of something that burned much faster than jet fuel. Shards of aluminum were ripped in a rose-petaled pattern that could only have come from a violent explosion.

It was a bomb.

But the Scots, who were officially in charge of the investigation, weren't yet ready to confirm such a conclusion. They wanted to be absolutely certain.

For four more days they delayed making a public announcement. Meanwhile each news program began with the same shot of the nose section of *Clipper Maid of the Seas* lying on its side in a Scottish meadow. CNN continued interviewing aviation experts. The experts pointed to schematics and cutaway drawings of the 747. They explained how the tired old bird had probably popped apart like a worn-out watch.

Not until the day after Christmas, nearly five days after the fall of Flight 103, did the truth come out. Flight 103 had not crashed because of a failure of her airframe. *Clipper Maid of the Seas* was destroyed by an explosive device stored in the forward cargo compartment. The

259 passengers and crew and the eleven people on the ground had been murdered.

The accident inquiry was now, additionally, a homicide investigation. No more airframe experts appeared on the news programs. They were replaced by experts on terrorism.

They had a memorial service for Jim MacQuarrie there in Lockerbie. According to his family's wishes, his remains were cremated.

The next day, Bob Gould checked in for his flight back to the United States. Under his arm he carried the box containing Jim MacQuarrie's ashes.

But he hadn't reckoned on British bureaucracy. As he stood red-eyed and drained at the departure counter at Heathrow Airport, clutching his box, he was confronted by a thin-haired, bespectacled customs agent. The agent raised both eyebrows. "See here," he said, "what do you think you're doing? You don't have permission to carry human remains out of the United Kingdom. You have to have authorization for that."

Gould stared at him. He couldn't believe this. After the spirit-numbing experience of Lockerbie, he was faced with a cement-headed obstructionist. Gould told them who he was and where he had been. He explained that he was carrying the ashes of the captain of Pan Am Flight 103 home to his family. He said that he had no intention, under any circumstances, of relinquishing custody of this box under his arm. It looked like a standoff that would quickly slip into a shouting match.

And then Gould witnessed a miracle.

The agent nodded curtly, and his bureaucratic eyebrows lowered. He conferred briefly with a colleague. And then, in one stroke, the agent sliced through half a millennium of Her Majesty's Royal Red Tape.

"Yes, sir," announced the agent. "Please accept our apologies. We wish you Godspeed and a swift journey."

Gould was on his way, box under his arm. Ten hours later, shivering in the New Hampshire night, he rang the doorbell of the MacQuarrie household.

*   *   *

In the shock and anger of Lockerbie, it was not surprising that nerves would be taut. A tabloid reporter was foolish enough to keep badgering one of the Pan Am team, a grizzled flight engineer. "Listen, sport, would you mind commenting on how this *accident* could have—"

A limit had been exceeded. The red-faced engineer whirled on the reporter. "Listen, asshole, quit calling this an *accident*. This was premeditated fucking murder. Do you understand?"

The reporter nodded agreeably, suddenly possessed of a clearer understanding. "Ah, yes, yes, I do. I think I get your meaning. . . ."

Now that they knew *what* had caused the fall of Flight 103, it was imperative to know precisely *how* such a heinous act had been committed. And by *whom*.

The investigators had delayed announcing the bomb evidence because they hoped to buy time. The saboteurs might make a mistake. They might leave a clue as to their identity if they thought the world didn't know it was a terrorist bombing.

It was a reasonable hope, but futile. The terrorists, whoever they were, had covered their tracks.

There was no shortage of suspects. Even before the bomb finding was announced, Scotland Yard's phones were ringing with calls from an assortment of loonies and extremist groups, all claiming credit for the fall of Flight 103. Psychics were phoning in to offer solutions to the crime.

It didn't take long, even before the forensic experts applied tests to the shredded metal, to figure out where the bomb had detonated. One fifty-foot section of the forward fuselage was missing from the assembled wreckage. A careful look at the severed nose and cockpit section showed that the nose and forward cabin had been neatly blown off the fuselage. The explosion had occurred in the forward baggage compartment, just behind the bulkhead connecting the nose section to the main cabin.

And that explained why no signal, not one sign of distress, had flashed down from Flight 103. The bomb had exploded next to the ship's main electronics bay, known as Station 41, the nerve center for the ships electrical, communications, and navigational equipment. In an instant, Flight 103's radios and radar transponder had been snuffed out. Down below, in the air traffic control center, the identifying blip on the radar screen had simply gone out like a failed bulb.

Forensic testing proved that the residue on certain shreds of metal came, in fact, from a Czech-made explosive substance called Semtex. The bomb had been contained in a Toshiba radio–cassette player, model RTF53D, which investigators determined had been transported in a Samsonite hard-sided suitcase. The weapon had been armed and detonated by a two-stop timer-barometer device that required both a specific cabin altitude and a certain elapsed time to blow up.

Which meant that the bombers hadn't intended to leave *any* evidence. Had Flight 103 not been delayed by the congested departure traffic at Heathrow Airport, the explosion would have occurred not over Scotland but farther along on the flight plan, over the North Atlantic. The true cause of the downing of Flight 103 might never have been learned.

The image was incessant: night after night on the evening news, the cockpit of *Clipper Maid of the Seas,* lying on its side in a Scottish meadow. Television viewers stared at the blue-and-white death capsule while the subliminal message etched itself into their consciousness: *Pan Am airplanes explode and crash. . . . The Doomsday Airline. . . . Fly Pan Am and you could end up as a bloated corpse in some foreign swamp. . . .*

Travelers stayed away in droves. Logic and loyalty and good sense had nothing to do with it. It was a gut reaction, an abhorrence of the televised images they had absorbed from Lockerbie. If you had to fly overseas, you'd best do it on KLM, or Lufthansa, or Swissair. Anyone. Any airline that didn't tempt terrorists.

Thus came the new year, 1989. The operating plan that Bob Gould had constructed was in place and working. The only trouble was, there were no passengers.

CHAPTER THIRTY

THE COYOTE'S LAST LEG

Did you hear about the new Tom Plaskett doll? You wind it
up and it does nothing for a year.
—*Joke reported in the* Wall Street Journal, *June 5, 1989*

You could stand in the back of a Pan Am jumbo jet, looking forward,
and see not a living, paying passenger. The cavernous passenger com-
partments of the 747s looked like abandoned warehouses.

The ghosts of Flight 103 were stalking the ticket counters. The
passenger loads that had begun, ever so haltingly, to pick up in 1988
vanished like the radar blip of *Clipper Maid of the Seas.*

Historically, Pan Am faced a cash crunch every winter during the
slack America-to-Europe tourist season. This year's shortfall amounted
to more than a crunch. Only by transferring its slots on previously
ordered Airbus A-320s to Braniff was Pan Am able to generate the
cash—$124 million—to meet its payroll at the beginning of 1989.

Worried employees were asking, "Why doesn't he do something?"

By *he* they meant, of course, the chairman. Granted, no one had
any particularly good ideas about *what* Tom Plaskett ought to be doing about Pan Am's condition. But they wanted *something* done.
Anything.

"I gave up a third of my wages and benefits," said an operations staffer, "for *this?* All we're doing is covering Plaskett's losses."

"Pan Am doesn't need a guy like Plaskett," declared a vice president from the Acker era. "What Pan Am needs now is a real fire-in-the-belly ass-kicker. And that ain't Tom Plaskett."

And that much seemed to be true: Tom Plaskett *didn't* have a fire in his belly. He was a corporate incarnation of Jimmy Carter. It was coming back to everyone now why he had been fired at Continental: Plaskett was too *slow-moving* for Frank Lorenzo's taste.

Then in June of 1989, plodding Tom Plaskett gave them all a huge surprise. He did something so uncharacteristic that people wondered if Mister Nice Guy might, in fact, have metamorphosed into a Skygod. It was a move so audacious even Juan Trippe would have been impressed.

Buy another airline?

When the news appeared in the business press that morning, Wall Street regarded it as a jolly good joke. The Financially Troubled Pan American? Here was an outfit out of money, burdened with debt, so strapped that it couldn't afford to buy a single new airplane, bidding to take over mighty Northwest Airlines.

Tom Plaskett formally presented Northwest with a takeover bid of $2.7 billion, which amounted to $110 per share of stock. And it was real money. Since April, Plaskett had been in marathon sessions with bankers and takeover strategists. Standing behind his bid were the likes of Bankers Trust, Morgan Guaranty Trust, Citicorp, and Prudential-Bache.

Wall Street stopped chuckling. *Hey, wait a minute . . . this looks real.* The caper was perhaps not so wacky after all. These were the eighties, the decade of the LBO and the corporate buccaneer. No one had ever accused Tom Plaskett of being a buccaneer, but here he was, throwing his weight around like a fire-breathing robber baron.

The reason the deal made sense—and the reason why the banks were willing to lend Plaskett the money—wasn't Pan Am's financial strength, which was appallingly nonexistent. Northwest itself was flush with cash and assets. Moreover, a computer analysis done by the banks showed that a merger of the two airlines would be a marriage made in heaven. According to the analysis, the merger would produce a total savings of more than $240 million annually, more than enough to make up for Pan Am's own shortfalls.

The trouble was, Pan Am wasn't the only player in the game. Northwest was a vulnerable takeover target, and other raiders were appearing on the horizon. And any such buyout would have to be approved by Northwest's board of directors, none of whom were jubilant about Pan Am's $883 million of debt and decrepit fleet of airplanes, including the oldest jumbos in the world.

But there was something appealing, if a bit quixotic, about the Pan Am bid. When overlaid with Pan Am's current structure, the Northwest system, particularly its Far East routes, presented a tantalizing facsimile of the old Imperial Airline. Even the cynical grunts in the Pan Am cockpits found themselves ruminating about the glory days they thought were behind them. By now, of course, they had been through too many such flights of fancy—white knights, would-be mergers—to get their hopes too high over this deal.

But still, in their secret hearts were the old dreams. *Imagine!* Pan Am, once again a heavyweight global carrier . . . it seemed too good to be true.

And, of course, it was.

For all Tom Plaskett's surprising boldness, Pan Am's hand simply wasn't strong enough. As romantically appealing as the Northwest–Pan Am marriage looked, this *was* the decade of the winner-take-all corporate predator. Such a predator was Alfred Checchi, a well-heeled takeover artist who plunked down a bid the Northwest directors decided they couldn't refuse. Al Checchi was the new owner of Northwest Airlines.

The disappointment settled like a pall of gloom over Pan Am. No one was blaming Plaskett for the failure, not even when it was divulged that he had spent some $23 million putting together the buyout package. Most of the grunts just shrugged and said, like a pilot in New York, "Hey, the little guy gave it a shot, didn't he? Better to go down kicking than to just roll over and die."

After the collapse of the Northwest initiative, there wasn't much more brave talk about Pan Am's "comeback." Even Plaskett was laying it on the line: Pan Am had one shot at survival—it had to sell, merge, or amalgamate with *somebody*.

With that assessment, Mister Nice Guy was redefining his role at Pan Am. He was not going to be the airline's savior. He was not a charismatic leader who would guide them back to glory. Tom Plaskett was just the bargaining agent.

Through it all, Plaskett was generally liked by the employees. He came around the crew rooms and employee lounges. He visited the cockpits on the shuttle to Washington. He listened to the employees' anxieties about the future.

You are correct, folks, he let them know. We are in deep financial effluvium. But we're in it together.

Oddly, that kind of siege mentality had a unifying effect among the workaday grunts. "Morale has never been higher," reported a flight attendants' union official. "It's the camaraderie you see when you're in the last lifeboat and you're bailing."

Another strange development was that *Pan Am was becoming a first-class operation.* Under Plaskett's administration, the airline improved its schedule performance, cleaned up its aging airplanes, renovated the terminals. The airline spent $31 million alone on the run-down Kennedy complex. Pan Am's abysmal on-time record, traditionally one of the worst in the industry, went from thirteenth to first place, flying over 80 percent of its flights on schedule. Broke or not, Pan Am was hauling more people across the Atlantic than any other airline, keeping its grip on 14 percent of the total market.

But the same old demon that plagued Pan Am wouldn't go away. Here it was, setting industry standards for leaving on time, delighting its passengers, even sweeping the halls and cleaning up the johns—and it was *still* losing $2 million a day.

Why couldn't Pan Am make money?

Well . . . actually, nobody could say. No one had ever delivered a simple, concise answer, any more than anyone had explained why Pan Am *made* money at one time. When Plaskett trotted out his cue cards and recited statistics about RPMs (revenue passenger miles) and load factors (percentage of seats filled) and yield (how much you were getting—or in Pan Am's case, *weren't* getting—from your product), it sounded like a lot of smoke from a number cruncher, which it was.

The audience listened politely, scratched their heads, and wondered: What the hell does it mean?

The truth was that almost *nobody* was making money flying the North Atlantic. Historically, the Pacific had been Pan Am's only real moneymaker, which was why, of course, United Airlines had bought it from Ed Acker in 1985. The Atlantic had become a cheap-fare market, with too many carriers flying too many seats for ridiculously low fares. The other major players on the Atlantic—United, American, TWA—fed their international flights from strong hub-and-spoke domestic systems—something Pan Am had never developed. The idea was that you *could* make money flying a passenger from New York to Europe *if* you also sold him a ticket to or from somewhere else in your system—Kansas City, Denver, Dallas . . .

Each time Pan Am was poised to build a true domestic system that fed its international web, it had, instead, done something egregiously inappropriate, like buying a regional airline (National, 1980), which it then proceeded to dismantle instead of expanding into a hub-and-spoke operation. Or building a nonfeeder "halo" operation (the Northeast Shuttle, 1987) that was disconnected from the rest of the airline.

Now it was too late. There was no money left to build anything. Even the shuttle was for sale.

Pan Am's summer of 1989 came and went, mostly without passengers. Almost all advance bookings had been wiped out by the disaster at Lockerbie.

But the traveling public's fear of terrorism was softening. Even CNN had stopped flashing the image of the blue-and-white death capsule in the Scottish meadow. The summer of 1990 was coming, and lo!—advance bookings were beginning to come in. After every bad break imaginable—could it be? Would there finally be a season without calamity?

Of course not.

No such luck for the world's most bedeviled airline. In August 1990, Saddam Hussein invaded Kuwait.

It was the crest of the travel season. Travelers had once again been lining up at the Pan Am ticket counters. Things had been looking, if not good, at least one hell of a lot better than at this time last year.

No more. A Middle East war was imminent. In the space of one televised glimpse of tanks rolling across the desert, fuel prices shot through the ceiling. Back was the specter of terrorism—the subliminal image of the death capsule in the meadow.

The crowds at the Pan Am ticket counters dispersed as if someone had discharged mustard gas. Would-be passengers put as much yardage between themselves and the Pan Am blue ball as their feet could take them.

It was the same scene all over again. From one cavernous end to the other of a 747 passenger cabin you could see scarcely a passenger. If anyone *had* to travel, he did it on an obscure, non-terrorist-tempting airline. Or he took a boat. Or he said to hell with it and stayed home to catch the war on CNN.

Instead of being a recovery year, 1990 was going down as the worst year in international airline history. Iraq refused to budge from its occupation of Kuwait, and the inevitability of war in the desert, with the possibility of losing Saudi Arabia's oil too, sent fuel prices off the scale.

The year 1990 was shaping up so badly it looked as though Pan Am wouldn't see the end of it. Something had to give. The airline couldn't pay its bills. Some bills, in fact, had gone unpaid for months. It was slash-and-burn time.

It was in this spirit that Tom Plaskett found himself in late summer sitting in a hotel conference room just outside Chicago's O'Hare Airport. Across from him was Stephen Wolf, a youngish, fast-burning former senior vice president for marketing at Pan Am from 1981 to 1982. He had taken an early departure and moved on to other plateaus. Now Steve Wolf was running United Airlines.

The presence of the two chief executives symbolized the contrast between the airlines. In a room full of business-suited executives, you could *feel* the vitality of Steve Wolf. He was tall, mustached, confident. Wolf was one of a handful of airline executives who, business reporters liked to write, possessed *vision*. Wolf had a plan that extended into the next century. A pity, they said, that Pan Am hadn't kept him.

All of which caused inevitable comparisons with Pan Am's chairman, Tom Plaskett, whose vision these days extended as far as next week's session with the creditors. Such comparisons were unfair, of course, since Plaskett was no more the cause of Pan Am's woes than Wolf was responsible for United's great success. But still, the distinction was there. Steve Wolf *looked* like a winner. Tom Plaskett looked like just what he was: a harried little man trying to get the best deal he could for his losing airline.

What Wolf wanted from Plaskett was nothing less than Pan Am's remaining crown jewel. The most prestigious route property still in Pan American's possession was its service to London's Heathrow Airport. United could not start up service to Heathrow on its own because of the inflexible *quid pro quo* that governed British-American access to each other's air terminals. British Airways had a specified number of slots and gates at Kennedy Airport, New York. In turn, Pan Am and TWA had similar slots and gates at Heathrow Airport, London. No other United States flag carriers had such rights. United's only entry to Heathrow was by acquiring the privilege from another carrier. Like Pan Am.

Which was why Wolf was sitting there in Chicago that day, smiling at Tom Plaskett. Pan American had been serving London for fifty-two years. Pan Am, in fact, had been the first United States airline to fly to the United Kingdom, beginning its service with the majestic Boeing B-314 flying boats.

Another volume of Pan Am history was about to end. In 1986, United Airlines had bought Pan Am's entire Pacific route system, closing out a half century of Pan American history. Now it was time to close out another.

There were details to be worked out, and many more such meetings before an agreement was signed and an announcement made. But Wolf and Plaskett had a deal: For $400 million Pan Am would sell its service to London from New York, Washington, Los Angeles, Seattle, and San Francisco. United would take over seven London-to-Europe routes served by Pan Am. United would also gain Pan Am's route from Washington to Paris, and it would obtain two 747-200 jumbos as well as spare parts and facilities in the United States and London.

*   *   *

Bob Gould was aghast. As a twenty-five-year pilot with Pan Am, he had a different view than Tom Plaskett had. He didn't think that selling off Pan Am's most valuable asset was the way to save the airline. Each time Pan Am had received an infusion of cash in return for a valuable property like the Pacific operation or the Pan Am Building, the airline had used the proceeds to fund new losses. There was no growth, just shrinkage.

Gould could see no future for Pan Am after the London sale. He saw only a vacuum. The Imperial Airline that he had joined as a new hire back in the sixties was gone.

So Gould resigned. A few days later, the announcement appeared in the press that he had been hired as the new president of Eastern Airlines, which was in bankruptcy. The court-appointed trustee of Eastern Airlines happened to be Pan Am's former vice-chairman and Bob Gould's old management mentor, Marty Shugrue.

In Skygod country, the report of the United sale was received like the news of an incoming Scud.

In the official employee news wire, Plaskett asked the troops to accept the sale as "a giant leap forward in strengthening Pan Am." It would be a new start for the Imperial Airline.

Giant leap. They had seen enough such leaps. Each one had left the airline with one of its parts missing. For years now they had watched Pan Am shed its assets, then squander the proceeds. The result was always the same—a smaller, weaker airline. And always with fewer employees.

A joke was making the rounds of the crew lounges. "Pan Am is like a coyote caught in a trap," went the tale. "It's chewed off three of its legs, and it's still in the trap."

The pilots' union filed a suit in federal court to prevent the sale. The union charged that Pan Am was violating the labor contract by not negotiating the transfer of an appropriate number of pilots to United along with the routes and airplanes.

With the Pacific sale in 1986, United had absorbed into its seniority list 410 Pan American airmen, all of whom went on the United seniority list according to their original date of hire at Pan Am. For most, it was an instant promotion in seniority and cockpit position. It was a *very* good deal for the transferred Pan Am pilots.

Too damned good, in the view of the United pilots. They were not about to allow another gaggle of refugees from Pan Am onto the upper regions of *their* seniority list. United had gone through a nasty strike by the pilots, and then experienced a buyout initiative by the same pilots. Collectively, the United pilots had become a formidable voice in the United executive suites. They didn't want any more Pan Am pilots on their seniority list. Just Pan Am routes and airplanes. Forget what had happened with the Pacific deal. That was history. These days United would acquire new pilots off the street, and they would start at the bottom of the list.

Which put an effective end to any illusions that ingenuous airmen still held about the international brotherhood of airline pilots. The protection of a union extended only as far as your own airline. In the case of mergers or acquisitions, it was every man for himself.

While the lawsuits and route applications and labor wrangling went on, Pan Am went on bleeding. The sale would take several months. It wasn't a simple transfer of assets, since the authority to service Heathrow required the approval of both the United States Department of Transportation and the British government, which had little interest in allowing a competitor the size of United Airlines into the same arena with their home team, British Airways.

Pan Am wobbled closer than ever to Tango Uniform. Without an infusion of cash, the airline wouldn't last long enough for the Heathrow sale to be consummated.

Something else had to go. Quickly. So Tom Plaskett reached up on the shelf and seized another Pan Am property.

For this one, history had already supplied a buyer.

In the autumn of 1989 the Berlin Wall tumbled. In the following year, to the astonishment of the world, the reunification of Germany proceeded at the speed of a *Blitzkrieg.*

It was because of the partition of Germany that Pan Am's Internal German Service had begun after World War II. For forty years the isolated city had been connected to the free world, via the three air corridors, by Pan American airplanes.

Now, unbelievably, Berlin was no longer isolated. There was no enemy. There was no more need for an Internal German Service. *Any-one* could fly into Berlin—even Lufthansa, Germany's monolithic flag carrier, which for nearly half a century had been barred by the Cold War pacts from flying into Berlin.

So it seemed pointless, at first glance, for Pan Am to offer to sell its Internal German Service to Lufthansa. Pan Am's exclusive Cold War license to fly the corridors across East Germany into isolated Berlin was an anachronism. There would soon be no Cold War, no East Germany, no corridors. Why would Lufthansa pay for something it could have for free?

But reunification was happening sooner than anyone had dreamed. Berlin was about to become once again a prominent European capital city, whether or not Lufthansa was ready. Lufthansa wasn't ready to step in and establish its own Berlin base. So for $150 million, Luft-hansa purchased Pan American's Internal German Service routes and facilities. The agreement included a lease arrangement by which, for several months, Pan Am airplanes and crews would continue to op-erate the service until Lufthansa could put together its own Berlin hub.

For old Pan Am Berlin hands, it amounted to the loss of their hometown.

The Last Flight—the final Pan Am trip into Berlin—was a hugely symbolic event, a handing back of the keys, so to speak.

Who would fly the Last Flight? The first word was that the system chief pilot, a pleasant fellow named Norm Davies, would come over from New York to command the ceremonial trip. But that went down badly with the old IGS hands. The Last Flight, they thought, ought to be flown by one of *them*—one of the old Berlin hands.

Davies already knew about the penchant of the IGS pilots for wild-cat work ethics. They could slow down, sit in, sick out—whatever it took to make their point. Davies wasn't dumb. With several generals, ambassadors, and his own CEO watching, it was not a time for a labor war with the grunts. So he conceded the point. One of the grunts could make the Last Flight.

* * *

Captain Hans Bernick could have been typecast for the role. Bernick looked like the actor Peter Graves. Urbane, multilingual, he fit perfectly into the Berlin operation. Bernick was a German who had been raised in China by missionary parents, orphaned in the revolution, smuggled into Hong Kong by mercenary pilots, then illegally landed in the United States, where he joined the Air Force. In the process, he learned to fly, became a citizen, and went to work for Pan American World Airways.

So Bernick, appropriately, would fly the Last Flight. It was even more appropriate, since it happened to be *his* last flight, at least as a captain. Bernick was turning sixty, the mandatory retirement age.

It was a round trip, from Berlin to Frankfurt and back. For the occasion Bernick did what every IGS captain dreamed about: He broke every rule he could.

One rule was that no unauthorized persons could ride in the cockpit. However, several pilots of a charter airline were trying to get to work in Frankfurt. Though the cabin had already been filled, Bernick wasn't leaving anybody behind. "Fine," said Bernick. "Put your bags in the cockpit."

"Where should we sit?"

"Where else? On your bags."

For the return flight to Berlin, he broke the same rule. He put his wife, Mai, in the cockpit.

In the Berlin terminal area, Bernick asked the air traffic controller, "How about a *Rundflug?*" He wanted to make a sightseeing tour around Berlin.

That was okay too. The controllers had gotten into the spirit of the occasion. "Berlin is yours, Clipper." It was a good night for breaking rules.

At an altitude of two thousand feet, they flew down the city's main artery, the Kurfürstendamm. Then they turned and flew down it the other way. Bernick flew a circle around Alexanderplatz, formerly the heart of East Berlin. It was a rare autumn night, clear and cool. The lights of Berlin glittered like Ganymede up close. The passengers loved it.

The best part—for Bernick—was the landing back at Tegel Airport. It was a grease job.

Inside the terminal, in the lounge behind gate 13, a party of sorts was in progress. Everyone was there—chief pilots, the Lufthansa crowd, Pan Amers both ground and air. Chairman Plaskett was there. He uttered some standard Plaskettudes about how bright Pan Am's future was. Old Berlin hands, past and present, had come from all over the globe. Most were feeling feisty and morose and a little mean.

". . . the best damn flying club in the world."

". . . shouldn't be selling out. We *built* this operation right up from the rubble."

"I've been here for twenty years. Berlin is, you know, *my home-town.*"

The party amounted to more of a wake than a celebration. They downed several crates of Berliner Kindl and talked about the glory days—Chicken Man and the AWARE days and the Deacon and the Great Strike and Beaver Man and the countless low-visibility approaches.

For some it was a good time to give Plaskett and his people a rough time about selling the Berlin operation. The trouble with that was, there was nobody—*really*—to be mad at. They wanted to argue that, goddammit, Pan Am *shouldn't* be selling out to Lufthansa. They wanted to continue the fantasy that Pan Am, by God's will and Allied decree and manifest destiny, had a right to be in Berlin forever.

But they knew better. History had dealt them a joker. Every day they flew over the meandering scar in the earth that used to be the Berlin Wall. They had seen the throat-rasping, eye-wetting zeal of Germans reuniting with Germans. The Cold War was indisputably over. Berlin was no longer an island. Like it or not, it was time for the *Ausländer* to pack up their flight kits and go home.

By the time the party broke up, it was past three in the morning. Everyone was properly soused, and anyway, the Kindl was gone. It was time to leave, because the Lufthansa ground staff had come in. They were taking down the Pan Am signs and schedules. They wanted to be ready for business first thing in the morning.

"What are you going to do when Pan Am shuts down?"

It was a question Martinside had taken to asking other pilots. The response was usually something like "Oh, I don't know. Get another job, I guess."

"What kind of job? Where?"

At this, a flash of annoyance. Pilots were uncomfortable talking about such things. It was like discussing your own funeral. "A flying job. I'd go to work flying for some other airline."

What the pilot meant was, he didn't want to think about it. Among most there was a deep-seated conviction that Pan Am wouldn't . . . not *really* . . . go Tango Uniform. Hell, for one thing, they *knew* the government wouldn't allow such a thing. Pan Am was just too vital to America's overseas presence. And all that baloney about astronomic losses—a million dollars a day, two million—well, they'd been hearing that twaddle for twenty-five years. How could that be true? If so, it added up to a number like the national debt. Why would Pan Am's creditors underwrite losses like that? Clearly those were *paper* losses, not real money. It had to be a charade to satisfy the banks and the IRS and to keep the unions from pushing for a raise, right?

For some, this line of thinking gave comfort. It made it easier to keep their heads in the sand. But there were a couple of grim precedents out there. Braniff had gone Tango Uniform back in the early eighties, dumping its legion of pilots out on the street. For a decade they turned up everywhere, wandering the backwaters of commercial aviation, flying nonscheds and cargo and start-up commuters. Those were the lucky ones. For many it was the end of their flying days altogether.

And now, most shockingly, Eastern Airlines. The fratricidal war and bloody death of Eastern sent a shudder through the Pan Am ranks. Every Pan Am pilot knew someone over there, an Eastern guy with a career and a life and a set of aspirations like his own, who had lost his job. Many had believed it would never happen. *Nah, not Eastern, for Christ's sake. Eastern is one of the oldest companies in the business, started by Rickenbacker himself. . . .*

But there it was. Tango Uniform.

Some of the tales were chilling. Former senior Eastern captains, accustomed to six-figure salaries, were losing airplanes, boats, cars, homes. Families were disintegrating. Divorce was devouring their community like a prairie fire. Over two dozen mature, accomplished, professional airline pilots, unable to cope with the chaos of their lives, had committed suicide.

So, thought a few realists over at Pan Am, maybe it *could* happen.

And if it did . . . if the very worst happened and I hit the street like an evicted squatter . . . *what am I gonna do?*

What Rob Martinside did, while Chairman Plaskett was handing over Pan Am's Heathrow routes to United Airlines, was look for a job. Most of the jobs he found were in Pacific Rim countries—Japan, Korea, Taiwan.

He was interviewed in Dallas by a company called Japan Air Services. It was a contract job, meaning that he would be retained for a finite time—five years—as an Airbus captain based in Tokyo. The salary was generous, considerably better than he made at Pan Am. The Japanese interviewers were polite, businesslike, utterly expressionless. They stared at Martinside as if he were a laboratory specimen.

After the interview he was given a check flight in a simulator. A Japanese check pilot sat in the jump seat. He observed without comment or the slightest change of expression.

A couple of weeks later they invited Martinside to Tokyo for a physical exam and an "orientation." He talked to one of the contract pilots already there.

"We're hired help," said the pilot, a former Eastern captain. "Behind all the bowing and shuffling, they're just tolerating us. We have no place at their table over here. Just remember that. Fly their airplanes, deposit the checks in the bank, go home when it's over. Play the game and you'll get on fine."

Martinside wasn't so sure. There were other jobs in other countries. Most were not so good—freight-hauling operations and start-up charter outfits where you earned about the same wages as a New York cabby.

The next month, Martinside received a formal offer of employment from the Japanese. They wanted him to report in five weeks. Martinside told them he wanted to think it over.

For a week he thought it over. Then he declined. He didn't know why. But, hell, Pan Am hadn't gone Tango Uniform yet. Now Martinside felt as if he were riding a raft in a rapids. It was too late to get out and walk. Besides, he wanted to stick around and see what happened.

It didn't take long. The next week something happened.

CHAPTER THIRTY-ONE

THE YAWNING ABYSS

PAN AM SEEKS CHAPTER ELEVEN SHIELD
—Header, Wall Street Journal, *January 9, 1991*

The article covered the entire page. The phones in Pan Am's public relations department rang all day. Was this it? *Tango Uniform?*

"Certainly not," declared the Pan Am spokesperson. "Pan Am definitely *isn't* going out of business. The schedule will fly exactly as published. And certainly, no one is being laid off."

Nothing, really, was changing. It was just, you know, a routine bankruptcy.

That was the party line. No one believed it, of course, least of all investors. Pan Am stock, which had once sold at $75 a share, bottomed that day, January 9, 1991, at 75 cents. Pan Am was, literally, a penny stock. Pan Am bonds, now junk grade, sold for 9 cents on the dollar.

The *real* news was that Pan Am had made it through the first week of 1991. In December the European consortium Airbus Industrie had yanked the leases on twenty-one Airbuses operated by Pan Am. Pan Am was nearly a year in arrears on the lease payments and wasn't able to give assurances that even the current payments could be made. The sale of routes to United, which was originally supposed to have netted $400 million—enough to survive this passengerless winter— had become mired in endless talks between the United States and Brit-

296

ish governments, whose blessings were needed to make the transfer.

In the meantime, Pan Am had run through its cash reserve, including the $150 million from Lufthansa for the IGS. Now it was January of 1991. There wasn't enough left in the kitty to make the mid-month payroll. A cessation of operations was imminent.

But no one wanted to see Pan Am go under. Not yet. Not until everyone had gotten what he wanted from the corpse.

The Bush administration certainly didn't want to see it—and that wasn't because of any maudlin sentiment for a pioneering American institution. The Reagan-Bush people had already proved that they weren't into saving airlines. But at this point they didn't want any more blood on their hands. They had already taken enough denunciation over Eastern Airlines, having been accused of coddling Frank Lorenzo and helping him bleed Eastern to death. Now Pan Am? No, if Pan Am was to go Tango Uniform, it had sure as hell better be somebody else's fault.

And United Airlines desperately wanted to keep Pan Am alive. United wanted the London operation, which was still hung up waiting on a decision from the administration as well as the British government. Pan Am *mustn't* be allowed to liquidate before closing that deal. After the routes were handed over to United, of course, then whatever happened to Pan Am was irrelevant.

Thus was formed an unlikely Save Pan Am coalition. During the first week of January, they put together a labyrinthine scheme: *If* Pan Am would agree to file Chapter Eleven, and *if* the Bush administration, in the form of the Department of Transportation, would give the go-ahead to the sale of the London operation to United, then Bankers Trust New York would provide to Pan Am $150 million in operating funds, $50 million of which would be guaranteed by United Airlines.

It wasn't a deal that filled everyone with happiness, but it saved them all the messiness of a dead airline on their hands. And for Tom Plaskett, it bought time. He could still shop around for a buyer.

There was something faintly . . . *humiliating* . . . about flying for a bankrupt airline. Especially for an airline that had soared as far and as high as Pan American World Airways. The tattered carpets in the Worldport, the fading paint on the airplanes, the understaffed check-in counters—it affronted the pilots' dignity. An Airbus captain in New York summed it up: "It's as if the queen mother was reduced to cleaning the johns."

The worst part was dealing with passengers—what few they had. Passengers figured that if the airline couldn't pay its bills, it might be skimping on things like fuel and maintenance.

"Captain, since the company is bankrupt, does that mean the airplanes don't get fixed like they used to?"

"No, sir. Our maintenance is the best in the business, just like always." *But these beat-up old airplanes need more than just fixing,* the captain felt like saying. *These clunkers need to be retired.*

"Pardon me, young man. Do you pilots have to work longer hours now that your airline is out of money?"

"Not at all, ma'am. Our duty limits are set by the FAA. We fly the same number of hours as we always have." *But we sure don't get paid like we ought to. We gave up a third of our compensation to save this goddam company.*

Sometimes the little old ladies would put on a Mother Teresa smile and pat the pilot on the arm. "We're all praying for your airline to make it, you know."

And *that* was the part they hated the most. *Screw* the little old ladies and their pieties. It was almost too much to bear . . . these patronizing ignoramuses . . . *praying* that Pan Am, the airline of the Skygods, would *make it.*

So they strode purposefully through the terminals, their heels clacking on the marble, eyes straight ahead. Things might be falling down around their heads. The bills might have gone unpaid. But, by God, Pan Am pilots could still comport themselves like Skygods.

It happened sometimes that a pilot in full Lord Nelson regalia—gold stripes, shiny brass wings, captain's hat with gilded visor—would be standing outside his hotel, awaiting his limo to the airport. Up would come a little old lady—the same one with the Mother Teresa smile—from Iowa or Oklahoma. "Excuse me, bellman," she would say. "Would you take my bags inside, please?"

This happened to Captain Eric Archer. Archer's handlebar mustache twitched slightly, and he drew himself up to full Skygodly height.

For a second he beamed his fearsome gaze—*the Look*—down the length of his imperious nose at the little old lady.

But only for a second. Archer was a *real* Skygod, which is to say, one in full possession of his dignity. He doffed his cap. "Why, certainly, madam," he said, and took the lady's bags inside. He cheerfully accepted the tip.

"We cannot absorb revenue loss without taking severe steps to lower our costs commensurate with the reduced revenue."

It was a classic Plaskettism, worthy of Yogi Berra. What the chairman meant was that he was pink-slipping another four thousand employees. Back in August when Iraq ventured into Kuwait and traffic slumped, Pan Am had eliminated two thousand jobs. Now, with this latest announcement, a full 20 percent of Pan Am's work force had become casualties of the Gulf War.

On January 17, 1991, international air traffic aboard American flag carriers virtually stopped. Desert Shield, the massive American and allied buildup on the border of Kuwait, was now Desert Storm. American warplanes were plastering Iraq.

The only good news for Pan Am about the war and the resultant fear of flying was CRAF—the military's Civil Reserve Air Fleet. Pan Am 747s and their crews were kept busy shuttling troops and supplies to the desert. But the rest of the Pan Am system looked like a ghost line. Passengers stayed home, mesmerized by the televised images of laser-guided bombs dismantling Baghdad.

It was the same old story. No passengers. Record losses. And no new cash, because the sale of the London operation to United *still* had not gone through. Even though the U.S. Department of Transportation had approved the transfer and the Department of Justice had cleared the transaction of antitrust problems, the British were still deliberating.

No government in the world was more protective of its flag carrier than the United Kingdom. Juan Trippe himself had battled for most of a decade for the right to land his flying boats in Britain. The British were exasperatingly skilled at doing nothing at all until so much time had passed it no longer mattered.

The coalition that had contrived to save Pan Am—the Bush administration, United Airlines, and Pan Am's major creditors—pointed indignant fingers across the ocean. The blood would be on British hands now. After fifty-two years of service to Britain, in time of peace and war, Pan Am was about to collapse because of British dithering.

Everything—routes, airplanes, typewriters, trash cans—was for sale. Most of all, Tom Plaskett wanted to sell the Northeast Shuttle—Ed Acker's creation—which was a marginal moneymaker on its own but had done nothing to augment Pan Am's troubled international business.

There were a few shoppers. A company in Portland, Oregon, named PacifiCorp declared an interest in buying the shuttle for $150 million and having it operated by Northwest. Another group based in Iowa and headed by a Pan Am pilot named Neil Sapp launched a quixotic effort of its own to take over the shuttle.

One of the most persistent shoppers—and most irritating—was TWA owner Carl Icahn. Icahn was like a horsefly around Tom Plaskett's head. Carl Icahn had bought out TWA and was managing it in much the same enervating fashion as Frank Lorenzo had run Continental and Eastern.

Like Lorenzo, Carl Icahn was a predatory creature, an animal of the roaring, deregulated eighties. What he lacked in hard cash he made up for in hubris. Although TWA was in scarcely better health than Pan Am, and even though Icahn was about to sell TWA's own London gates to American Airlines, Icahn was talking about building a merged TWA–Pan Am airline into a new American megacarrier. He was offering $1.50 per share for Pan Am's outstanding 150 million shares, and an additional $1 per share in subordinated notes.

Pan Am and TWA? The notion brought ironic smiles to those who remembered Juan Trippe's own frustrated merger talks with TWA when it was controlled by Howard Hughes. Virtually every CEO since Trippe had fantasized about such a merger. It was a tantalizing prospect—a single American flag carrier that would span virtually the entire planet.

The trouble was, it was too late. It would be a marriage of the enfeebled. And no one in the industry took Carl Icahn seriously as a builder of such an enterprise. Icahn's style was to buy on the cheap, in a highly leveraged takeover, and then sell off assets to fund his huge indebtedness.

These days Tom Plaskett was ignoring Icahn's phone calls. And that was making Icahn furious. "Plaskett will go down in history," Icahn told the *Wall Street Journal,* "as the General Custer of the airlines." Almost every day's business paper carried a revised condition of Icahn's bid to buy out Pan Am. Pan Am would have to file Chapter Eleven before Icahn would make a deal. The shuttle would have to be included. And, oh, yes, that damn obstructionist Plaskett would have to go.

In March 1991, Her Majesty's Government saw fit to grant approval to the transfer of Pan Am's London operation to United Airlines.

And so it was done. Thus $290 million found its way into Pan Am's empty coffers.

During that same month, after a hundred hours of ground war, Kuwait was retaken. Desert Storm was over. Spring was coming. Another travel season was at hand.

Screwed again!

It was the most frequent utterance, or words to that effect, when the pilots read the item on the company wire.

Forty-two airmen would go to United.

Forty-two! No one could believe it.

The route sale to United was a done deal. United would take possession of everything associated with Pan Am's Heathrow operation —routes, gates, offices, vehicles, *two* 747-200 jumbo jets.

The only unresolved issue had been, *how many pilots?*

The Pan Am pilots contended that, based on the number of crews it took to service the routes being sold, 351 airmen should be transferred from Pan Am to United Airlines. The United pilots, who wanted to see no more senior Pan Am refugees added to their roster, insisted that the number ought to be only what it took to fly the two 747s— about forty.

The matter had gone before a federal arbitrator named Arthur

Fishbein. Fishbein listened to both arguments, and then decided. Part of his decision was based on what he saw happening at the two airlines. Pan Am was the Incredible Shrinking Airline. United was expanding. It was the old "expectations" formula carried forward from the National acquisition. The Pan Am pilots *shouldn't* have high expectations.

Forty-two. That was the number of pilots the arbitrator figured should go with the two 747s being transferred. Never mind the rest of the routes being sold that would be flown by *United* pilots.

It was a crushing defeat for the Pan Am pilots. Even the United pilots were shocked at their success. United had just captured Pan Am's premier routes, a prize that everyone knew would create employment for *several hundred* United Airlines pilots.

It was almost a repeat of the sale to Lufthansa wherein Pan Am had cashed in one of its crown jewels, an operation flown by Pan Am pilots for over forty years. Not one airman had gone with the sale.

Now London. The pieces of Pan Am were being peddled like furniture in a garage sale. And no pilots went with the pieces.

The news spewed like a cloud of swamp gas through the cockpits and crew rooms. There was talk of mutiny. Plaskett had sold them out, they said. The chairman had it in his power—*in his responsibility to his people*—to negotiate a fair number of employees to go with the routes. And he wasn't doing it. People were not part of the equation.

And what about the Air Line Pilots Association, the union to which both Pan Am and United pilots paid serious dues? What the hell was a union for, asked the enraged Pan Amers, if not to protect the careers and livelihoods of its members?

Such questions were academic. The pilots already knew the facts about unions and airlines. ALPA was unable to do anything to save their jobs. As a national union, ALPA had no clout in merger affairs, because it subsisted on dues money from its member airline pilots. And of all ALPA's member councils, none paid more dues or wielded more clout than the United Airlines council.

Pan Am, in the big picture, didn't really count.

Rumors flew, literally, at the speed of light. They flashed between passing jetliners over the North Atlantic.

"Rumor check," a voice would say on 131.4, the company frequency.

From somewhere in the night sky a voice from another airplane would answer. "Here's the latest. We're being bought out by the Yellow Cab Company."

Someone else would jump in. "I heard it was Greyhound Bus."

"Nah. They don't want to bring us up to their pay scale."

There might be as many as half a dozen airplanes exchanging wild stories, six miles above the ocean. They spoke what was foremost on their minds.

"Furlough letters are out."

"Already got mine. After this trip, I'm outa here."

"Where to?"

"Anywhere. American's hiring. So are Delta and United."

These were the young guys talking—*real* new hires. They would be the first to be furloughed. It was hard on them, being out of a job. But they were also the ones who could get jobs elsewhere. The *old* new hires were the ones who were unhirable.

"Someone said he heard a team from Delta was looking over the property yesterday in New York. Does that mean Delta is buying us?"

No one answered. In the darkened cockpits over the North Atlantic, pilots were shaking their heads. That was *really* a wild one. Of all the rumors, that was the wildest.

CHAPTER THIRTY-TWO

DELTA

For those who go to Delta, it's a sunny day. For those who get furloughed, it's raining like hell. For those who will stay with Pan Am, it's . . . cloudy.
—PAN AM CAPTAIN BOB FERREL, *ALPA officer*

To the astonishment of everyone, the rumor contained truth.

Delta? It caused a lot of head-scratching in the airline business. Why would an outfit like Delta Airlines, Southern and conservative, slow-moving as the Chattahoochee in August, do something so uncharacteristic as take on down-at-the-heels, teetering-on-the-brink-of-decrepitness Pan American?

Because Delta Airlines was an awakening giant. Since its beginning back in 1928 as a crop-dusting outfit in Monroe, Louisiana, Delta had expanded in shrewd, cautious increments. By the end of the 1980s, after the first decade of deregulation, Delta had grown into the third-largest airline in the country. Delta was one of the first airlines to construct a hub-and-spoke system, concentrating its activity at "hubs" like Atlanta, Dallas, Cincinnati, and Salt Lake City, with feeder routes—"spokes"—radiating outward to its hundreds of satellite destinations.

The "Big Three"—American, United, and Delta—had all prospered under deregulation, developing hub-and-spoke networks, frequent-flier programs, computer reservations systems, and sophis-

304

ticated yield management strategies that enabled them to overwhelm their regional competitors. While American and United, both flush with cash, spent over a billion dollars buying up the routes of Pan Am, TWA, Continental, and Eastern, Delta had held back.

"We sit around quietly doing our thing," Delta's president, Whit Hawkins, liked to say, "while the rest of them go around killing each other."

But now, down in Atlanta, the thought was occurring that perhaps they had sat around long enough. It was catch-up time. "Slowness is their hallmark," said Ed Greenslet, an airline consultant, about Delta's management, "but when they make a move, it's a considered move and it has a lot of internal logic."

The logic in this instance was that Delta had no choice. Delta *had* to break out of its carefully constructed domestic shell and become a player in the global arena. It was the only way it could stay abreast of rivals American and United, which had just captured, respectively, the London Heathrow rights of TWA and Pan Am. With the collapse of communism, the markets of Europe were changing with each morning's headlines.

To begin building a European operation from scratch was not feasible. It would take decades, even if Delta could somehow get the reciprocal government concessions, an event as likely as a return of the Zeppelins.

In April 1991, Delta had a $476 million stock offering, its first since 1962. The purpose was to raise money for expansion. And here was the Pan Am European system, already in place. It was a turnkey deal. All Delta had to do was change the paint schemes on the airplanes and print new schedules.

Delta didn't even have to hire more pilots. They went with the package.

In the crew rooms and cockpits of the Financially Troubled Pan American, there were smiles. The broadness of the smiles was directly proportional to the seniority of the smilers.

Delta was talking about taking seven hundred pilots. Naturally, that meant Pan Am's *senior* seven hundred pilots, right?

Sure. That much, at least, seemed cast in stone. After all, seniority

was the name of the game in the airline business. How an *entire* seniority list merged into another airline's seniority list was sometimes
controversial, as in the National and Pan Am merger in 1980. But
within one's own airline, one's relative position on the list never
changed. Since back when Christ was a copilot, *everything* had been
done by seniority. You could bitch about not having it. You could
stew over the senior pilots getting the plums and the juniors getting
the dregs. But everyone agreed it was the only fair system. All you had
to do was wait your turn. Sooner or later even you, given enough
patience, would be senior. It was a tyrannical, frustrating system, but
no one had ever come up with a scheme that was more fair.

And then came an announcement that struck the Pan Am pilots
like a bolt of summer lightning: *Delta wasn't taking the senior pilots!*

In the crew rooms around the Pan Am system you could hear a
single great blowing sound. It was the breath whooshing from the
lungs of the Skygods.

Delta didn't want the lumbering old 747s, Pan Am's senior flagships. Or the senior pilots who flew them. Delta Airlines wanted Pan
Am's newer and more efficient Airbus A-310s. And since Delta was
buying the Northeast Shuttle, it wanted the 727s that were used on
the shuttle. To operate this fleet of two- and three-engine jetliners,
Delta naturally wanted the crews who were already trained and qualified to fly them. Never mind that most of these—captains and copilots—came from the midlevels of the seniority list and, in the case
of the junior copilots, right off the bottom.

In short, to hell with seniority.

Which made the jumbo pilots red-faced, hyperventilating, eye-
bulging *furious. What was going on here?* Here they were, the *senior*
captains in the whole damn airline. *Skygods,* by temperament, seniority, and divine right. And here someone was spouting this ant-brained
blather about the *junior* pukes, some of them fuzzy-cheeked new hires,
being the ones transferred with Pan Am's most historic routes—and
guaranteed a secure job forever after. Could this be true?

Well, yes . . . actually . . . that's the way it was going down.

Oh, the outrage! It was the fine, bubbling fury of the impotent
victim. Someone was stealing their careers, patting them on the head,
telling them to go their merry way. Don't make a fuss. Have a nice
life. What the Skygods really wanted now was to have their hands

wrapped around the windpipes of the bastards who were doing this to them.

And that was the problem. Who were the bastards?

The most convenient culprit was ALPA—the Air Line Pilots Association—their own union, which had given them the seniority system to start with and which now, in the view of the most senior Pan Am pilots, was allowing the system to be ripped to shreds and fed to the hogs.

The left-behind Skygods formed a committee and pooled funds and hired a law firm. There was righteous talk about injunctions and lawsuits and shutting the bastards down. It didn't change anything, at least for the moment, but it made them feel better. But only a little.

Meanwhile, the sellout to Delta went ahead with the unstoppability of a Mississippi flood. Delta was in a hurry, because rival bidders were putting together their own, larger offers for the bankrupt airline. Tom Plaskett was in a hurry for the standard reason: Pan Am was out of money.

The airline was still managing to lose two to three million dollars every day. Gone was the take from the Lufthansa sale, and gone were the long-awaited proceeds of the London sale to United. Pan Am's cash on hand amounted to less than $40 million, which it had preserved mainly by not paying bills.

Plaskett was in a bigger hurry even than the airline's unsecured creditors, who could see their investments being repaid for pennies on the dollar. After the first outcry from the creditors committee, Delta's opening offer of $260 million had been upped to $310 million.

Plaskett and Delta chairman Ron Allen had already made an agreement in principle, but the price still didn't suit the unsecured creditors committee. Throughout July and into August, they haggled in the bankruptcy court, nudging the ante ever skyward. Delta revamped its offer five times, offering a bigger cash infusion, rescinding it, briefly taking on United Airlines as an investment partner, then shedding it, all the while facing down challenges from TWA and American.

On the morning of August 12, 1991, in the court of New York bankruptcy judge Cornelius Blackshear, Tom Plaskett unloaded most of Pan Am's remaining assets to Delta Airlines for $416 million in cash and the assumption of $389 million worth of liabilities.

To some, it still seemed like too good a deal for Delta. Several unsuccessful bidders, notably Carl Icahn, screamed that their own bids were being ignored. But Icahn's bids were backed mostly by paper and pledges, with little hard cash. Delta was not only waving real money, it was immediately advancing $80 million of debtor-in-possession funding to keep Pan Am in operation.

Even better, Delta was agreeing to invest in what was now being called the "restructured" Pan Am, the remaining sliver of the airline that would be based in Miami and fly to Latin America. Delta would own 45 percent of the Restructured Pan Am, and the creditors would hold the other 55 percent. And this was enough to persuade Cornelius Blackshear, the bankruptcy judge, as well as the creditors committee, to give the go-ahead.

After the agreements had been signed, Tom Plaskett and Ron Allen, Delta's chairman, posed for photographs and appeared on televised business news programs. Was Plaskett being offered a job in the restructured airline? "It hasn't been discussed," said Plaskett.

Allen was beaming about Delta's new acquisition. "Now we go to work," he told the reporters.

Allen wanted Delta to begin operating the shuttle in September. On November 1 the North Atlantic operation was supposed to switch to Delta colors. And on December 1 the Restructured Pan Am was supposed to emerge from bankruptcy, under its new operating plan.

The *Wall Street Journal* carried a full-page ad:

PAN AM NOW HAS A FUTURE.
WE THANK EVERY ONE OF YOU WHO HELPED
MAKE IT POSSIBLE.

In a long paean signed by Tom Plaskett, the chairman assured the world:

"While the restructured Pan Am is a smaller airline, it will still be a financially sound carrier to what many see as major economic growth areas of the world: Latin America and the Caribbean. . . ."

The Restructured Pan Am . . .

It had a brave, proud ring to it. But no one was kidding himself.

This was not the old Imperial Airline, nor even the old Financially Troubled Pan Am. The Restructured Pan Am was going to be a little island-hopping, Latino-flavored, steel-drum outfit, propped up by Delta Airlines. For Delta, it was a trial balloon to see whether it made sense for Delta to commit bigger resources to a South American expansion.

For the pilots it was a time of mad scrambling for position. The lifeboats were leaving, and it was every man for himself. To go to Delta, you had to be on the A-310 Airbus. Or else you had to be one of the senior 727 pilots who would go with the shuttle.

Since Delta was taking more A-310 pilots than Pan Am currently had assigned, more would have to be trained. And since training time was short and expensive, first priority went to those who had *ever* been on the A-310, since it would be quicker and cheaper to requalify them. The next priority went to pilots who were holding assignments to the Airbus but had not yet been trained.

Suddenly, a rating on the Airbus equated to a secure old age in the airline business.

It was like the last flight out of Saigon. Grab any slot, pull any string, climb aboard anything that was leaving town. Get on the List. Pilots hounded the office, begging for a training slot. They pulled every company and union string they had ever heard of. One pilot, when told he wasn't supposed to be in that Airbus class, threatened to chain himself to the simulator. *Get on the List.*

A few actually turned Delta down, choosing to stay with the Restructured Pan Am. It had little to do with sentiment. They were mostly pilots pushing the mandatory retirement age of sixty. Pan Am was one of the few airlines that allowed retired captains to continue working as flight engineers. Flight engineers were not pilots, by job definition. They sat at their own panel in the cockpit and monitored aircraft systems—pressurization, fuel, hydraulics. They were not bound by the federally mandated age sixty retirement rule that applied to pilots; they could keep on working into their twilight years.

But not at Delta. Delta's policy was that captains retired at age sixty. Period. They didn't come back in any form, even as flight engineers.

*   *   *

Rob Martinside was one of the lucky ones. He was among the seven hundred, roughly a third of the original Pan Am pilots, who made the List. Another seven hundred or so would remain with what was left of Pan Am, the Restructured Pan Am. The bottom third, the most junior who happened also not to be on the Airbus, were furloughed.

Those on the List were invited to Atlanta for a four-day Delta "orientation." With his fellow inductees, Martinside stepped off the shuttle bus one October morning at the Delta headquarters complex. And then he stopped, his mouth open. He stared at the magnificent training building, filled with simulators and modern classrooms. He gazed in wonder at the sprawling administrative buildings. The place looked like the Doral Country Club.

Martinside felt like a ghetto kid on his first trip to the suburbs. He looked at his fellow Pan Amers stepping off the bus. Their mouths were open too.

Someone in the group summed it up: *"Holy shit . . ."*

No doubt about it. Delta was doing well, and it showed. It slowly came home to the Pan Am pilots that the other two megacarriers, United and American, were probably doing just as well. The Big Three—Delta, American, United—had been prepared for deregulation. During the turbulent eighties, while Pan Am was squandering its opportunities and assets, the Big Three had made smart choices. Or lucky ones. Either way, it amounted to the same thing.

On the day of the transfer, Rob Martinside put on his new uniform. It was much like the Pan Am naval-style uniform he'd worn for twenty-six years. The black double-breasted coat had two rows of brass buttons. The sleeves bore four gold stripes. The cap was black instead of white.

He checked in that evening for his flight to Europe. He felt like a kid on his first day in a new school. All the former Pan Amers looked self-conscious in their new brass-buttoned, black-hatted uniforms.

In the parking lot he passed an old friend from his new-hire days, now a 747 captain, who was staying behind with the Restructured Pan Am. The old friend looked at him curiously, eyeing the new uniform. He didn't stop to talk.

Martinside hoped the feeling would go away soon. It was something very much like . . . *guilt*. And it was making him angry.

Here he was, a survivor. He'd gotten a toehold in the lifeboat and been saved. Now he could look back and see his old colleagues of the past quarter century. They'd been through it all together—the Clipper skippers and the SST fizzle and AWARE and the Great Strike and Lockerbie and Chapter Eleven.

Now this. It wasn't the way they had expected it to end.

CHAPTER THIRTY-THREE

TANGO UNIFORM

What Pan Am looked like was a black hole.

—DELTA AIRLINES EXECUTIVE *to the*
Wall Street Journal, *December 5, 1991*

In the sunless bowels of the Pan Am flight training academy, Harry Shepard cursed the A-300 simulator. He had to keep reminding himself that it *was* only a simulator—nothing more than a big, three-axis, hydraulic-powered, $2 million Nintendo game.

Shepard sat in the left seat, straining to keep the flight director bars on his instrument panel crossed. It was a slippery damn simulator. Like most such training devices, it was a microsecond slower in control response than a real airplane.

Shepard was going through A-300 training because he wasn't one of the fortunates taken by Delta. He had been a 747 captain. Now he was downgrading to an Airbus A-300. He hated it.

During the coffee break he noticed something odd. Outside on the maintenance ramp, there seemed to be more parked airplanes—Pan Am airplanes—than usual. Coveralled mechanics were going from airplane to airplane stuffing plugs into the engine intakes and exhausts, affixing covers to the probes on the fuselage. It looked like they were pickling them for storage.

312

Shepard tried not to think about it. He had other things on his mind today. Like the damn A-300 simulator.

Midway through the next period a call came from the training office: "Shut it down, guys. Gather up your bags and manuals and leave the building."

"Why?"

"Why do you think?" The secretary's voice was cracking. "We're closing down. We've got fifteen minutes to leave the building."

Shepard and his training partner exchanged glances. *Closing down? You mean . . . ?* Privately, each had expected it. Shepard had known since he saw the parked airplanes.

They gathered their approach plates, their checklists, their cockpit paraphernalia. No one spoke.

The front door was already locked. A uniformed security guard had attached a chain and padlock.

"How do we get out?"

"I dunno," said the guard. "Try the side door."

They found the side door. It was a fire escape. There was a two-foot drop from the door ledge to a plat of shrubs outside.

Harry Shepard stood in the knee-high shrubs and looked back inside the building. All of them, pilots, instructors, secretaries, were standing in line, waiting their turn to hop out the side door into the plat of shrubs.

So this is it, he thought. This is what it's like. All in all, it seemed like a damned undignified way to end your career.

In their darkest ruminations, the grunts used to wonder how it would look. They didn't have to wonder anymore. Today they were seeing it: *Tango Uniform.*

It was a tableau of failure. Concrete ramps awash with parked airplanes. Idle tractors, tugs, trucks, left where they were last used. Passenger lounges empty as ghost towns, littered with used newspapers, useless timetables. Stunned faces, some weeping, some contorted with anger.

The end had come suddenly, though the warning signs had been there for anyone to see. On September 1 the Northeast Shuttle was

transferred to Delta. On November 1 the North Atlantic operation
and the Frankfurt hub were transferred. What was left, the little Latin
American operation everyone was now calling Pan Am II, was supposed to emerge from bankruptcy in the first week of December.

It never made it.

Part of the takeover arrangement had been that Delta would cover
$80 million of Pan Am's operating losses during the transition period.
During the autumn of 1991, Pan Am roared through the $80 million
like a prairie fire. To preserve its investment, Delta kicked in another
$35 million. That, too, was vaporized. There seemed to be no end in
sight.

Alarm bells were going off in Atlanta.

The biggest problem was that no one was buying tickets on Pan
Am II. Advance bookings were appallingly absent. It was as though
the nation's travel agents, on whom the airline depended for its customers, had already peered into their computer screens and read Pan
Am's obituary. *You want to fly on Pan Am? Well . . . maybe . . . you
ought to think about booking on American . . . or Avianca. . . . You
don't want to worry about getting stuck down there. . . . Remember
when Eastern and Braniff went under . . . all those passengers stranded
with no way to get home. . . .*

At a November 26 meeting, Pan Am's chief financial officer, Rolf
Andresen, reported to Delta executives and Pan Am's creditors that
traffic was down. Revenues were running behind projections. *Way*
behind.

Wary glances flashed among the silent Delta executives.

Then the Pan Am management people and the creditors went on
to explain how they would deal with the shortfall. They would just
have to lower reserves. And they might try to obtain "concessions
from suppliers, employees, and others who had a stake in the airline."

Nothing was said, but a limit had been reached. Clearly, the Pan
Am II enterprise was turning into a bottomless pit. The Delta team
packed their briefcases and hurried back to Atlanta.

The next week, thirty-three days after the transfer to Delta, they
met again in the court of U.S. bankruptcy judge Cornelius Blackshear.
It was December 3, the day the new Pan Am was scheduled to shed
its Chapter Eleven protection.

In an apologetic tone, Delta lawyer Lawrence M. Handelsman told the court that after a "weekend of agony" his client had made a decision. Delta had decided not to pump any more money into Pan Am. "The world has changed," said Handelsman. That seemed to be his explanation. Twice more he said it, as if the point needed emphasizing. *The world has changed.*

And so it had.

The next morning, Thursday, December 4, 1991, Pan Am's offices opened for business. And then they closed again. There was no more business. Without the infusion of any more Delta money, Pan Am II was extinct. Tango Uniform.

Pan Am II's president, Russell Ray, who had been on the job only a few weeks, told the press, "I am distressed that this effort has failed."

He wasn't nearly as distressed as Pan Am's creditors—and employees. Before the day was over, recriminations were landing like mortar shells. "You can't tell me an airline as big and smart and sophisticated as Delta, that has known more about Pan Am than Pan Am does since April and that has been involved in every decision, that they wake up one night and say 'the world has changed,' " said Henry Miller, investment banker at Prudential Securities.

Most industry observers, though, accepted Delta's side of the story. In retrospect, the pullout seemed inevitable. "I think their offer was for real," said L. John Eichner, chairman of Simat, Helliesen & Eichner, an airline consulting firm. "I'm not questioning their good faith, just their competence."

Did Delta's fiscally temperate management, in cutting a deal that would eventually amount to $1.7 billion, suddenly develop cold feet? "They're looking into the future," said Henry Miller, "and they're very scared about what they see as the prospects for the business."

The day after the shutdown, Pan Am's creditors filed a ten-count lawsuit against Delta for breach of contract for $2.5 billion in damages. "This was deliberate," said Leon Marcus, the outspoken attorney for the creditors committee. "They dropped the bomb on all these employees and the traveling public."

In Barbados, sitting in the cockpit of the Boeing 727 *Clipper Goodwill*, Captain Mark Pyle watched the Pan Am station manager walking toward the airplane. Pyle could tell by the manager's face that it was bad news.

All the news these days was bad. Pyle and his crew already knew before they left New York that Delta Airlines had withdrawn from the Restructured Pan Am deal. The news was only bound to get worse.

Pyle read the Teletype message the manager handed him. In curt language it declared that as of nine o'clock that morning the airline had ceased operations.

Pyle went back to the cabin to tell the flight attendants. Each of the women had been flying for Pan Am, or for National, for over twenty years. They all broke down in tears.

The manager wanted to know if they would fly the airplane back to Miami. He said he would find a way to buy fuel. Not only were their revenue passengers stranded there in Barbados, many of the now-unemployed Pan Am staff wanted to return to the United States.

For Pyle it would be one of his last Skygodly decisions. He was a new captain, and he'd waited eighteen years to get there. He was a former instructor, now a check pilot, and a dedicated company man. He liked to run his airplane by the book.

"How long will it take?" he asked.

"Maybe two hours."

Pyle had to laugh. What could they do? Fire him? "We'll wait," he said. "We'll wait as long as it takes."

Two hours later, when the passengers and employees were aboard, they took off for Miami.

A hundred miles out, the flight engineer, Chuck Freeman, made radio contact with Pan Am operations. Then he turned to the captain. He was choking back tears. "Mark . . . we're the last flight . . . *the final flight*. They want us to make a low pass."

Another decision, probably his last. *Low pass?* And then it occurred to him: *This is a historic moment.* A low pass? Absolutely.

So that's what he did. Low. He brought *Clipper Goodwill* right down the centerline of runway 12, low enough for the folks on the ground to count the rivets.

They turned downwind, landed, and taxied toward the gate. It was like a victory parade.

Vehicles—police, fire trucks, security cars, tow trucks—lined the taxiway. Television crews followed the taxiing airplane. Ramp workers came to attention and saluted. Water cannons fired streams over the slowly moving jetliner. All the Pan Am personnel at the gate were standing at attention as Pyle brought the jet to a stop.

Pyle shook hands with Chuck Freeman and Bob Knox, the twenty-three-year-veteran first officer. They had just flown the final trip of a Pan American Clipper.

And that made them unique. It made them—in effect—the last of the Skygods.

In Manhattan the Primitives still remembered their old enemy, Juan Trippe. They were *forced* to remember him, even in death, because the great slab he had erected stood there just as it always had, astraddle Park Avenue. And his daily reminder to them still perched atop the slab, smacking them in the eye each morning.

The old man was gone, and now even his Imperial Airline was extinct. But there it was anyway, every morning, that damn reminder in letters fifteen feet high: PAN AM.

For several more months it stayed up there, lurid and presumptuous, chiding them like a rebuke from Trippe's grave. The absurdly tall letters and the globe-shaped logo still conjured the old man's fantasies:

Supersonic transports . . . lunar flight . . . Clipper ships sailing to the stars . . .

And then one morning they looked up—and it was gone. The logo and the tall letters, PAN AM, had been removed. In their place would be erected the name of the insurance company that owned the building.

The old Skygod and his airline were officially dead. The Primitives had won.

INDEX

Accidentals, 55–56, 58
accidents:
  Clipper ships and, 19–20, 25, 96
  flight training and, 60–61, 66
  of Johnstad, 258–260
  Skygods and, 90–91, 103–116
Acker, C. Edward, 286, 300
  background of, 216, 221
  as CEO, 215–223, 236, 239, 241, 243–
    248, 257–258, 261–265, 266
Acker, Sandy, 222
Affourtit, Dan, 268
Airbus Industries, 246, 282, 296, 306,
  312
Air Florida, 212, 216–217, 220, 221, 255
Air Force, U.S., 4, 5, 6, 8, 30, 31, 33, 35,
  56–57, 71, 77, 163–164, 252, 278
Air France, 151
Airline Deregulation Act (1978), 179–180,
  186–187, 193
airline industry:
  deregulation of, 179–180, 186–187,
    193, 247, 253, 304–305, 310
  founding tycoons of, 10, 32, 190
  jet development and, 27–38, 39–40, 61
  origins of, 12–17
  subsidization of, 13, 167–168, 175–177
  traffic growth in, 4, 40, 73, 182–183,
    184–185, 269–270
  traffic slumps in, 93, 135, 180, 281,
    282, 286–287
  see also domestic airlines; foreign
    airlines
airline mergers, 13, 15

between Pan Am and domestic carriers,
  139–141, 168, 187–189, 193–197,
  198–205, 208, 283–284, 303, 304–
  311
Air Line Pilots Association (ALPA), 30,
  64, 90, 202, 236, 237, 243, 247, 255,
  256, 263, 271, 302
Airmail (Kelly) Act (1925), 13
airmail service, 13, 14–17, 29, 176, 179
Air National Guard, 62, 252
Airplane Heads, 55–56, 58
Allen, Bill, 76
  Boeing 707 and, 34–38
  Boeing 747 and, 69–71, 77, 123,
    131
Allen, Ron, 307
American Airlines, 4, 28, 30, 40, 132,
  133, 134, 139–140, 142, 145, 164,
  173, 174, 182, 188, 267, 286, 304–
  305, 310
American Consulting Engineers Council,
  192
American Overseas Airlines, 133, 155
Anderson, Ira, 113
Anderson, Robert B., 94
Andresen, Rolf, 314
Archer, Eric, 298–299
Army Air Corps, U.S., 14
Arneson, Don, 224, 229
Arnold, Henry "Hap," 14, 15
Atlantic, Gulf and Caribbean Air Lines,
  15
Aviation Corporation of America, 14, 15
Avritt, Jerry, 272, 273

AWARE, 177–180, 181, 182, 189, 196, 216, 248
Axelsson, Kurt, 254

Baker, George Ted, 190–191, 192, 236
Bali, 110–111
Bancroft, Steve, 20–21
Bankers Trust, 283, 297
Beasley, Terry, 175–177
Beaver Man, 160
Belluschi, Pietro, 43
Berlin, 111, 151
Berliner Zeitung, 158
Berlin Wall, 151, 154, 290
Bernick, Hans, 204, 292
black boxes, 106, 108, 111
"black hole" syndrome, 107
Blackshear, Cornelius, 307–308, 314
Bledsoe, Roger, 204–205
Boeing Airplane Company, 4, 127, 199
   jet development by, 30–38, 69–79
   Pan Am's relationship with, 35, 130
Boeing B-29 bomber, 30, 57, 72
Boeing B-52 bomber, 31, 163
Boeing B-247, 38
Boeing B-307 Stratoliner, 35
Boeing B-314 *Pacific Clipper*, 21–22
Boeing B-314 *Yankee Clipper*, 19–20, 96
Boeing B-377 Stratocruiser, 18, 30, 35, 72
Boeing Dash Eighty, 30–31
Boeing 707 *Clipper America*, 39
Boeing 707 *Clipper Rising Sun*, 103–104
Boeing 707 jetliner, 3, 39–40, 60, 65, 66, 67, 69, 70, 72, 79, 81, 94–95, 124–125, 126, 133, 152, 203, 252
   accidents involving, 90, 91, 103–116
   development of, 30–38
Boeing 727 *Clipper Goodwill*, 315–317
Boeing 727 jetliner, 111, 152, 154, 157, 199, 204, 211, 306, 309
Boeing 737 jetliner, 220
Boeing 747 *Clipper Constitution*, 130
Boeing 747 *Clipper Juan T. Trippe*, 207
Boeing 747 *Clipper Maid of the Seas*, bombing of, 116*n*, 271–281
Boeing 747 *Clipper Westwind*, 164–166
Boeing 747 *Clipper Young America*, 129–130
Boeing 747 jetliner, 85, 98, 126, 136–137, 140, 169, 175, 179, 187, 203, 204, 211, 270, 288, 299, 301, 302
   accidents involving, 111–112, 116
   bombing of, 116*n*, 271–281
   development of, 69–79
   engines of, 71–75, 122–123, 129–131, 144
   first commercial flight of, 129–130
   hijackings of, 111–112, 269
   Pan Am's financial losses and, 95, 122–123, 144, 146, 180, 182, 207, 282
   size of crew on, 225
   SP model, 246
Boggs, Cale, 5, 63

Bond, Al "Chicken Man," 149–150, 151, 161
Borger, John, 46, 71, 75
Borman, Frank, 194
Born, Marc, 254
Braniff, Inc., 258, 261–262, 264
Braniff Airlines, 4, 131, 132, 134, 139, 140, 142, 185, 188, 255, 258, 294
Braniff International, 216, 217, 221, 282
Brewster, Owen, 96
British Airways, 185, 288, 290
Brock, Horace, 23
Brunie, Henry, 41
Bush administration, 297, 299

Caldwell, Cy, 16–17
Caribbean, 12, 14, 139, 217
Carney, Robert, 192
Carter, Jimmy, 186, 194, 283
Carter administration, 185, 186, 188
Chandler, Norman, 94
Checchi, Alfred, 284
check pilots, 88, 239–240, 250
chief pilots, 24, 39, 113, 129, 156, 157, 158, 160–161, 239–240, 248, 268, 291
Citicorp, 283
Civil Aeronautics Act (1935), 48
Civil Aeronautics Board (CAB), 10, 131–134, 138, 139, 167, 169, 170, 175, 179, 180, 181, 186–187, 193, 194–195, 196
Civil Reserve Air Fleet (CRAF), 169, 278, 299
Clair, Kathleen, 48, 49, 99
Clarke, Arthur C., 55
Clipper Club, 164, 222
Clipper ships:
   accidents involving, 19–20, 25, 96
   America, 39
   American, 29
   China, 19, 24, 39, 73
   Clipper II, 96
   Hawaii, 20
   Pacific, 21–22
   Samoan, 25
   Yankee, 19–20, 96
   see also flying boats
Cloud Club, 33, 41
CNN, 277, 278, 287
Cogliani, Lou, 80–82, 90, 103–104, 115
Coleman, William, 265
Colonial Air Transport, 13–14
Colussy, Dan, 143, 166, 210
Comet jetliner, 30, 39
Concorde SST, 46, 47, 49–50, 171
Congress, U.S., 132, 133, 167, 170, 175, 179
   SST program killed by, 44–47, 127
Continental Airlines, 133, 134, 139, 142, 267, 283, 300, 305
copilots (first officers), 105, 181, 250

CRAF (Civil Reserve Air Fleet), 169, 278, 299
Crilly, Bill, 147
Crooker, John, 132
Cuba, 14–17, 191
Curtiss, Glenn, 11

David, Donald, 94
Davies, Norm, 291
Davis, Frank, 138, 147
de Gaulle, Charles, 47
Delta Airlines, 4, 140, 143, 173, 182, 185, 188
    Pan Am purchased and shut down by, 303, 304–308, 312–317
Democratic Party, 48, 50, 51, 131, 133, 134, 168
Demura, John, 230–231
Denham, Mike, 5, 63, 66
Denison, George, 143
Diedrich, Joe, 167
DME (distance-measuring equipment), 103
domestic airlines, 98, 170, 173
    home offices of, 4, 40
    overseas routes awarded to, 131–134, 139, 175, 176, 185
    Pan Am mergers with, 139–141, 168, 187–189, 193–197, 198–205, 208, 283–284, 303, 304–311
Doppler navigation system, 126
Douglas, Donald, 31, 32, 36, 37
Douglas Aircraft, 4, 30, 31, 33, 36, 37–38
Douglas DC-3 transport, 36, 37–38
Douglas DC-4 transport, 18
Douglas DC-6 transport, 18, 28, 30, 31
Douglas DC-7 transport, 28, 31
Douglas DC-8 jetliner, 31, 36, 37, 40, 70, 133, 252
Douglas DC-10 jetliner, 173
Doyle, Frank, 138, 146, 147
Drasin, Tamara, 20
Drexel Burnham Lambert, 257
Dryer, Pat, 228–229
Dulles Airport, 129, 141
Duncan, Jim, 268, 269
Dutch rolls, 65, 66

Earhart, Amelia, 20
Eastern Airlines, 4, 10, 30, 52, 133, 139, 140, 187, 190, 192, 194–195, 289, 294, 297, 300, 305
Eastern Air Transport, 13
Eastern Shuttle, 265
Eichner, L. John, 315
Eisenhower, Dwight D., 50
Eisenhower administration, 46, 52, 131
electronic guide paths, 154–155
Eleuthera Island, 124–125
engines:
    failure of, 258–260
    see also specific engines

Evarts, Bob, 105
Export-Import Bank, U.S., 176

FAA (Federal Aviation Agency/Administration), 46, 52, 77, 112
Faded Aristocracy, 142–143, 146
Fairchild FC-2 float planes, 16–17
FAM 4 (Key West–Havana airmail route), 14–17
Farnham, Bob, 83–84, 86–87
Federal Aviation Administration (FAA), 46, 52, 77, 112
Federal Aviation Agency, see Federal Aviation Administration
Fenton, Will, 82–83
Ferrel, Bob, 304
Ferris, Richard, 243, 244, 245
Fishbein, Arthur, 301–302
Flanagan, Tom, 210
Flanigan, Peter, 141
flight attendants, 87, 248, 270
    see also Independent Union of Flight Attendants; stewardesses
flight engineers, 64, 114, 181, 250, 309
Flight Engineers International Association, 64, 236, 241
Flight 103, bombing of, 116n, 271–281
flight simulators, 66, 312–313
Florida Airways, 15
Flower, Scott, 46
flying boats, 18–19, 29, 35, 73
    see also Clipper ships
Flying Tiger Airlines, 117, 134
Fokker, Tony, 13–14, 30
Fokker trimotor transport planes, 13–14, 15, 16
Ford, Bob, 21–22
Ford, Henry, 14
Ford administration, 168, 169, 170, 179, 181
foreign airlines, 93, 176, 179, 248
    U.S. routes awarded to, 185
Forrestal, James, 52
Forster, Dave, 65, 66–67
Freeman, Chuck, 316, 317
frequent-flier programs, 267
Froman, Jane, 20
fuel price levels, 167, 172, 179, 183, 287
furloughing, 125–126, 181–182, 212, 250, 251–254

Garrett, Bob, 193
Gates, John, 53
Gaugler, Jack, 225
General Dynamics, 98
General Electric engines, 71, 200
Germany, Federal Republic of (West Germany), 151, 153, 154
Germany, reunification of, 290–291
Gibson, Hud, 115
Giere, Bernie, 252, 253
Gill, Lewis B., 203–204
Gilson, Art, 158–161, 231

Glover, W. Irving, 15
Goldsmith, Sir James, 257
Gould, Bob, 219, 247, 263, 267–268, 274–277, 279–280, 281, 289
Gray, Harold, 53, 78
  background and career of, 95–96
  cancer of, 98, 134–135
  character of, 96–97, 122, 137, 163
  as Pan Am's CEO, 51, 93, 95, 97–99, 122–123, 132
  retirement of, 135
Great Britain, 47, 151, 299–300, 301
Grebey, C. Raymond, 237–238, 239, 263
Greenslet, Ed, 305
Gropius, Walter, 43
Gruenther, Alfred, 78, 147
Gulf United Corporation, 216, 221
Gulf War, 286–287, 299, 301
Gwinn, Bill, 74–75

Halaby, Najeeb, 95, 123, 125, 162–163, 166, 181, 223
  background of, 51–52
  opposition to, 97, 98, 135, 137–138, 142, 144, 146–148
  as Pan Am's CEO, 135, 136–148, 206
  SST program and, 46, 47, 48–49, 50
  as test pilot, 51–52, 136–137
  Washington lobbying by, 53, 97, 132–133, 134, 135
Hambleton, John, 13, 14
Handelsman, Lawrence M., 314–315
Harmon Trophy, 24
Havens, Clyde, 105–106
Hawaii, 134, 138, 167
Hawkins, Whit, 305
Heathrow Airport, 279, 288, 290, 295, 301, 305
Heinemann, Milt, 72
hijackings, 111–112, 269
Hilton International Hotels, 140
Hoover, Herbert, 129
Horner, Jack, 71
Hotchkiss, Jim, 175–177
House of Representatives, U.S., 254
Howard, William R., 265
Hoyt, Richard F., 15
Hughes, Howard, 140, 300

Icahn, Carl, 300–301, 308
ILS (instrument landing system), 107
Independent Union of Flight Attendants, 218, 236, 241
Ingalls, Dave, 78
instrument approaches, 154–155
Intercontinental Hotels, 10, 53, 171, 209, 210, 211, 225, 244, 265
Internal German Service, 220, 232–234, 235–236, 240–241, 297
  antics of pilots based in, 149–161
  end of, 290–293
International Air Transport Association, 37

International Air Transportation Fair Competitive Practices Act (1975), 179
International Herald Tribune, 175
Iran, 168–172
Iran Air, 168–169

Jackson, Henry "Scoop," 127
James, Chuck, 62
Japan Air Services, 295
Jet Capital Corporation, 192
jets:
  commercial introduction of, 8, 27–30, 39–40, 61, 192
  U.S. development of, 30–38, 69–79
JFK Airport, see Kennedy Airport
Johnson, Lyndon B., 49, 53, 65, 67, 75–78, 118, 131–132, 134
Johnson administration, 53, 75–78, 134, 139, 168, 185
Johnstad, Errol, 255–256
Johnston, Tex, 31
Joint Labor Council, 257, 264
jumbo jets, see Boeing 747 jetliner
Justice Department, U.S., 140–141, 168, 195, 299

Kahn, Alfred E., ix, 186–187, 194
Karachi, 269
KC-97 tanker, 57
Kelly (Airmail) Act (1925), 13
Kendall, Donald, 265
Kennedy, John F., 45, 46–47, 48–49, 50
Kennedy, Joseph P., 48, 134
Kennedy, Vern, 224
Kennedy administration, 45, 46–47, 50, 131
Kennedy airport, 288
  Pan Am's facilities at, 4, 123, 222, 285
Kerkorian, Kirk, 257–258
Kerrigan, John, 239
Key West–Havana airmail route (FAM 4), 14–17
Khomeini, Ayatollah Ruhollah, 172
Kinkel, Don, 113
Knight, Richard, 138
Knox, Bob, 317
Kraft, Chuck, 5, 62
Kubrick, Stanley, 55

La Guardia Airport, 22, 265
landing and handling fees, 179
Landis, James M., 10
Latin America, 14, 29, 107, 131, 139, 308, 309, 314
Lawrence, Harding, 140
Leet, James, 138, 143, 147
Lehman, Robert, 94, 95
LeMay, Curtis, 57
Leonard, Archie, 143
Leslie, John, 97
Lewis, Roger, 97–98
Lindbergh, Anne Morrow, 29, 175

Lindbergh, Charles A., 23, 24, 27, 31,
    84–86, 95, 147
  death of, 174–175
  early Pan Am work of, 29, 30
  SST opposed by, 45, 78
  in World War II, 28–29, 30
Littlefield, Gus, 254
load factors, 285
Lockheed Aircraft, 30, 46, 147, 167, 175
Lockheed C-5A, 71, 77
Lockheed Constellations, 28, 30
Lockheed Elektra propjet, 30, 31
Lockheed L-1011 Tri-Star jetliner, 187,
    199–200, 211, 247
Lockheed Sirius floatplane, 29
London, 272
  United's purchase of Pan Am's opera-
    tions in, 288, 295, 296–297, 301,
    305, 307
Long Island Airways, 12–13
Lorenzo, Frank, 192–193, 195–197, 209,
    267, 283, 297, 300
Luce, Clare Boothe, 96
Luce, Henry, 96
Lufthansa, 185, 291, 293, 297, 302

McDivitt, Les, 249
McDonnell Douglas DC-10 jetliner, 199–
    200, 209, 247
Mach numbers, 82
McKee, Mark, 78
McNamara, Robert, 47, 77–78, 117
MacQuarrie, Jim, 237, 239, 241, 255,
    256, 271–274, 276, 277, 279
Magnuson, Warren, 127
Mahanor, Bob, 87
Marcus, Leon, 315
Marine Corps, U.S., 4, 8, 62
Maritime Commission, 48
Martin M-130 Hawaii Clipper, 20
Martinside, Rob, 104–105, 107, 127,
    224, 293, 294–295
  as check pilot, 240
  childhood of, 58
  as copilot, 82, 84–87, 114–115, 117–
    121
  at Delta, 310–311
  in Germany, 152
  hiring of, 3, 6, 7–8, 64
  Lindbergh and, 84–86
  as pilot, 228, 231–234
  seniority of, 204
  Southall affair and retention hearing of,
    88–90, 91
  training period of, 55, 57–58, 60, 64–
    65, 66, 67, 68
  in Vietnam, 117–121
Master of Ocean Flying Boats, see
  Skygods
Maximum Skygods, 255–256, 263
Maytag, Bud, 191–192, 193, 197
Meany, George, 127
Messerschmitt, Willy, 29

Metropolitan Life Insurance Company,
    208
Meyer, C. E., 246
Miami Airport, 192
military reserves, 62–64
Miller, Henry, 315
Miller, Sam, 39
Mirka, Hans, 265
Mitchell, Billy, 14–15
Mitchell, John, 140, 258
Montgomery, John K., 14
Morgan Guaranty Trust, 283
Moscow, 125, 167
Muhammad Reza Shah Pahlavi, 168–172
Mullikin, Walt, 158
Musick, Edwin, 23–25, 96

National Airlines, 133, 139, 185, 209,
    236
  founding and growth of, 190–192
  Pan Am's merger with, 188–189, 193–
    197, 198–205, 208, 247, 253, 306
national air races, 256, 258–260
National Air Taxi, 190
navigators, 64, 126
Navy, U.S., 4, 6, 8, 12, 15, 51–52, 57,
    62, 64, 123–124
Neubaur, Al, 109–110
Neumann, Gerard, 71
Nevada Air National Guard, 62
new hires, 18, 25, 26, 54–68
  Airplane Heads vs. Accidentals, 55–56,
    58
  AWARE and, 177–180
  definition of, 54, 61–62
  furloughing of, 125–126, 181–182,
    250, 251–254
  hiring of, 3–9, 59, 61, 64, 67
  look of, 3–4, 87
  military backgrounds of, 3, 4–5, 7, 8,
    56, 62–63
  in military reserves, 62–64
  promoted to pilots, 67–68, 227–234
  salaries of, 62, 64
  Skygods' relationship with, 80–91,
    113–114, 158–161
  stewardesses and, 87–89
  training of, 55–68
  in Vietnam, 117–118
  see also copilots; seniority of pilots
New York, N.Y., 141–142, 181
New York Times, 44, 49, 173, 176–177
Nixon, Edward, 258
Nixon, Pat, 129
Nixon, Richard M., 134, 141, 168, 181,
    258
Nixon administration, 139, 140–141,
    167–168, 185
nondirectional radio beacon (NDB),
    110
nonscheduled carriers, 135, 252
North, Dave, 254
North American B-45 bomber, 58

North American B-70 supersonic bomber, 46
North Atlantic, 8, 131, 139, 192
  airlines' financial losses on, 286
  first jetliner crossing of, 39
  jets developed for crossing of, 31, 32, 38
  Pan Am's market share in, 27, 133, 185, 270
Northeast Airlines, 143
Northeast (Pan Am) Shuttle, 257, 262, 264–265, 286, 300, 306, 313–314
Northwest Airlines, 131, 134, 185, 246, 248, 300
  Pan Am's attempted purchase of, 283–284
Nyalis, Frank, 158

oil shocks, 167, 179, 184–185
Operations Review Group, 108–109, 112, 114
Organization of Petroleum Exporting Countries (OPEC), 167, 172

Pacific Division, 96, 114, 243–248, 286, 288
Pacific Ocean, 8, 20, 131–134, 181
PacifiCorp, 300
Pagnotta, John, 276–277
Pago Pago, 24–25, 108–109
Pan Am Building, 10, 48, 78, 92
  construction of, 40–43
  Pan Am sign on, 43, 317
  sale of, 207–208, 244, 289
Pan American World Airways (Pan Am):
  accounting chaos at, 166
  Atlantic Division of, 96
  aviation firsts of, 6, 8, 21–22, 39
  board of directors of, 32, 51, 78–79, 94–95, 146–148, 166, 171, 206, 209–210, 219, 247, 261–262, 264, 265
  college graduates as new managers at, 142–143
  death of, 99, 293–295, 312–317
  domestic routes sought by, 50, 138–139, 176–177, 179–180, 181, 187
  domestic strategy of, 217–218, 247, 286
  earnings of, 93, 123, 182, 184
  employee concessions and givebacks at, 218–219, 237–239, 256–258, 262–264, 268
  employees' campaign on behalf of, 173–180, 181, 182
  employee stock ownership plan at, 218–219
  federal government's relationship with, ix, 16, 48, 50, 53, 96–97, 98, 131–135, 138–139, 140–141, 167–168, 169–170, 176–181, 185–186, 297
  final flight for, 315–317
  financial losses of, 135, 144, 146, 173–

174, 180, 207–209, 218, 220–221, 236, 244, 269, 282–283, 285, 296–298, 299, 307
  flight operations review and standardization of, 108–109, 112–116, 269
  founding of, 10, 14–15
  German base of, see Internal German Service
  Iranian deal with, 168–172
  Key West–Havana airmail route and, 14–17
  logo of, 3, 8, 42, 198–199, 200, 207, 317
  1985 strike at, 235–242, 245, 247, 269
  1960s expansion of, see new hires
  office of the president of, 138, 143, 146
  on-time record of, 285
  operating revenues of, 40, 73, 93
  operational philosophy of, 22–23
  Overseas Division of, 96
  Pacific Division of, 96, 114, 243–248, 265, 286, 288
  restructuring of, 210, 308–309
  route system changes at, 166–167, 180–181, 182, 217–218
  safety record of, 112, 116, 151
  sales of assets of, 207–208, 243–248, 265, 286–289, 296–297, 299–302, 303, 304–308, 313–314
  stock prices of, 123, 257, 296
  vice-presidential proliferation at, 166
  wartime services of, 117–121, 169, 299
Pan Am Express, 257, 262
Pan Am (Northeast) Shuttle, 257, 262, 264–265, 286, 300, 306, 313–314
Pan Am World Services, 210, 257
Paris, 39, 166, 181, 288
Parker, Cliff, 205
Parker, Jack, 265
Parsell, Red, 232–233
Penn Central, 147, 175, 207
Perry, Bud, 278
Pfaff, Bob, 84–86
Phillips, Larry, 234
pilots:
  Acker's relationship with, 215–216, 223
  baggage carrying by, 224–225
  check, 88, 239–240, 250
  chief, 24, 39, 113, 129, 156, 157, 158, 160–161, 239–240, 248, 268, 291
  conservatism of, 150
  corporate assets sales and transfer of, 248–250, 289–290, 301–302, 305–307
  hotel routine of, 225–227
  mandatory retirement of, 309
  necktie-cutting ritual of, 229, 234
  salaries of, 152, 199, 218, 223, 262
  of single vs. multiengine planes, 5, 7, 63
  standardization and, 114–116
  stewardesses' relationships with, 5, 87–89
  Trippe's relationship with, 19, 22

union of, *see* Air Line Pilots Association
women as, 254
see also seniority of pilots; Skygods
Pipkin, Mike, 254
Plaskett, Tom:
  character of, 266–267
  as Pan Am's CEO, 266–267, 269, 282–290, 293, 295, 297, 300–301, 307
Player, Willis, 92, 146, 169
Post, Wiley, 24
Pratt & Whitney, 28, 32, 130, 199
Pratt & Whitney J-57 engines, 30, 31–32, 33, 34, 36
Pratt & Whitney J-75 engines, 32–34, 36, 37, 38, 71
Pratt & Whitney JT-3D fan-jet engines, 73, 85
Pratt & Whitney JT-9D fan-jet engines, 74, 122–123, 129–131, 144
Priester, Andre, 22–23, 46, 96
Primitives, 27, 28, 39, 42, 43, 44, 49, 92, 207, 317
Pritzker, Jay A., 258, 261–262, 263, 264
propeller efficiency, 23
Proxmire, William, 44, 45, 47, 175, 177–178, 179, 248
Prudential-Bache, 283
Pryor, Sam, 74, 78
Pyle, Mark, 315–317

Qantas, 179
Quesada, Pete, 46, 52

Ray, Russell, 315
Rehman, Tom, 104
Rentschler, Fred, 32–33, 34, 71
Republican Party, 50, 51, 132, 133, 134, 167
Rickenbacker, Eddie, 10, 30, 52, 190, 294
Rockefeller, James, 94
Rockefeller, Laurance, 52
Rockefeller, Nelson, 43
Rockefeller, Stillman, 147
Rockefeller, William A., 13
Rock Sound, 124–125
Rolex Company, 162
Rolls-Royce Aero, 145, 164
Rolls-Royce engines, 33, 34, 71, 199, 247
Roosevelt, Franklin D., 30, 48, 50
runways, 15–16, 18–19, 28

SAC (Strategic Air Command), 57, 163–164
San Francisco, Calif., 113–114, 181
San Francisco International Airport, 3, 55, 111
Sapp, Neil, 300
SCADTA (Sociedad Colombo-Alemana de Transportes), 14
Schoenfeld Airport, 151
Schultz, Ed, 21
Scroggin, Charlie, 58–59
Seawell, William T., 147, 223, 265

background of, 145, 163, 164
character of, 162–163, 164, 266
hiring of, 145–146
as Pan Am's CEO, 147, 162–172, 177, 178, 180, 182–183, 184, 187–188, 189, 193, 195–197, 198, 200, 205, 206, 207–210, 216, 217, 219
retirement of, 210, 212
Selph, Rich, 177–178, 248–249, 250
Semtex, 281
seniority of pilots, 67, 124, 125
  in Pan Am–Delta deal, 305–307
  in Pan Am–National merger, 188–189, 196–197, 198, 200–205, 212, 306
  in Pan Am–United deals, 248–250, 290, 301–302
  and promotion of new hires, 227–228, 229
Shaffer, Ed, 157–158
Sheeline, Paul, 210, 265
Shepard, Harry, 249, 312–313
Shugrue, Martin R., ix, 123–127, 243, 247, 260, 268
  Braniff deal opposed by, 261–265
  in labor negotiations, 218, 237
  as management trainee, 126–127
  Pan Am titles held by, 254, 262–263
Sikorsky S-42B *American Clipper*, 29
Sikorsky S-42B *China Clipper*, 19, 24, 39, 72
Sikorsky S-42B *Clipper II*, 96
Sikorsky S-42B *Samoan Clipper*, 25
Simat, Helliesen & Eichner, 245
Simon, Charles, 195
Simon, William, 170
Skadden, Arps, Slate, Meagher & Flom, 257
Skygods, 6, 18–26, 298–299
  accidents involving, 90–91, 103–116
  AWARE ignored by, 180
  idiosyncrasies of, 19–22, 114–115
  Maximum, 255–256, 263
  new hires' relationships with, 80–91, 113–114, 158–161
  Pan Am–Delta deal and, 306–307
  on seniority list, 227–228, 229
  uniforms and title of, 19, 26
Smith, Connie, 62
Smith, C. R., 10, 28, 30, 40
Smith, Denny, 253–254
snapback provisions, 238, 239
sound barrier, 52
Southall, Frank, 88, 89, 91
Southall, Jill, 88–89
South America, *see* Latin America
Soviet Union, 47, 125, 151
Spaatz, Carl, 14, 15
space travel, commercial potential of, 8–9, 55, 211
Spater, George, 139
standardization, 114–116
STANINE test, 6
Stanton, Frank, 147

stewardesses, 109–110
    flying incident involving, 157–158
    pilots' relationships with, 5, 87–89
    union of, *see* Independent Union of
        Flight Attendants
Strategic Air Command (SAC), 57, 163–
    164
Sullivan, R.O.D., 19–20
Supersonic Transport (SST) planes, 8–9,
    70, 78
    killing of U.S. program for, 44–50,
        127–128, 175, 211
    see also Concorde SST
swept-wing aircraft, 29

Taft, Ron, 62
Tango Uniform, 262, 294, 296, 312–317
    definition of, 255
Teamsters, 236
Tegel Flughafen, 233, 235, 292
Tempelhof Flughafen, 153, 154, 157
terrorism, 111–112, 116*n*, 269, 271–281,
    286
Terry, Juanita, 11
Texas International, 193–194, 195
Tillinghast, Charles, 139, 140–141
Towers Financial Corporation, 258
Transportation Department, U.S., 170,
    290, 297, 299
Transport Workers Union, 236, 239, 241
Trans Texas Airlines, 192
Transway International, 216
Trippe, Betty, 206
Trippe, Juan, 10–17, 26, 122, 132, 137,
    139, 140, 142, 146, 148, 163, 185,
    186, 222, 223, 283, 299, 317
    background of, 11–12
    corporate growth credo of, 12, 27
    death of, 206–207
    as dissembler and manipulator, 10–11,
        31, 32–38, 48–49, 50, 69–70
    early career of, 13–17
    Halaby hired by, 50–51, 52–53, 144
    jet development and, 27–28, 30, 31–38,
        39–40, 69–79, 123, 131
    nautical fetish of, 19
    Pan Am Building and, 40–43
    Pan Am titles held by, 15, 39, 51, 94,
        95, 96
    pilots' relationship with, 19, 22
    private 707 service for, 124–125
    retirement and succession of, 92–95,
        97–99
    SST program and, 44–50
Truman, Harry S., 50, 133
Truman administration, 131
Tubbs, Fred, 60–61
TU-144 SST, 47
turboprop planes, 28, 61
TWA, 35, 117, 131, 133, 179, 185, 192,
    246, 269, 286, 300, 305

home office of, 4, 40
Pan Am's proposed mergers with, 139,
    140–141, 168, 187
round-the-world rights of, 134
route-swap between Pan Am and, 180–
    181, 182
2001: A Space Odyssey, 54–55

uniforms, 19, 26, 156, 199, 231–232,
    310–311
United Aircraft Corporation, 30, 32, 71
United Airlines, 10, 59, 133, 139, 140,
    142, 173, 174, 182, 185, 188, 265,
    304, 310
    Pan Am's London service bought by,
        288, 295, 296–297, 299, 301, 305,
        307
    Pan Am's Pacific Division bought by,
        243–248, 265, 286, 288

Vance, Cyrus, 94, 147
Van Houten, George, 157, 158
Vienna, 166–167, 181
Vietnam War, 63–64, 76, 117–121, 127
Volcker, Paul, 258

Waddell, Jack, 136
Wall Street Journal, 44, 49, 125, 166,
    167, 184, 185, 194, 195, 210–211,
    239, 245, 257–258, 264, 269, 282,
    296, 308, 312
Waltrip, Bill, 210, 217
Washington, D.C., 141–142
Watson, Arthur, 94
Watson, Tom, 147
Waugh, Jim, 113
Webb, Everette, 129
Weeks, Bob, 129
Western Airlines, 134
Whitbeck, J. E., 16–17
White, Ivan, 60
white knights, 256–258
Whitney, Cornelius "Sonny," 13, 14
Wilson, Charles E. "Engine Charlie," 52
Winkler, Walt, 278
Wiser, F. C. "Bud," 143
Wolf, Stephen, 287–288
Wolfson, Erwin, 41–42, 207
Wood, Everett, 155–156
Wood, Jim, 56–57, 62, 80–82, 103,
    104–105, 108, 127, 149–150, 152,
    159, 161, 215, 227, 228, 231, 240
World Airways, 117
World War I, 12
Wright, Wilbur, 11
Wright Aeronautical Corporation, 15
Wright brothers, 11

Yale University, 11, 12, 13, 51, 78, 96